The Lone Ranche

by

Captain Mayne Reid

Double 9
BOOKS

The Lone Ranche
by Captain Mayne Reid

Copyright © 2023

All Rights reserved.

ISBN: 978-93-59393-15-5

Published by

DOUBLE 9 BOOKS

2/13-B, Ansari Road
Daryaganj, New Delhi – 110002
info@double9books.com
www.double9books.com
Tel. 011-40042856

ABOUT THE AUTHOR

Thomas Mayne Reid(Captain Mayne Reid)(4 April 1818 - 22 October 1883) was an Irish-American author who battled in the Mexican-American Conflict (1846-1848). His many deals with American life depict a provincial approach in the American states, the horror of slave work, and the lives of American Indians "Captain," Reid composed adventure books likened to those by Frederick Marryat and Robert Louis Stevenson and set in the American West, Mexico, South Africa, the Himalayas, and Jamaica. He was a fan of Master Byron. His novels contain action that takes place primarily in untamed locations. He was a truly prolific author, with over 60 titles published in his lifetime, including both fiction and non-fiction.

CONTENTS

Chapter One.
A Tale of the Staked Plain.

"Hats Off!"

Within the city of Chihuahua, metropolis of the northern provinces of Mexico—for the most part built of mud—standing in the midst of vast barren plains, o'ertopped by bold porphyritic mountains—plains with a population sparse as their timber—in the old city of Chihuahua lies the first scene of our story.

Less than twenty thousand people dwell within the walls of this North Mexican metropolis, and in the country surrounding it a like limited number.

Once they were thicker on the soil; but the tomahawk of the Comanche and the spear of the Apache have thinned off the descendants of the *Conquistadores*, until country houses stand at wide distances apart, with more than an equal number of ruins between.

Yet this same city of Chihuahua challenges weird and wonderful memories. At the mention of its name springs up a host of strange records, the souvenirs of a frontier life altogether different from that wreathed round the history of Anglo-American borderland. It recalls the cowled monk with his cross, and the soldier close following with his sword; the old mission-house, with its church and garrison beside it; the fierce savage lured from a roving life, and changed into a toiling *peon*, afterwards to revolt against a system of slavery that even religion failed to make endurable; the neophyte turning his hand against his priestly instructor, equally his oppressor; revolt followed by a deluge of blood, with ruinous devastation, until the walls of both *mission* and military *cuartel* are left tenantless, and the redskin has returned to his roving.

Such a history has had the city of Chihuahua and the settlements in its neighbourhood. Nor is the latter portion of it all a chronicle of the olden time. Much of it belongs to modern days; ay, similar scenes are transpiring even now. But a few years ago a stranger entering its gates would have seen nailed overhead, and whisked to and fro by the wind, some scores of objects similar to one another, and resembling tufts of hair, long, trailing, and black, as if taken from the manes or tails of horses. But it came not thence; it was human hair; and the patches of skin that served to keep the bunches together had been stripped from human skulls! They were *scalps* — the scalps of Indians, showing that the Comanche and Apache savages had not had it all their own way.

Beside them could be seen other elevated objects of auricle shape, set in rows or circles like a festooning of child peppers strung up for preservation. No doubt their procurement had drawn tears from the eyes of those whose heads had furnished them, for they were human ears!

These ghastly souvenirs were the *bounty warrants* of a band whose deeds have been already chronicled by this same pen. They were the trophies of "Scalp Hunters" — vouchers for the number of Indians they had killed.

They were there less than a quarter of a century ago, waving in the dry wind that sweeps over the plains of Chihuahua. For aught the writer knows, they may be there still; or, if not the same, others of like gory record replacing or supplementing them.

It is not with the "Scalp Hunters" we have now to do — only with the city of Chihuahua. And not much with it either. A single scene occurring in its streets is all of Chihuahuaense life to be depicted in this tale.

It was the spectacle of a religious procession — a thing far from uncommon in Chihuahua or any other Mexican town; on the contrary, so common that at least weekly the like may be witnessed. This was one of the grandest, representing the story of the Crucifixion. Citizens of all classes assisted at the ceremony, the soldiery also taking part in it. The clergy, of course, both secular and regular, were its chief supports and propagators. To them it brought bread, and if not butter — since there is none in Chihuahua — it added to their incomes and influence, by the sale of leaden crosses, images of the Virgin Mother, and the numerous sisterhood of saints. In the *funcion* figured the usual Scripture characters: — The Redeemer conducted to the place of Passion; the crucifix, borne on the shoulders of a brawny, brown-skinned Simon; Pilate the oppressor; Judas the betrayer — in short, every prominent personage spoken of as having been present on that occasion when the Son of Man suffered for our sins.

There is, or was then, an American hotel in Chihuahua, or at least one conducted in the American fashion, though only a mere *posada*. Among its guests was a gentleman, stranger to the town, as the country. His dress and general appearance bespoke him from the States, and by the same tokens it could be told that he belonged to their southern section. He was in truth a Kentuckian; but so far from representing the type, tall, rough, and stalwart, usually ascribed to the people "Kaintuck," he was a man of medium size, with a build comparable to that of the Belvidere Apollo. He had a figure tersely set, with limbs well knitted; a handsome face and features of amiable cast, at the same time expressing confidence and courage. A costly Guayaquil hat upon his head, and coat to correspond, bespoke him respectable; his *tout ensemble* proclaimed him a man of leisure; while his air and bearing were unmistakably such as could only belong to a born gentleman.

Why he was in Chihuahua, or whence he had come to it, no one seemed to know or care. Enough that he was there, and gazing at the spectacular procession as it filed past the posada.

He was regarding it with no eye of wonderment. In all likelihood he had seen such before. He could not have travelled far through Mexico without witnessing some ceremony of a similar kind.

Whether interested in this one or no he was soon notified that he was not regarding it in the manner proper or customary to the country. Standing half behind one of the pillars of the hotel porch, he had not thought it necessary to take off his hat. Perhaps placed in a more conspicuous position he would have done this. Frank Hamersley—for such was his name—was not the sort of man to seek notoriety by an exhibition of bravado, and, being a Protestant of a most liberal creed, he would have shrunk from offending the slightest sensibilities of those belonging to an opposite faith—even the most bigoted Roman Catholic of that most bigoted land. That his "Guayaquil" still remained upon his head was due to simple forgetfulness of its being there; it had not occurred to him to uncover.

While silently standing with eyes turned towards the procession, he observed scowling looks, and heard low growlings from the crowd as it swayed slowly past. He knew enough to be conscious of what this meant; but he felt at the same time disinclined to humiliate himself by a too facile compliance. A proud American, in the midst of a people he had learned to despise—their idolatrous observances along with them—no wonder he should feel a little defiant and a good deal exasperated. Enough yielding, he thought, to withdraw farther back from behind the pillar, which he did.

It was too late. The keen eye of a fanatic had been upon him—one who appeared to have authority for meting out chastisement. An officer, bearded and grandly bedizened, riding at the head of a troop of lancers, quickly wheeled his horse from out of the line of march, and spurred him towards the porch of the posada. In another instant his bared blade was waving over the hatted head of the Kentuckian.

"*Gringo! alto su sombrero! Abajo! a sus rodillas!*" ("Off with your hat, greenhorn! Down upon your knees!") were the words that came hissing from the moustached lips of the lancer.

As they failed to beget compliance, they were instantly followed by a blow from the blade of his sabre. It was given sideways, but with sufficient sleight and force to send the Guayaquil hat whirling over the pavement, and its wearer reeling against the wall.

It was but the stagger of a sudden and unexpected surprise. In another instant the "gringo" had drawn a revolving pistol, and in yet another its bullet would have been through the brain of the swaggering aggressor, but for a third personage, who, rushing from behind, laid hold of the Kentuckian's arm, and restrained the firing.

At first it seemed to Hamersley the act of another enemy; but in a moment he knew it to be the behaviour of a friend—at least a pacificator bent upon seeing fair play.

"You are wrong, Captain Uraga," interposed he who had intermeddled, addressing himself to the officer. "This gentleman is a stranger in the country, and not acquainted with our customs."

"Then it is time the heretico should be taught them, and, at the same time, respect for the Holy Church. But what right, Colonel Miranda, have you to interfere?"

"The right, first of humanity, second of hospitality, and third that I am your superior officer."

"Bah! You mistake yourself. Remember, señor coronel, you are not in your own district. If it was in Albuquerque, I might take commands from you. This is the city of Chihuahua."

"Chihuahua or not, you shall be made answerable for this outrage. Don't imagine that your patron, Santa Anna, is now Dictator, with power to endorse such base conduct as yours. You seem to forget, Captain Uraga, that you carry your commission under a new regime—one that holds itself responsible, not only to fixed laws, but to the code of decency—responsible also for international courtesy to the great Republic of which, I believe, this gentleman is a citizen."

"Bah!" once more exclaimed the bedizened bully. "Preach your *palabras* to ears that have time to listen to them. I shan't stop the procession for either you or your Yankee protégé. So you can both go to the devil."

With this benevolent permission the captain of lancers struck the spurs into his horse, and once more placed himself at the head of his troop. The crowd collected by the exciting episode soon scattered away—the sooner that the strange gentleman, along with his generous defender, had disappeared from the portico, having gone inside the inn.

The procession was still passing, and its irresistible attractions swept the loiterers along in its current—most of them soon forgetting a scene which, in that land, where "law secures not life," is of too frequent occurrence to be either much thought of or for long remembered.

Chapter Two.
A Friend in Need.

The young Kentuckian was half frenzied by the insult he had received. The proud blood of his republican citizenship was boiling within his veins. What was he to do?

In the agony of his dilemma he put the question to the gentleman who, beyond all doubt, had restrained him from committing manslaughter.

The latter was an entire stranger to him—never seen him before. He was a man of less than thirty years of age, wearing a broad-brimmed hat upon his head, a cloth jacket, slashed *calzoneras,* and a red crape scarf around his waist—in short, the *ranchero* costume of the country. Still, there was a military bearing about him that corresponded to the title by which the lancer captain had addressed him.

"Caballero," he said in reply, "if your own safety be of any consequence to you I should advise you to take no further notice of the incident that has arisen, however much it may have exasperated you, as no doubt it has done."

"Pardon me, señor; but not for all the world would I follow your advice—not for my life. I am an American—a Kentuckian. We do not take blows without giving something of the same in return. I must have redress."

"If you seek it by the law I may as well warn you, you won't have much chance of finding it."

"I know that. The law! I did not think of such a thing. I am a gentleman; I suppose this Captain Uraga supposes himself to be the same, and will not refuse to give me the usual satisfaction."

"He may refuse, and very likely will, on the plea of your being a stranger—only a barbarian, a *Tejano* or *gringo,* as he has put it."

"I am alone here—what am I to do?"

The Kentuckian spoke half in soliloquy, his countenance expressing extreme chagrin.

"*Fuez, señor!*" responded the Mexican colonel, "if you're determined on a *desafio* I think I might arrange it. I feel that I am myself a little compromised by my interference; and if you'll accept of me for your second, I think I can answer for it that Captain Uraga will not dare to deny us."

"Colonel Miranda—your name, I believe—need I attempt to express my thanks for so much generosity? I cannot—I could not. You have removed the very difficulty that was in my way; for I am not only a stranger to you, but to every one around. I arrived at Chihuahua but yesterday, and do not know a soul in the place."

"Enough; you shall not be disappointed in your duel for the want of a second. As a preliminary, may I ask if you are skilled in the use of the sword?"

"Sufficiently to stake my life upon it."

"I put the question, because that is the weapon your adversary will be certain to choose. You being the challenger, of course he has the choice; and he will insist upon it, for a reason that may perhaps amuse you. It is that we Mexican gentlemen believe you Americans somewhat *gauche* in the handling of the rapier, though we know you to be adepts in the use of the pistol. I take Captain Gil Uraga to be as thorough a poltroon as ever wore epaulettes, but he will have to meet you on my account; and he would perhaps have done so anyhow—trusting to the probability of your being a bad swordsman."

"In that he may find himself disappointed."

"I am glad to hear it; and now it only needs to receive your instructions. I am ready to act."

The instructions were given, and within two hours' time Captain Gil Uraga, of the Zacatecas Lancers, was in receipt of a challenge from the Kentuckian—Colonel Miranda being its bearer.

With such a voucher the lancer officer could not do otherwise than accept, which he did with cooler confidence for the very reason Miranda had made known. A *Tejano*, was his reflection—what should he know of the sword?

And swords were the weapons chosen.

Had the captain of Zacatecas Lancers been told that his intended adversary had spent a portion of his life among the Creoles of New Orleans, he would have been less reliant on the chances likely to turn up in his favour.

We need not describe the duel, which, if different from other encounters of the kind, was by being on both sides bitter, and of deadly intent. Suffice it to say, that the young Kentuckian displayed a skill in swordsmanship sufficient to disarrange several of Gil Uraga's front teeth, and make an ugly gash in his cheek. He had barely left to him sufficient command of his mouth to cry "Basta!" and so the affair ended.

"Señor Hamersley," said the man who had so effectively befriended him, after they had returned from the encounter, and were drinking a bottle of Paso wine in the posada, "may I ask where you intend going when you leave Chihuahua?"

"To Santa Fé, in New Mexico; thence to the United States, along with one of the return caravans."

"When do you propose starting?"

"As to that, I am not tied to time. The train with which I am to cross the plains will not be going for six months to come. I can get to Santa Fé by a month's travel, I suppose?"

"Less than that. It is not a question of how soon you may arrive there, but when you leave here. I advise you to start at once. I admit that two days is but a short time to see the sights of even so small a place as Chihuahua. But you have witnessed one of them—enough, I should say. If you take my advice you will let it content you, and kick the Chihuahua-ense dust from your feet before another twenty-four hours have passed over your head."

"But why, Colonel Miranda?"

"Because so long as you remain here you will be in danger of losing your life. You don't know the character of the man with whom you have crossed swords. I do. Although wearing the uniform of an officer in our army, he is simply a *salteador*. A coward, as I told you, too. He would never have met you if he had thought I would have given him a chance to get out of it. Perhaps he might have been tempted by the hopes of an easy conquest from your supposed want of skill. It would have given him something to boast about among the dames of Chihuahua, for Captain Gil deems himself no little of a lady-killer. You have spoilt his physiognomy for life; and, depend upon it, as long as life lasts, he will neither forget nor forgive that. I shall also come in for a share of his spite, and it behoves both of us to beware of him."

"But what can he do to us?"

"Caballero, that question shows you have not been very long in this country, and are yet ignorant of its customs. In Mexico we have some callings not congenial to your people. Know that stilettoes can here be purchased cheaply, with the arms of assassins to use them. Do you understand me?"

"I do. But how do you counsel me to act?"

"As I intend acting myself—take departure from Chihuahua this very day. Our roads are the same as far as Albuquerque, where you will be out of reach of this little danger. I am returning thither from the city of Mexico, where I've had business with the Government. I have an escort; and if you choose to avail yourself of it you'll be welcome to its protection."

"Colonel Miranda, again I know not how to thank you. I accept your friendly offer."

"Reserve your thanks till I have done you some service beyond the simple duty of a gentleman, who sees another gentleman in a dilemma he had no hand in creating. But enough, señor; we have no time to spend in talking. Even now there may be a couple of poignards preparing for us. Get your things ready at once, as I start two hours before sunset. In this sultry weather we are accustomed to travel in the cool of the evening."

"I shall be ready."

That same afternoon, two hours before the going down of the sun, a party of horsemen, wearing the uniform of Mexican dragoons of the line, issued from the *garita* of Chihuahua, and took the northern road leading to Santa Fé, by El Paso del Norte. Colonel Miranda, his ranchero dress changed for the fatigue uniform of a cavalry officer, was at its head, and by his side the stranger, whose cause he had so generously and gallantly espoused.

Chapter Three.
The Colonel Commandant.

Six weeks have elapsed since the day of the duel at Chihuahua. Two men are standing on the *azotea* of a large mansion-like house close to the town of Albuquerque, whose church spire is just visible through the foliage of trees that shade and surround the dwelling. They are Colonel Miranda and the young Kentuckian, who has been for some time his guest; for the hospitality of the generous Mexican had not terminated with the journey from Chihuahua. After three weeks of toilsome travel, including the traverse of the famed "Dead Man's Journey," he was continuing to extend it in his own house and his own district, of which last he was the military commandant, Albuquerque being at the time occupied by a body of troops, stationed there for defence against Indian incursions.

The house on whose roof the two men stood was that in which Colonel Miranda had been born—the patrimonial mansion of a large estate that extended along the Rio del Norte, and back towards the Sierra Blanca, into territories almost unknown.

Besides being an officer in the Mexican army, the colonel was one of the *ricos* of the country. The house, as already said, was a large, massive structure, having, like all Mexican dwellings of its class, a terraced roof, or *azotea*. What is also common enough in that country, it was surmounted by a *mirador*, or "belvedere." Standing less than half a mile distant from the soldier's *cuartel*, the commandant found it convenient to make use of it as his headquarters. A small guard in the *saguan*, or covered entrance below, with a sentinel stationed outside the gate in front, indicated this.

There was no family inside, wife, woman, or child; for the colonel, still a young man, was a bachelor. Only *peons* in the field, grooms and other servants around the stables, with domestics in the dwelling—all, male and female, being Indians of the race known as "Indios mansos"—brown-skinned and obedient.

But though at this time there was no living lady to make her soft footsteps heard within the walls of the commandant's dwelling, the portrait of a lovely girl hung against the side of the main *sola*, and on this his American guest had more than once gazed in silent admiration. It showed signs of having been recently painted, which was not strange, since it was the likeness of Colonel Miranda's sister, a few years younger than himself—at the time on a visit to some relatives in a distant part of the Republic. Frank Hamersley's eyes never rested on it without his wishing the original at home.

The two gentlemen upon the housetop were leisuring away the time in the indulgence of a cigar, watching the water-fowl that swam and plunged on the bosom of the broad shallow stream, listening to the hoarse croakings of pelicans and the shriller screams of the *guaya* cranes. It was the hour of evening, when these birds become especially stridulent.

"And so you must go to-morrow, Señor Francisco?" said his host, taking the cigaritto from between his teeth, and looking inquiringly into the face of the Kentuckian.

"There is no help for it, colonel. The caravan with which I came out will be leaving Santa Fé the day after to-morrow, and there's just time for me to get there. Unless I go along with it, there may be no other opportunity for months to come, and one cannot cross the plains alone."

"Well, I suppose I must lose you. I am sorry, and selfishly, too, for, as you see, I am somewhat lonely here. There's not one of my officers, with the exception of our old *medico*, exactly of the sort to be companionable. True, I have enough occupation, as you may have by this time discovered, in looking after our neighbours, the *Indios bravos*, who, knowing the skeleton of a regiment I've got, are growing saucier every day. I only wish I had a score or two of your stalwart trappers, who now and then pay a visit to Albuquerque. Well, my sister will soon be here, and she, brave girl, has plenty of life in her, though she be but young. What a joyous creature she is, wild as a mustang filly fresh caught. I wish, Don Francisco, you could have stayed to make her acquaintance. I am sure you would be delighted with her."

If the portrait on the wall was anything of a faithful likeness, Hamersley could not have been otherwise. This was his reflection, though, for certain reasons, he did not in speech declare it.

"It is to be hoped we shall meet again, Colonel Miranda," was his ingenious rejoinder. "If I did not have this hope, I should now be parting from you with greater regret. Indeed, I have more than a presentiment we shall meet again; since I've made up my mind on a certain thing."

"On what, Don Francisco?"

"On returning to New Mexico."

"To settle in the country?"

"Not exactly that; only for a time—long enough to enable me to dispose of a cargo of merchandise in exchange for a bag of your big Mexican dollars."

"Ah! you intend to become one of the prairie merchants, then?"

"I do. That intention has been the cause of my visiting your country. I am old enough to think of some calling, and have always had a fancy for the adventurous life of the prairie trader. As I have sufficient means to stock a small caravan for myself, I think now of trying it. My present trip has been merely one of experiment and exploration. I am satisfied with the result, and, if no accident arise, you may see me back on the Del Norte before either of us be twelve months older."

"Then, indeed, is there a hope of our meeting again. I am rejoiced at it. But, Señor Don Francisco," continued his host, changing to a serious tone, "a word lest I might forget it—a word of counsel, or warning, I may call it. I have observed that you are too unsuspicious, too regardless of danger. It does not all lie upon the prairies, or among red-skinned savages. There is as much of it here, amid the abodes of our so-called civilisation. When you are travelling through this country bear your late antagonist in mind, and should you at any time meet, beware of him. I have given you some hints about the character of Gil Uraga. I have not told you all. He is worse than you can even imagine. I know him well. Do you see that little house, out yonder on the other side of the river?"

Hamersley nodded assent.

"In that hovel he was born. His father was what we call a *pelado*—a poor devil, with scarce a coat to his back. Himself the same, but something worse. He has left in his native place a record of crimes well known, with others more than suspected. In short, he is, as I have told you, a robber. No doubt you wonder that such a man should be an officer in our army. That is because you are ignorant of the state of our service—our society as well. It is but the result of constantly recurring changes in our political system. Still you may feel surprise at his holding this commission, with the patriotic party—the pure one—in power, as it now is. That might be inexplicable even to myself, since I know that he will be traitor to our cause when convenient to him. But I also know the explanation. There is a power, even when the party exercising it is not in the ascendant—an influence that works by sap and secrecy. It is that of our hierarchy. Gil Uraga is one of its tools, since it exactly suits his low instincts and treacherous training. Whenever the day is ripe for a fresh *pronunciamento* against our liberties—if we are so unfortunate as to have one—he will be amongst the foremost of the traitors. *Carrai*! I can think of him only with disgust and loathing. Would you believe it, señor, that this fellow, now that epaulettes have been set on his shoulders—placed there for some vile service—has the audacity to aspire to the hand of my sister? Adela Miranda standing in bridal robes by the side of Gil Uraga! I would rather see her in her shroud!"

Hamersley's bosom heaved up as he listened to the last words, and with emotion almost equalling that which excited his host. He had just been thinking about the portrait upon the wall, and how beautiful the original must be. Now hearing her name coupled with that of the ruffian whose blow he had felt, and whose blood he had spilled, he almost regretted not having ended that duel by killing his adversary outright.

"But surely, Colonel Miranda," he said at length, "there could be no danger of such an event as that you speak of?"

"Never, so long as I live. But, amigo, as you have learnt, this is a strange land—a country of quick changes. I am here to-day, commanding in this district, with power, I may almost say, over the lives of all around me. To-morrow I may be a fugitive, or dead. If the latter, where is she, my poor sister, going to find the arm that could protect her?"

Again the breast of Hamersley heaved in a convulsive manner. Strange as it might appear, the words of his newly-made friend seemed like an appeal to him. And it is just possible some such thought was in the mind of the Mexican colonel. In the strong man by his side he saw the type of a race who can protect; just such an oak as he would wish to see his sister extend her arms tendril-like around, and cling on to for life.

Hamersley could not help having vague and varied misgivings; yet among them was one purpose he had already spoken of—a determination to return to Albuquerque.

"I am sure to be back here," he said, as if the promise was meant to tranquillise the apprehensions of the colonel. Then, changing to a more careless tone, he added,—

"I cannot come by the spring caravans; there would not be time enough to make my arrangements. But there is a more southern route, lately discovered, that can be travelled at any season. Perhaps I may try that. In any case, I shall write you by the trains leaving the States in the spring, so that you may know when to expect me. And if, Colonel Miranda," he added, after a short reflective pause, in which his countenance assumed a new and graver form of expression, "if any political trouble, such as you speak of, should occur, and you may find it necessary to flee from your own land, I need not tell you that in mine you will find a friend and a home. After what has happened here, you may depend upon the first being true, and the second hospitable, however humble."

On that subject there was no further exchange of speech. The two individuals, so oddly as accidentally introduced, flung aside the stumps of their cigars; and, clasping hands, stood regarding one another with the gaze of a sincere, unspeakable friendship.

Next morning saw the Kentuckian riding away from Albuquerque towards the capital of New Mexico, an escort of dragoons accompanying him, sent by the Mexican colonel as a protection against marauding Indians.

But all along the road, and for months after, he was haunted with the memory of that sweet face seen upon the *sola* wall; and instead of laughing at himself for having fallen in love with a portrait, he but longed to return, and look upon its original—chafing under an apprehension, with which the parting words of his New Mexican host had painfully inspired him.

Chapter Four.
A Pronunciamento.

A little less than a quarter of a century ago the Navajo Indians were the terror of the New Mexican settlements. It was no uncommon thing for them to charge into the streets of a town, shoot down or spear the citizens, plunder the shops, and seize upon such women as they wanted, carrying these captives to their far-off fastnesses in the land of Navajoa.

In the *canon* de Chelley these savages had their headquarters, with the temple and *estufa*, where the sacred fire of *Moctezuma* was never permitted to go out; and there, in times past, when Mexico was misruled by the tyrant Santa Anna, might have been seen scores of white women, captives to the Navajo nation, women well born and tenderly brought up, torn from their homes on the Rio del Norte, and forced to become the wives of their red-skinned captors—oftener their concubines and slaves. White children, too, in like manner, growing up among the children of their despoilers; on reaching manhood to forget all the ties of kindred, with the *liens* of civilised life—in short, to be as much savages as those who had adopted them.

At no period was this despoliation more rife than in the time of which we write. It had reached its climax of horrors, day after day recurring, when Colonel Miranda became military commandant of the district of Albuquerque; until not only this town, but Santa Fé, the capital of the province itself, was menaced with destruction by the red marauders. Not alone the Navajoes on the west, but the Apaches on the south, and the Comanches who peopled the plains to the east, made intermittent and frequent forays upon the towns and villages lying along the renowned Rio del Norte. There were no longer any outlying settlements or isolated plantations. The grand *haciendas*, as the humble *ranchos*, were alike lain in ruins. In the walled town alone was there safety for the white inhabitants of Nuevo Mexico, or for those Indians, termed *mansos*, converted to Christianity, and leagued with them in the pursuits of civilisation. And, indeed, not much safety either within towns—even in Albuquerque itself.

Imbued with a spirit of patriotism, Colonel Miranda, in taking charge of the district—his native place, as already known—determined on doing his best to protect it from further spoliation; and for this purpose had appealed to the central government to give him an increase to the forces under his command.

It came in the shape of a squadron of lancers from Chihuahua, whose garrison only spared them on their being replaced by a troop of like strength, sent on from the capital of the country.

It was not very pleasant to the commandant of Albuquerque to see Captain Gil Uraga in command of the subsidy thus granted him. But the lancer officer met him in a friendly manner, professing cordiality, apparently forgetful of their duelling feud, and, at least outwardly, showing the submission due to the difference of their rank.

Engaged in frequent affairs with the Indians, and expeditions in pursuit of them, for a while things seemed to go smoothly enough.

But as Adela Miranda had now returned home, and was residing with her brother, in the interludes of tranquillity he could not help having some concern for her. He was well aware of Uraga's aspirations; and, though loathing the very sight of the man, he was, nevertheless, compelled to tolerate his companionship to a certain extent, and could not well deny him the *entrée* of his house.

At first the subordinate bore himself with becoming meekness. Mock humility it was, and soon so proved itself. For, as the days passed, rumours reached the distant department of New Mexico that the old tyrant Santa Anna was again returning to power. And, in proportion as these gained strength, so increased Gil Uraga's confidence in himself, till at length he assumed an air of effrontery—almost insolence—towards his superior officer; and towards the sister, in the interviews he was permitted with her, a manner significantly corresponding.

These were few, and still less frequent, as his brusque behaviour began to manifest itself. Observing it, Colonel Miranda at length came to the determination that the lancer captain should no longer enter into his house—at least, by invitation. Any future relations between them must be in the strict execution of their respective military duties.

"Yes, sister," he said, one afternoon, as Adela was buckling on his sword-belt, and helping to equip him for the evening parade, "Uraga must come here no more. I well understand the cause of his contumacious behaviour. The priest party is again getting the ascendency. If they succeed, heaven help poor Mexico. And, I may add, heaven help us!"

Drawing the girl to his bosom with a fond affectionate embrace, he gave her a brother's kiss. Then, striding forth, he sprang upon a saddled horse held in waiting, and rode off to parade his troops on the *plaza* of Albuquerque.

A ten minutes' trot brought him into their presence. They were not drawn up in line, or other formation, to receive him. On the contrary, as he approached the *cuartel*, he saw strange sights, and heard sounds corresponding. Everything was in confusion—soldiers rushing to and fro, uttering seditious cries. Among these were "Viva Santa Anna!"

"Viva el General Armijo!"

"Viva el *Coronel* Uraga!"

Beyond doubt it was a *pronunciamento*. The old regime under which Colonel Miranda held authority was passing away, and a new one about to be initiated.

Drawing his sword and putting spur to his horse, he dashed in among the disaffected men.

A few of the faithful ran up, and ranged themselves by his side.

Then commenced a struggle, with shouting, shooting, sabring, and lance-thrusts. Several fell—some dead, some only disabled; among the last, Colonel Miranda himself, gravely wounded.

In ten minutes it was all over; and the commandant of Albuquerque, no longer commanding, lay lodged in the garrison *carcel*; Captain Gil Uraga, now colonel, replacing him as the supreme military officer of the district.

While all around ran the rumour that Don Antonio Lopes de Santa Anna was once more master of Mexico; his satellite, Manuel Armijo, again Governor of Santa Fé.

Chapter Five.
"Why comes he not?"

"What delays Valerian? What can be keeping him?"

These questions came from Adela Miranda, on the evening of that same day, standing in the door of her brother's house, with eyes bent along the road leading to Albuquerque. Valerian was her brother's baptismal name, and it was about his absence she was anxious.

For this she had reasons—more than one. Though still only a young girl, she quite understood the political situation of the Mexican Republic; at all times shifting, of late more critical than usual. In her brother's confidence, she had been kept posted up in all that transpired in the capital, as also the district over which he held military command, and knew the danger of which he was himself apprehensive—every day drawing nigher and nigher.

Shortly after his leaving her she had heard shots, with a distant murmur of voices, in the direction of the town. From the *azolea*, to which she had ascended, she could note these noises more distinctly, but fancied them to be salutes, vivas, and cheers. Still, there was nothing much in that. It might be some jubilation of the soldiery at the ordinary evening parade; and, remembering that the day was a *fiesta*, she thought less of it.

But, as night drew down, and her brother had not returned, she began to feel some slight apprehension. He had promised to be back for a dinner that was long since due—a repast she had herself prepared, more sumptuous than common on account of the saint's day. This was it that elicited the anxious self-asked interrogatories.

After giving utterance to them, she paced backward and forward; now standing in the portal and gazing along the road; now returning to the *sola de comida*, to look upon the table, with cloth spread, wines decanted, fruits and flowers on the épergne—all but the dishes that waited serving till Valerian should show himself.

To look on something besides—a portrait that hung upon the wall, underneath her own. It was a small thing—a mere photographic carte-de-visite. But it was the likeness of one who had a large place in her brother's heart, if not in her own. In hers, how could it? It was the photograph of a man she had never seen—Frank Hamersley. He had left it with Colonel Miranda, as a souvenir of their short but friendly intercourse.

Did Colonel Miranda's sister regard it in that light? She could not in any other. Still, as she gazed upon it, a thought was passing through her mind somewhat different from a sentiment of simple friendship. Her brother had told her all—the circumstances that led to his acquaintance with Hamersley; of the duel, and in what a knightly manner the Kentuckian had carried himself; adding his own commentaries in a very flattering fashion. This, of itself, had been enough to pique curiosity in a young girl, just escaped from her convent school; but added to the outward semblance of the stranger, by the sun made lustrous—so lustrous inwardly—Adela Miranda was moved by something more than curiosity. As she stood regarding the likeness of Frank Hamersley she felt very much as he had done looking at hers—in love with one only known by portrait and repute.

In such there is nothing strange nor new. Many a reader of this tale could speak of a similar experience.

While gazing on the carte-de-visite she was roused from the sweet reverie it had called up by hearing footsteps outside. Someone coming in through the *saggan*.

"Valerian at last!"

The steps sounded as if the man making them were in a hurry. So should her brother be, having so long delayed his return.

She glided out to meet him with an interrogatory on her lips.

"Valerian?"—this suddenly changing to the exclamation, "*Madre de Dios!* 'Tis not my brother!"

It was not, but a man pale and breathless—a *peon* of the establishment—who, on seeing her, gasped out,—

"Señorita! I bring sad news. There's been a mutiny at the cuartel—a *pronunciamento*. The rebels have had it all their own way, and I am sorry to tell you that the colonel, your brother—"

"What of him? Speak! Is he—"

"Not killed, *nina*; only wounded, and a prisoner."

Adela Miranda did not swoon nor faint. She was not of the nervous kind. Nurtured amid dangers, most of her life accustomed to alarms from Indian incursions, as well as revolutionary risings, she remained calm.

She dispatched messengers to the town, secretly, one after another; and, while awaiting their reports, knelt before an image of the Virgin, and prayed.

Up till midnight her couriers went, and came. Then one who was more than a messenger—her brother himself!

As already reported to her, he was wounded, and came accompanied by the surgeon of the garrison, a friend. They arrived at the house in hot haste, as if pursued.

And they were so, as she soon after learnt.

There was just time for Colonel Miranda to select the most cherished of his *penates*; pack them on a *recua* of mules, then mount, and make away.

They had scarce cleared the premises when the myrmidons of the new commandant, led by the man himself, rode up and took possession of the place.

By this time, and by good luck, the ruffian was intoxicated—so drunk he could scarce comprehend what was passing around him. It seemed like a dream to him to be told that Colonel Miranda had got clear away; a more horrid one to hear that she whom he designed for a victim had escaped from his clutches.

When morning dawned, and in soberer mood he listened to the reports of those sent in pursuit—all telling the same tale of non-success—he raved like one in a frenzy of madness. For the escape of the late Commandant of Albuquerque had robbed him of two things—to him the sweetest in life—one, revenge on the man he heartily hated; the other, possession of the woman he passionately loved.

Chapter Six.
Surrounded.

A plain of pure sand, glaring red-yellow under the first rays of the rising sun; towards the east and west apparently illimitable, but interrupted northward by a chain of table-topped hills, and along its southern edge by a continuous cliff, rising wall-like to the height of several hundred feet, and trending each way beyond the verge of vision.

About half-distance between this prolonged escarpment and the outlying hills six large "Conestoga" waggons, locked tongue and tail together, enclosing a lozenge-shaped or elliptical space—a *corral*—inside which are fifteen men and five horses.

Only ten of the men are living; the other five are dead, their bodies lying a-stretch between the wheels of the waggons. Three of the horses have succumbed to the same fate.

Outside are many dead mules; several still attached to the protruding poles, that have broken as their bodies fell crashing across them. Fragments of leather straps and cast gearing tell of others that have torn loose, and scoured off from the perilous spot.

Inside and all around are traces of a struggle—the ground scored and furrowed by the hoofs of horses, and the booted feet of men, with here and there little rivulets and pools of blood. This, fast filtering into the sand, shows freshly spilled—some of it still smoking.

All the signs tell of recent conflict. And so should they, since it is still going on, or only suspended to recommence a new scene of the strife, which promises to be yet more terrible and sanguinary than that already terminated.

A tragedy easy of explanation. There is no question about why the waggons have been stopped, or how the men, mules, and horses came to be killed. Distant about three hundred yards upon the sandy plain are other men and horses, to the number of near two hundred. Their half-naked bodies of bronze colour, fantastically marked with devices in chalk-white, charcoal-black, and vermillion red—their buckskin breech-clouts and leggings, with plumes sticking tuft-like above their crowns—all these insignia show them to be Indians.

It is a predatory band of the red pirates, who have attacked a travelling party of whites—no new spectacle on the prairies.

They have made the first onslaught, which was intended to stampede the caravan, and at once capture it. This was done before daybreak. Foiled in the attempt, they are now laying siege to it, having surrounded it on all sides at a distance just beyond range of the rifles of those besieged. Their line forms the circumference of a circle of which the waggon clump is the centre. It is not very regularly preserved, but ever changing, ever in motion, like some vast constricting serpent that has thrown its body into a grand coil around its victim, to close when ready to give the fatal squeeze.

In this case the victim appears to have no hope of escape—no alternative but to succumb.

That the men sheltered behind the waggons have not "gone under" at the first onslaught is significative of their character. Of a surety they are not common emigrants, crossing the prairies on their way to a new home. Had they been so, they could not have "corralled" their unwieldy vehicles with such promptitude; for they had started from their night camp, and the attack was made while the train was in motion—advantage being taken of their slow drag through the soft, yielding sand. And had they been but ordinary emigrants they would not have stood so stoutly on the defence, and shown such an array of dead enemies around them. For among the savages outside can be seen at least a score of lifeless forms lying prostrate upon the plain.

For the time, there is a suspension of hostilities. The red men, disappointed by the failure of their first charge, have retreated back to a safe distance. The death-dealing bullets of the whites, of which they have had fatal proof, hold them there.

But the pause is not likely to be for long, as their gestures indicate. On one side of the circle a body of them clumped together hold counsel. Others gallop around it, bearing orders and instructions that evidently relate to a changed plan of attack. With so much blood before their eyes, and the bodies of their slain comrades, it is not likely they will retire from the ground. In their shouts there is a ring of resolved vengeance, which promises a speedy renewal of the attack.

"Who do you think they are?" asks Frank Hamersley, the proprietor of the assaulted caravan. "Are they Comanches, Walt?"

"Yis, Kimanch," answers the individual thus addressed; "an' the wust kind o' Kimanch. They're a band o' the cowardly Tenawas. I kin tell by thar bows. Don't ye see that thar's two bends in 'em?"

"I do."

"Wal, that's the sort o' bow the Tenawas carry—same's the Apash."

"The Indians on this route were reported friendly. Why have they attacked us, I wonder?"

"Injuns ain't niver friendly—not Tenawas. They've been riled considerably of late by the Texans on the Trinity. Besides, I reck'n I kin guess another reezun. It's owin' to some whites as crossed this way last year. Thar war a scrimmage atween them and the redskins, in the which some squaws got kilt—I mout say murdered. Thar war some Mexikins along wi' the whites, an' it war them that did it. An' now we've got to pay for their cussed crooked conduk."

"What's best for us to do?"

"Thar's no best, I'm afeerd. I kin see no chance 'cept to fight it out to the bitter eend. Thar's no mercy in them yells—ne'er a morsel o' it."

"What do they intend doing next, think you?"

"Jest yet 'taint easy to tell. Thar's somethin' on foot among 'em—some darned Injun trick. Clar as I kin see, that big chief wi' the red cross on his ribs, air him they call the Horned Lizard; an' ef it be, thar ain't a cunniner coon on all this contynent. He's sharp enough to contrive some tight trap for us. The dose we've gin the skunks may keep 'em off for a while—not long, I reck'n. Darnation! Thar's five o' our fellows wiped out already. It looks ugly, an' like enuf we've all got to go under."

"Don't you think our best way will be to make a dash for it, and try to cut through them. If we stay here they'll starve us out. We haven't water enough in the waggons to give us a drink apiece."

"I know all that, an' hev thort o' 't. But you forget about our hosses. Thar's only two left alive—yours and myen. All the rest air shot or stampedoed. Thurfor, but two o' us would stand a chance o' gettin' clar, an' it slim enough."

"You are right, Walt; I did not think of that I won't forsake the men, even if assured of my own safety—never!"

"Nobody as knows you, Frank Hamersley, need be tolt that."

"Boys!" cries out Hamersley, in a voice that can be heard all through the corral; "I needn't tell you that we're in a fix, and a bad one. There's no help for us but to fight it out. And if we must die, let us die together."

A response from eight voices coming from different sides—for those watching the movements of the enemy are posted round the enclosure—tells there is not a craven among them. Though only teamsters, they are truly courageous men—most of them natives of Kentucky and Tennessee.

"In any case," continues the owner of the caravan, "we must hold our ground till night. In the darkness there may be some chance of our being able to steal past them."

These words have scarce passed the lips of the young prairie merchant, when their effect is counteracted by an exclamation. It comes from Walt Wilder, who has been acting as guide to the party.

"Dog-goned!" he cries; "not the shadder o' a chance. They ain't goin' to give us till night. I knewed the Horned Lizard 'ud be after some trick."

"What?" inquire several voices.

"Look whar that lot's stannin' out yonder. Can't ye guess what they're at, Frank Hamersley?"

"No. I only see that they have bows in their hands."

"An' arrers, too. Don't you obsarve them wroppin' somethin' round the heads o' the arrers—looks like bits o' rags? Aye, rags it air, sopped in spittles and powder. They're agoin' to set the waggons afire! They air, by God!"

Chapter Seven.
Fiery Messengers.

The teamsters, each of whom is watching the post assigned to him, despite the danger, already extreme, see fresh cause of alarm in Wilder's words. Some slight hope had hitherto upheld them. Under the protection of the waggons they might sustain a siege, so long as their ammunition lasts; and before it gave out some chance, though they cannot think what, might turn up in their favour. It was a mere reflection founded on probabilities still unscrutinised—the last tenacious struggle before hope gives way to utter and palpable despair. Hamersley's words had for an instant cheered them; for the thought of the Indians setting fire to the waggons had not occurred to any of the party. It was a thing unknown to their experience; and, at such a distance, might be supposed impossible.

But, as they now look around them, and note the canvas tilts, and light timbers, dry as chips from long exposure to the hot prairie sun; the piles of dry goods—woollen blankets, cotton, and silk stuffs—intended for the stores of Chihuahua, some of which they have hastily pulled from their places to form protecting barricades—when they see all this, and then the preparations the Indians are engaged in making, no wonder that they feel dismay on Walt Wilder shouting out, "They're agoin' to set the waggons afire!"

The announcement, although carrying alarm, conveys no counsel. Even their guide, with a life-long experience on the prairies, is at a loss how they ought to act in this unexpected emergency. In the waggons water there is none—at least not enough to drown out a conflagration such as that threatened; and from the way the assailants are gesturing the traders can predict that ere long, a shower of fiery shafts will be sent into their midst. None of them but have knowledge sufficient to admonish them of what is intended. Even if they had never set foot upon a prairie, their school stories and legends of early life would tell them. They have all read, or heard, of arrows with tinder tied around their barbs, on fire and spitting sparks, or brightly ablaze.

If any are ignorant of this sort of missile, or the mode of dispatching it on its mischievous errand, their ignorance is not destined longer to continue. Almost as soon as Wilder has given utterance to the warning words, half a score of the savages can be seen springing to the backs of their horses, each bearing a bow with a bunch of the prepared arrows. And before a single preventive step can be taken by the besieged traders, or any counsel exchanged between them, the pyrotechnic display has commenced.

The bowmen gallop in circles around the besieged enclosure, their bodies concealed behind those of their horses—only a leg and an arm seen, or now and then a face for an instant, soon withdrawn. Not exactly in circles but in spiral rings—at each turn drawing closer and nearer, till the true distance is attained for casting the inflammatory shafts.

"Stand to your guns, men!" is the hurried command of the guide, backed by a kind of encouragement from the proprietor of the caravan.

"Now, boys!" adds the guide, "ye've got to look out for squalls. Keep two an' two of ye thegither. While one brings down the hoss, t' other take care o' the rider as he gits unkivered. Make sure afore ye pull trigger, an' don't waste so much as the snappin' o' a cap. Thar goes the first o' the fire works!"

As Wilder speaks, a spark is seen to shoot out from one of the circling cavaliers, which rising rocket-like into the air, comes in parabolic curve towards the corral.

It falls short some twenty yards and lies smoking and sputtering in the sand.

"They han't got thar range yit," cries the guide; "but this child hez got his—leastwise for that skunk on the clay-bank mustang. So hyar goes to rub him off o' the list o' fire shooters."

And simultaneous with the last word is heard the crack of Wilder's rifle.

The young prairie merchant by his side, supposing him to have aimed only at the Indian's horse, has raised his own gun, ready to take the rider as soon as uncovered.

"No need, Frank," shouts the guide, restraining him. "Walt Wilder don't waste two charges o' powder that way. Keep yur bullet for the karkidge o' the next as comes 'ithin range. Look yonder! I know'd I'd fetch him out o' his stirrups—tight as he's tried to cling to 'em. Thar he goes to grass!"

Hamersley, as the others on the same side of the corral, were under the belief that the shot had been a miss; for the Indian at whom it was aimed still stuck to his horse, and was carried for some distance on in curving career.

Nor did the animal show any sign of having been hit. But the rider did. While engaged in the effort of sending his arrow, the savage had exposed his face, one arm, and part of the other. Ere he could withdraw them, Walt's bullet had struck the arm that supported him, breaking the bone close to the elbow-joint. He has clung on with the tenacity of a shot squirrel, knowing that to let go will be certain death to him. But, despite all his efforts, the crippled arm fails to sustain him; and, with a despairing cry, he at length tumbles to the ground. Before he can rise to his feet, his body is bored by a leaden messenger from one of the men watching on that side, which lays him lifeless along the sand.

No cheer of triumph ascends from among the waggons; the situation of those who defend them is too serious for any idle exhibition. The man who has fired the last shot only hastens to re-load, while the others remain mute and motionless—each on the look-out for a like opportunity.

The fall of their comrade has taught the freebooters a lesson, and for a time they make their approach with more caution. But the shouts of those standing spectators in the outer circle stimulate them to fresh efforts, as the slightest show of cowardice would surely cause them to be taunted. Those entrusted with the fiery arrows are all young warriors, chosen for this dangerous service, or volunteers to perform it. The eyes of their chief, and the braves of the tribe, are upon them. They are thirsting for glory, and hold their lives as of little account, in the face of an achievement that will gain them the distinction most coveted by an Indian youth—that which will give him rank as a warrior, and perhaps some day raise him to a chieftaincy.

Stimulated by this thought, they soon forget the check caused by the fall of their comrade; and, laying aside caution, ride nearer and nearer, till their arrows, one after another, hurtle through the air, and dropping like a continuous shower of spent rocket-sticks upon the covers of the corralled waggons.

Several of them fall to shots from the barricade, but then places are supplied by fresh volunteers from the outer circle; and the sparkling shower is kept up, till a curl of smoke is seen soaring above the white tilts of the waggons, and soon after others at different places and on different sides of the enclosure.

As yet the besieged have not seen this. The powder-smoke puffing up from their own guns, discharged in quick repetition, obscures everything in a thick, sulphurous cloud; so that even the white covers of the waggons are scarce distinguishable, much less the spots where it has commenced smoking.

Not long, however, till something besides smoke makes itself visible, as also audible. Here and there flames flicker up, with a sharp crackling noise, which continues. The one is not flashes from the guns, nor the other a snapping of percussion-caps.

Wilder, with eyes turning to all points, is the first to perceive this.

"We're on fire, boys!" he vociferates; "on fire everywhar!"

"Great God! yes! What are we to do?" several ask, despairingly.

"What air we to do?" shouts the guide, in response. "What kin we do, but fight it out to the death, an' then die! So let us die, not like dogs, but as men—as Americans!"

Chapter Eight.
Knife, Pistol, and Hatchet.

The brave words had scarce passed from Walt Wilder's lips when the waggons became enveloped in a cloud of smoke. From all sides it rolled into the corral till those inside could no longer see one another.

Still through the obscurity rang their cries of mutual encouragement, repeating the determination so tersely expressed.

They knew they had no water by which to extinguish the fast-threatening flames; yet in that moment of emergency they thought of an expedient. There were shovels in the waggons; and laying hold of these, they commenced flinging sand over the places that had caught fire, with the intent to smother the incipient blaze. Left alone, and with time, they might have succeeded. But they were not left alone, for the savages, seeing the advantage they had gained, were now fast closing for a final charge upon the corral, and the implements of industry had to be abandoned.

These were thrown despairingly aside; and the besieged, once more grasping their rifles, sprang back into the waggons—each with eager eye searching for an assailant. Though themselves half blinded by the smoke, they could still see the enemy outside; for the Indians, grown confident by the *coup* they had made, were now riding recklessly near. Quick came the reports of rifles—faster and more frequent than ever; fast as ten men, all practised marksmen, could load and fire. In less than sixty seconds nearly a score of savages dropped to the death-dealing bullets, till the plain appeared strewn with dead bodies.

But the crisis had come—the time for a general charge of the whole band; and now the dusky outside ring was seen gradually contracting towards the corral—the savages advancing from all sides, some on foot, others on horseback, all eager to secure the trophy of a scalp.

On they came, violently gesticulating, and uttering wild vengeful shouts.

With the besieged it was a moment for despair. The waggons were on fire all around them, and in several places flames were beginning to flicker up through the smoke. They no longer thought of making any attempt to extinguish them. They knew it would be idle.

Did they think of surrender? No—not a man of them. That would have been equally idle. In the voices of the advancing foe there was not an accent of mercy.

Surrender! And be slain afterwards! Before which to be tortured, perhaps dragged at the horse's tail, or set up as a target for the Tenawa sharpshooters to practise at. No! They would have to die anyhow. Better now than then. They were not the men to offer both cheeks to the insulter. They could resign sweet life, but death would be all the sweeter with corpses of Indians lying thickly around them. They would first make a hecatomb of their hated foes, and then fall upon it. That is the sort of death preferred by the prairie man—hunter, trapper, or trader—glorious to him as the cannon-furrowed field to the soldier. That is the sort of death of which Walt Wilder spoke when he said, "Let us die, not like dogs, but as men—as Americans!"

By this time the smoke had completely enveloped the waggons, the enclosed space between, and a fringe of some considerable width around them. But a still darker ring was all around—the circle of savage horsemen, who from all sides were galloping up and dismounting to make surer work of the slaughter. The warriors jostled one another as they pressed forward afoot, each thirsting for a scalp.

The last throe of the conflict had come. It was no longer to be a duel at a distance—no more a contest between rifle-bullets and barbed arrows; but the close, desperate, hand-to-hand contest of pistol, knife, spear, club, and hatchet.

The ten white men—none of them yet *hors de combat*—knew well what was before them. Not one of them blanched or talked of backing. They did not even think of surrender. It would have been too late to sue for mercy, had they been so inclined.

But they were not. Attacked without provocation, and treacherously, as they had been, their fury was stronger than their fear; and anger now nerved them to frenzied energy of action.

The savages had already closed around the waggons, clustering upon the wheels, some like snakes, wriggling through the spaces left undefended. Rifles ceased to ring; but pistols cracked—repeating pistols, that dealt death at every shot, sending redskin after redskin to the happy hunting grounds. And by the pistol's flash blades were seen gleaming through the smoke—now bright, anon dimmed, and dripping blood.

For every white man that fell, at least three red ones went down upon the sand.

The unequal contest could not long continue. Scarce ten minutes did it last, and but for the obscuring smoke five would have finished it. This was in favour of the assailed, enabling them to act with advantage against the assailants. Such a quick, wholesale slaughter did the white men make with their revolvers that the savages, surprised and staggered by it, for a moment recoiled, and appeared as if again going to retreat.

They did not—they dared not. Their superior numbers—the shame of being defeated by such a handful of foes—the glory of conquest—and, added to it, an angry vengeance now hot in their hearts—all urged them on; and the attack was renewed with greater earnestness than ever.

Throughout every scene in the strife Frank Hamersley had comported himself with a courage that made his men feel less fear of death, and less regret to die by his side. Fighting like a lion, he had been here, and there, and everywhere. He had done his full share of slaving.

It was all in vain. Though standing in the midst of thick smoke, unseeing and unseen, he knew that most of his faithful men had fallen. He was admonished of this by their less frequent responses to his cries of encouragement, telling him the struggle was close upon its termination. No wonder his fury was fast giving place to despair. But it was no craven fear, nor any thought of escape. His determination not to be taken alive was strong as ever.

His hand still firmly clasped his bowie-knife, its blade dripping with the blood of more than one enemy; for into the body of more than one had he plunged it. He clutched it with the determination still farther to kill—to take yet another life before parting with his own.

It was hopeless, useless slaughter; but it was sweet. Almost insane with anger, he thought it sweet.

Three dusky antagonists lay dead at his feet, and he was rushing across the corral in search of a fourth. A giant figure loomed up before him, looking more gigantic from the magnifying effect of the smoke. It was not that of a savage; it was Walt Wilder.

"Dead beat!" hoarsely and hurriedly muttered the guide. "We must go under, Frank. We're boun' to go under, if we don't—"

"Don't what, Walt?"

"Git away from hyar."

"Impossible."

"No. Thar's still a chance, I think—for us two anyways. There ain't many o' the others left, an' ef thar war, we can't do 'em any good now. Our stayin' 'ud be no use—no use dyin' along wi' 'em; while ef we get clar, we mout live to revenge 'em. Don't ye see our two horses are still safe? Thar they air, cowerin' clost in agin one o' the waggons. 'Tain't much kit? I admit; still thar's a shadder. Come, Frank, and let's try it."

Hamersley hesitated. It was at thought of deserting even the last of his faithful followers, who had sacrificed, or were still sacrificing, their lives in his service. But, as the guide had truly said what good could he do them by staying and getting killed? And he might survive to avenge them!

The last reflection would have decided him! But Wilder had not waited for him to determine. While speaking the urgent words, he laid his huge hand upon Hamersley's shoulder and half led, half dragged him in the direction of the horses. "Keep hold o' yur rifle, though it air empty," hurriedly counselled the guide. "If we shed get away, it will be needed. We mout as well go under hyar as be upon the pararira without a gun. Now mount!"

Almost mechanically the young Kentuckian climbed upon the back of the horse nearest to him—his own. The guide had not yet mounted his; but, as could be seen through the smoke, was leaning against the wheel of one of the waggons. In an instant after Hamersley perceived that the vehicle was in motion, and could hear a slight grating noise as the tire turned in the sand. The great Conestoga, with its load had yielded to the strength of the Colossus.

In another instant he had sprung upon his horse's back and riding close to Hamersley, muttered in his ear, "Now I've opened a crack atween two o' the wehicles. Let's cut out through it. We kin keep in the kiver o' the smoke as far as it'll screen us. You foller, an' see that ye don't lose sight o' me. If we must go under in the eend, let it be out on the open plain, an' not shut up hyar like badgers in a barr'l. Follow me clost, Frank. Now or niver!"

Almost mechanically the young Kentuckian yielded obedience; and in ten seconds after the two horsemen had cleared the waggon clump, with the shouting crowd that encircled it and were going at full gallop across the sand-strewn plain.

Chapter Nine.
Quarrelling over Scalps.

Nearly simultaneous with the departure of the two horsemen came the closing scene of the conflict. Indeed it ended on the instant of their riding off. For of their comrades left behind there was not one upon his feet— not one able to fire another shot, or strike another blow. All lay dead, or wounded, among the waggons; some of the dead, as the wounded, clasping the handle of a knife whose blade reeked with blood, or a pistol from whose muzzle the smoke was still oozing.

But soon among the whites there were no wounded, for the hovering host, having closed in from all sides, leaped from their horses, swarmed over the barrier between, tomahawking the last that showed signs of life, or thrusting them with their long lances, and pinning them to the sand. Through the body of every white man at least a half-dozen spear-blades were passed, while a like number of savages stood exultingly over, or danced triumphantly around it.

And now ensued a scene that might be symbolised only among wild beasts or fiends in the infernal regions. It was a contest for possession of the scalps of those who had fallen—each of the victors claiming one. Some stood with bared blades ready to peel them off, while others held out hands and weapons to prevent it. From the lips of the competitors came shouts and expostulations, while their eyes flashed fire, and their arms rose and fell in furious gesticulations.

Amidst their demoniac jargon could be heard a voice louder than all, thundering forth a command. It was to desist from their threatening strife and extinguish the flames that still flared up over the waggons. He who spoke was the one with the red cross upon his breast, its bars of bright vermilion gleaming like fire against the sombre background of his skin. He was the chief of the Tenawa Comanches—the Horned Lizard—as Wilder had justly conjectured.

And as their chief he was instantly obeyed. The wranglers, one and all, promptly suspended their disputes; and flinging their weapons aside, at once set to carrying out his orders.

Seizing upon the shovels, late dropped from the hands of their now lifeless antagonists, and plying them to better purpose, they soon smothered the flame, and the smoke too, till only a thin drift stole up through the sand thrown thickly over it.

Meanwhile a man, in appearance somewhat differing from the rest, was seen moving among them.

Indian in garb and guise, savage in his accoutrements, as the colour of his skin, he nevertheless, showed features more resembling races that are civilised. His countenance was of a cast apparently Caucasian, its lineaments unlike those of the American aboriginal; above all, unlike in his having a heavy beard, growing well forward upon his cheeks, and bushing down below the chin.

True, that among the Comanche Indians bearded men are occasionally met with—*mestizos*, the descendants of renegade whites. But none paraded as he, who now appeared stalking around the ruined caravan. And there was another individual by his side, who had also hair upon his cheeks, though thinner and more straggling; while the speech passing between the two was not the guttural tongue of the Tenawa Comanches, but pure Mexican Spanish.

Both were on foot, having dismounted; he with the heavy beard leading, the other keeping after as if in attendance.

The former flitted from one to another of those who lay slain; in turn stooping over each corpse, and scrutinising it—to some giving but a cursory glance, to others more careful examination—then leaving each with an air of disappointment, and a corresponding exclamation.

At length, after going the complete round of the dead, he faced towards his satellite, saying,—

"*Por dios*! he don't appear to be among them! What can it mean? There could be no doubt of his intention to accompany the caravan. Here it is, and here we are; but where is he? *Carajo*! If he has escaped me, I shall feel as if I'd had all this trouble for nothing."

"Think of the precious plunder," rejoined the other. "These grand *carretas* are loaded with rich goods. Surely they don't count for nothing."

"A fig for the goods! I'd give more for his scalp than all the silks and satins that were ever carried to Santa Fé. Not that I'd care to keep such a trifle. The Horned Lizard will be welcome to it, soon as I see it stripped from his skull. That's what I want to see. But where is it? Where is he? Certainly not among these. There isn't one of them the least like him. Surely it must be his party, spoken of in his letter? No other has been heard of coming by this route. There they lie, all stark and staring—men, mules, and horses—all but him."

The smoke has thinned off, only a thin film still wafting about the waggons, whose canvas tilts, now consumed, expose their contents—some of them badly burnt, some but slightly scorched. The freebooters have commenced to drag out boxes and bales, their chief by a stern command having restrained them from returning to take the scalps of the slain. All has been the work of only a few moments—less than ten minutes of time—for it is scarce so much since Wilder and Hamersley, stealing out between the wheels, rode off under cover of the cloud.

By this he with the beard, speaking Spanish, has ceased to scrutinise the corpses, and stands facing his inferior, his countenance showing an air of puzzled disappointment, as proclaimed by his repeated speeches.

Once again he gives speech to his perplexity, exclaiming:

"*Demonios!* I don't understand it. Is it possible that any of them can have got away?"

As he puts the question there comes a shout from outside, seeming to answer it. For it is a cry half in lamentation—a sort of wail, altogether unlike the charging war-whoop of the Comanches. Acquainted with their signals, he knows that the one he has heard tells of an enemy trying to escape.

Hurrying outside the corral, he sees two mounted men, nearly a mile off, making in the direction of the cliffs. And nearer, a score of other men, in the act of mounting, these being Indians, who have just caught sight of the fugitives, and are starting to pursue.

More eager than any, he rushes direct to his horse, and, having reached, bestrides him at a spring. Then, plunging deep the spur, he dashed off across the plain towards the point where the two men are seen making away. Who both may be he knows not, nor of one need he care; but of one he does, feeling sure it is the same for whom he has been searching among the slain.

"Not dead yet, but soon shall be!"

So mutters he, as with clenched teeth, bridle tight-drawn, and fingers firmly clasping the butt of a double-barrelled pistol, he spurs on after the two horsemen, who, heading straight for the cliff, seem as if they had no chance to escape; for their pursuers are closing after them in a cloud, dark as the dreaded "norther" that sweeps over the Texan desert, with shout symbolising the clangour that accompanies it.

Chapter Ten.
A Brave Steed Abandoned.

In making his bold dash, Walt Wilder was not acting without a preconceived plan. He had one. The smoke, with its covering cloud, might be the means of concealment, and ultimate salvation; at all events, it would cover their retreat long enough to give them a start of the pursuers, and then the speed of their horses might possibly be depended upon for the rest.

They at first followed this plan, but unfortunately soon found that it would not long avail them. The smoke was not drifting in the right direction. The breeze carried it almost straight towards the line of the cliffs, while their only chance was to strike for the open plain. At the cliffs their flight would be stopped.

So far the smoke had favoured them. Thick and stifling in the immediate vicinity of the waggons, it enabled them to slip unobserved through the ruck of savages. Many of these, still mounted, had seen them pass outward, but through the blue film had mistaken them for two of their own men. They perhaps knew nothing of there having been horses inside the corral, and did not expect to see any of their caged enemies attempting to escape in that way. Besides, they were now busy endeavouring to extinguish the fires, all resistance being at an end.

As yet there was no sign of pursuit, and the fugitives rode up with the projecting *nimbus* around them. In the soft sand their horses' hoofs made no noise, and they galloped towards the cliff silent as spectres.

On reaching its base, it became necessary for them either to change the direction of their flight, or bring it to a termination. The bluff towered vertically above them, like a wall of rude masonwork. A cat could not have scaled it, much less horse, or man. They did not think of making the attempt.

And now, what were they to do? Ride out from the smoke-cloud, or remain under its favouring shelter? In either case they were sure of being discovered and pursued. It would soon clear off, and they would be seen from the waggons. Already it was fast thinning around them; the Indians having nearly extinguished the fires in order to save the treasure, which had no doubt been their chief object for attacking the caravan. Soon there would be no smoke—and then?

The pursued men stayed not to reflect further. Delay would only add to their danger; and with this thought urging them on, they wheeled their horses to the left, and headed along the line of the bluff. Six seconds after they were riding in a pure atmosphere, under clear dazzling sunlight.

But it gave them no delight. A yell from the savages told them they were seen, and simultaneously with the shout, they perceived a score of horsemen spurring from the crowd, and riding at full speed towards them.

They were both splendidly mounted, and might still have had a fair chance of escape; but now another sight met their eyes that once more almost drove them to despair.

A promontory of the cliff, stretching far out over the sandy plain, lay directly in their track. Its point was nearer to the pursuers than to them. Before they could reach, and turn it, their retreat would be intercepted.

Was there still a chance to escape in the opposite direction?

Again suddenly turning, they galloped back as they had come; again entered the belt of smoke; and, riding on through it, reached the clear sunlight beyond.

Again a torturing disappointment. Another promontory—twin to the first—jutted out to obstruct them.

There was no mystery in the matter. They saw the mistake they had made. In escaping under cover of the cloud they had gone too far, ridden direct into a deep embayment of the cliff!

Their pursuers, who had turned promptly as they, once more had the advantage. The outlying point of rocks was nearer to them, and they would be almost certain to arrive at it first.

To the fugitives there appeared no alternative but to ride on, and take the chance of hewing their way through the savages surrounding—for certainly they would be surrounded.

"Git your knife riddy, Frank!" shouted Wilder, as he dug his heels into his horse's side and put the animal to full speed. "Let's keep close thegither—livin' or dead, let's keep thegither!"

Their steeds needed no urging. To an American horse accustomed to the prairies there is no spur like the yell of an Indian; for he knows that along with it usually comes the shock of a bullet, or the sting of a barbed shaft.

Both bounded off together, and went over the soft sand, silent, but swift as the wind.

In vain. Before they could reach the projecting point, the savages had got up, and were clustering around it. At least a score, with spears couched, bows bent, and clubs brandishing, stood ready to receive them.

It was a gauntlet the pursued men might well despair of being able to run. Truly now seemed their retreat cut off, and surely did death appear to stare them in the face.

"We must die, Walt," said the young prairie merchant, as he faced despairingly toward his companion.

"Maybe not yet," answered Wilder, as with a searching glance, he directed his eye along the façade of the cliff.

The red sandstone rose rugged and frowning, full five hundred feet overhead. To the superficial glance it seemed to forbid all chance either of being scaled, or affording concealment. There was not even a boulder below, behind which they might find a momentary shelter from the shafts of the pursuers. For all that, Wilder continued to scan it, as if recalling some old recollection.

"This must be the place," he muttered. "It is, by God!" he added more emphatically, at the same time wrenching his horse around, riding sharp off, and calling to his companion to follow him.

Hamersley obeyed, and rode after, without knowing what next. But, in another instant, he divined the intent of this sudden change in the tactics of his fellow fugitive. For before riding far his eyes fell upon a dark list, which indicated an opening in the escarpment.

It was a mere crack, or chine, scarce so wide as a doorway, and barely large enough to admit a man on horseback; though vertically it traversed the cliff to its top, splitting it from base to summit.

"Off o' yur hoss!" cried Wilder, as he pulled up in front of it, at the same time flinging himself from his own. "Drop the bridle, and leave him behind. One o' 'em'll be enough for what I want, an' let that be myen. Poor critter, it air a pity! But it can't be helped. We must hev some kiver to screen us. Quick, Frank, or the skunks will be on to us!"

Painful as it was to abandon his brave steed, Hamersley did as directed without knowing why. The last speeches of the guide were somewhat enigmatical, though he presumed they meant an important signification.

Slipping down from his saddle, he stood by his horse's side, a noble steed, the best blood of his own State, Kentucky, famed for its fine stock.

The animal appeared to know that its master was about to part from it. It turned its head towards him; and, with bent neck, and steaming nostrils, gave utterance to a low neigh that, while proclaiming affection, seemed to say, "Why do you forsake me?"

Under other circumstances the Kentuckian would have shed tears. For months he and his horse had been as man and man together in many a long prairie journey—a companionship which unites the traveller to his steed in liens strong as human friendship, almost as lasting, and almost as painful to break. So Frank Hamersley felt, as he flung the bridle back on the animal's withers—still retaining hold of the rein, loth to relinquish it.

But there was no alternative. Behind were the shouting pursuers quickly coming on. He could see their brandished spears glancing in the sun glare. They would soon be within reach, thrusting through his body; their barbed blades piercing him between the ribs.

No time for sentiment nor dallying now, without the certainty of being slain.

He gave one last look at his steed, and then letting go the rein, turned away, as one who, by stern necessity, abandons a friend, fearing reproach for what he does, but without the power to explain it.

For a time the abandoned steed kept its place, with glances inquiringly sent after the master who had forsaken it. Then, as the yelling crew came closer behind, it threw up its head, snorted, and tore off with trailing bridle.

Hamersley had turned to the guide, now also afoot, but still retaining hold of his horse, which he was conducting towards the crack in the cliff, with all his energies forcing it to follow him; for the animal moved reluctantly, as though suspecting danger inside the darksome cleft.

Still urging it on, he shouted back to the Kentuckian, "You go first, Frank! Up into the kanyon, without losin' a second's time. Hyar, take my gun, an' load both, whiles I see to the closin' o' the gap."

Seizing both guns in his grasp, Hamersley sprang into the chine, stopping when he got well within its grim jaws.

Wilder went after, leading his steed, that still strained back upon the bridle.

There was a large stone across the aperture, over which the horse had to straddle. This being above two feet in height, when the animal had got its forelegs over Wilder checked it to a stand. Hitherto following him with forced obedience, it now trembled, and showed a strong determination to go back. There was an expression, in its owner's eye it had never seen before—something that terribly frayed it. But it could not now do this, though ever so inclined. With its ribs close pressing the rocks on each side, it was unable to turn; while the bridle drawn firmly in front hindered it from retiring.

Hamersley, busily engaged in loading the rifles, nevertheless found time to glance at Wilder's doings, wondering what he was about.

"It air a pity!" soliloquised the latter, repeating his former words in similar tones of commiseration. "F'r all that, the thing must be done. If thar war a rock big enough, or a log, or anythin'. No! thar ain't ne'er another chance to make kiver. So hyar goes for a bit o' butcherin'."

As the guide thus delivered himself, Hamersley saw him jerk the bowie knife from his belt, its blade red and still reeking with human gore. In another instant its edge was drawn across the throat of the horse, from which the blood gushed forth in a thick, strong stream, like water from the spout of a pump. The creature made a last desperate effort to get off, but with its forelegs over the rocks and head held down between them, it could not stir from the spot. After a convulsive throe or two, it sank down till its ribs rested upon the straddled stone; and in this attitude it ended its life, the head after a time drooping down, the eyes apparently turned with a last reproachful look upon the master who had murdered it!

"It hed to be did; thar war no help for it," said Wilder, as he hurriedly turned towards his companion, adding: "Have you got the guns charged?"

Hamersley made answer by handing him back his own rifle. It was loaded and ready. "Darn the stinkin' cowarts!" cried the guide, grasping the gun, and facing towards the plain. "I don't know how it may all eend, but this'll keep 'em off a while, anyhow."

As he spoke he threw himself behind the body of the slaughtered steed, which, sustained in an upright position between the counterpart walls, formed a safe barricade against the bullets and arrows of the Indians. These, now riding straight towards the spot, made the rocks resound with exclamations of surprise—shouts that spoke of a delayed, perhaps defeated, vengeance.

They took care, however, not to come within range of that long steel-grey tube, that, turning like a telescope on its pivot, commanded a semicircle of at least a hundred yards' radius round the opening in the cliff.

Despite all the earnestness of their vengeful anger, the pursuers were now fairly at bay, and for a time could be kept so.

Hamersley looked upon it as being but a respite—a mere temporary deliverance from danger, yet to terminate in death. True, they had got into a position where, to all appearance, they could defend themselves as long as their ammunition lasted, or as they could withstand the agony of thirst or the cravings of hunger. How were they to get out again? As well might they have been besieged in a cave, with no chance of sortie or escape.

These thoughts he communicated to his companion, as soon as they found time to talk.

"Hunger an' thirst ain't nothin' to do wi' it," was Wilder response. "We ain't a goin' to stay hyar not twenty minutes, if this child kin manage it as he intends ter do. You don't s'pose I rushed into this hyar hole like a chased rabbit? No, Frank; I've heern o' this place afore, from some fellers thet, like ourselves, made *caché* in it from a band o' pursuin' Kimanch. Thar's a way leads out at the back; an' just as soon as we kin throw dust in the eyes o' these yellin' varmints in front, we'll put straight for it. I don't know what sort o' a passage thar is—up the rocks by some kind o' raven, I b'lieve. We must do our best to find it."

"But how do you intend to keep them from following us? You speak of throwing dust in their eyes—how, Walt?"

"You wait, watch an' see. You won't hev yur patience terrifically tried: for thar ain't much time to spare about it. Thar's another passage up the cliffs, not far off; not a doubt but these Injuns know it; an' ef we don't make haste, they'll git up thar, and come in upon us by the back door, which trick won't do, nohowsomdever. You keep yurself in readiness, and watch what I'm agoin' to do. When you see me scoot up back'ards, follor 'ithout sayin' a word."

Hamersley promised compliance, and the guide, still kneeling behind the barricade he had so cruelly constructed, commenced a series of manoeuvres that held his companion in speechless conjecture.

He first placed his gun in such a position that the barrel, resting across the hips of the dead horse, projected beyond the tail. In this position he made it fast, by tying the butt with a piece of string to a projecting part of the saddle. He next took the cap from his head—a coonskin it was—and set it so that its upper edge could be seen alongside the pommel, and rising about three inches above the croup. The ruse was an old one, with some new additions and embellishments.

"It's all done now," said the guide, turning away from the carcase and crouching to where his comrade awaited him. "Come on, Frank. If they don't diskiver the trick till we've got time to speed up the clift, then thar's still a chance for us. Come on, an' keep close arter me!"

Hamersley went, without saying a word. He knew that Wilder, well known and long trusted, had a reason for everything he did. It was not the time to question him, or discuss the prudence of the step he was taking. There might be danger before, but there was death—sure death—behind them.

Chapter Eleven.
A Descent into Darkness.

In less than a dozen paces from its entrance the chine opened into a wider space, again closing like a pair of callipers. It was a hollow of elliptical shape—resembling an old-fashioned butterboat scooped out of the solid rock, on all sides precipitous, except at its upper end. Here a ravine, sloping down from the summit-level above, would to the geologist at once proclaim the secret of its formation. Not so easily explained might seem the narrow outlet to the open plain. But one skilled in the testimony of the rocks would detect certain ferruginous veins in the sandstone that, refusing to yield to the erosion of the running stream, had stood for countless ages.

Neither Walt Wilder nor the young Kentuckian gave thought to such scientific speculations as they retreated through the narrow gap and back into the wider gorge. All they knew or cared for was that a gully at the opposite end was seen to slope upward, promising a path to the plain above.

In sixty seconds they were in it, toiling onward and upward amidst a chaos of rocks where no horse could follow—loose boulders that looked as if hurled down from the heavens above or belched upward from the bowels of the earth.

The retreat of the fugitives up the ravine, like their dash out of the enclosed corral, was still but a doubtful effort. Neither of them had full confidence of being able eventually to escape. It was like the wounded squirrel clutching at the last tiny twig of a tree, however unable to support it. They were not quite certain that the sloping gorge would give them a path to the upper plain; for Wilder had only a doubtful recollection of what some trapper had told him. But even if it did, the Indians, expert climbers as they were, would soon be after them, close upon their heels. The ruse could not remain long undetected.

They had plunged into the chasm as drowning men grasp at the nearest thing afloat—a slender branch or bunch of grass, a straw.

As they now ascended the rock-strewn gorge both had their reflections, which, though unspoken, were very similar. And from these came a gleam of hope. If they could but reach the summit-level of the cliff! Their pursuers could, of course, do the same; but not on horseback. It would then be a contest of pedestrian speed. The white men felt confidence in their swiftness of foot; in this respect believing themselves superior to their savage pursuers. They knew that the Comanches were horse Indians—a significant fact. These centaurs of the central plateaux, scarce ever setting foot upon the earth, when afoot are almost as helpless as birds with their wings plucked or pinioned.

If they could reach the crest of the cliff, then all might yet be well; and, cheered by this reflection, they rushed up the rock-strewn ravine, now gliding along ledges, now squeezing their bodies between great boulders, or springing from one to the other—in the audacity of their bounds rivalling a brace of bighorns.

They had got more than half-way up, when cries came pealing up the glen behind them. Still were they hidden from the eyes of the pursuers. Jutting points of rock and huge masses that lay loose in the bed of the ravine had hitherto concealed them. But for these, bullets and arrows would have already whistled about their ears, and perhaps put an end to their flight. The savages were near enough to send either gun-shot or shaft, and their voices, borne upward on the air, sounded as clear as if they were close at hand.

The fugitives, as already said, had reached more than halfway up the slope, and were beginning to congratulate themselves on the prospect of escape. They even thought of the course they should take on arriving at the summit-level, for they knew that there was an open plain above. All at once they were brought to a stop, though not by anything that obstructed their path. On the contrary, it only seemed easier; for there were now two ways open to them instead of one, the ravine at this point forking into two distinct branches. There was a choice of which to take, and it was this that caused them to make a stop, at the same time creating embarrassment.

The pause, however, was but for a brief space of time—only long enough to make a hasty reconnoissance. In the promise of an easy ascent there seemed but little difference between the two paths, and the guide soon came to a determination.

"It's a toss up atween 'em," he said; "but let's take the one to the right. It looks a little the likest."

Of course his fellow-fugitive did not dissent, and they struck into the right-hand ravine; but not until Walt Wilder had plucked the red kerchief from his head, and flung it as far as he could up the left one, where it was left lying in a conspicuous position among the rocks.

He did not say why he had thus strangely abandoned the remnant of his head-gear; but his companion, sufficiently experienced in the ways and wiles of prairie life, stood in no need of an explanation.

The track they had now taken was of comparatively easy ascent; and it was this, perhaps, that had tempted Wilder to take it. But like most things within the moral and physical world, its easiness proved a delusion. They had not gone twenty paces further up when the sloping chasm terminated. It debouched on a little platform, covered with large loose stones, and there rested after having fallen from the cliff above. But at a single glance they saw that this cliff could not be scaled.

They had entered into a trap, out of which there was no chance of escape or retreat without throwing themselves back upon the breasts of their pursuers.

The Indians were already ascending the main ravine. By their voices it could be told that they had reached the point where it divided; for there was a momentary suspension of their cries, as with the baying of hounds thrown suddenly off the scent.

It would not be for long. They would likely first follow up the chasm where the kerchief had been cast, but, should that also prove a *cul-de-sac*, they would return and try the other.

The fugitives saw that it was too late to retrace their steps. They sprang together upon the platform, and commenced searching among the loose rocks, with a faint hope of finding some place of concealment.

It was but a despairing sort of search, again like two drowning men who clutch at a straw.

All at once an exclamation from the guide called his companion to his side. It was accompanied by a gesture, and followed by words low muttered.

"Look hyar, Frank! Look at this hole! Let's git into it!"

As Hamersley came close he perceived a dark cavity among the stones, to which Wilder was pointing. It opened vertically downward, and was of an irregular, roundish shape, somewhat resembling the mouth of a well, half-coped with slabs.

Dare they enter it? Could they? What depth was it?

Wilder took up a pebble and flung it down. They could hear it descending, not at a single drop, but striking and ricochetting from side to side.

It was long before it reached the bottom and lay silent. No matter for that. The noise made in its descent told them of projecting points or ledges that might give them a foothold.

They lost not a moment of time, but commenced letting themselves down into the funnel-shaped shaft, the guide going first.

Slowly and silently they went down—like ghosts through the stage of a theatre—soon disappearing in the gloom below, and leaving upon the rock-strewn platform no trace to show that human foot had ever trodden it.

Chapter Twelve.
A Storm of Stones.

Fortunately for the fugitives, the cavity into which they had crept was a shaft of but slight diameter, otherwise they could not have gone down without dropping far enough to cause death, for the echoes from the pebbles betokened a vast vertical depth.

As it was, the void turned out to be somewhat like that of a stone-built chimney with here and there a point left projecting. It was so narrow, moreover, that they were able to use both hands and knees in the descent, and by this means they accomplished it.

They went but slowly, and took care to proceed with caution. They knew that a false step, the slipping of a foot or finger, or the breaking of a fragment that gave hold to their hands, would precipitate them to an unknown depth.

They did not go farther than was necessary for quick concealment. There was noise made in their descent, and they knew that the Indians would soon be above, and might hear them. Their only hope lay in their pursuers believing them to have gone by the left hand path to the plain above. In time the Indians would surely explore both branches of the ravine, and if the cunning savages should suspect their presence in the shaft there would be no hope for them. These thoughts decided them to come to a stop as soon as they could find foothold.

About thirty feet from the top they found this, on a point of rock or ledge that jutted horizontally. It was broad enough to give both standing room, and as they were now in the midst of amorphous darkness, they took stand upon it.

The Indians might at any moment arrive on the platform above. They felt confident they could not be seen, but they might be heard. The slightest sound borne upwards to the ears of the savages might betray them, and, knowing this, they stood still, scarce exchanging a whisper, and almost afraid to breathe.

It was not long before they saw that which justified their caution—the plumed head of a savage, with his neck craned over the edge of the aperture, outlined conspicuously against the blue sky above. And soon half a dozen similar silhouettes beside it, while they could hear distinctly the talk that was passing overhead.

Wilder had some knowledge of the Comanche tongue, and could make out most of what was being said. Amidst exclamations that spoke of vengeance there were words in a calmer tone—discussion, inquiry, and conjecture.

From these it could be understood that the pursuers had separated into two parties, one following on the false track, by the path which the guide had baited for them, the other coming direct up the right and true one.

There were bitter exclamations of disappointment and threats of an implacable vengeance; and the fugitives, as they listened, might have reflected how fortunate they had been in discovering that unfathomed hole. But for it they would have already been in the clutches of a cruel enemy.

However, they had little time for reflection. The talk overhead at first expressed doubts as to their having descended the shaft, but doubts readily to be set at rest.

The eyes of the Indians having failed to inform them, their heads were withdrawn; and soon after a stone came tumbling down the cavity.

Something of this kind, Wilder had predicted; for he flattened himself against the wall behind, and stood as "small" as his colossal frame would permit, having cautioned his companion to do the same.

The stone passed without striking them, and went crashing on till it struck on the bottom below.

Another followed, and another; the third creasing Hamersley on the breast, and tearing a couple of buttons from his coat.

This was shaving close—too close to be comfortable. Perhaps the next boulder might rebound from the wall above and strike one or both of them dead.

In fear of this result, they commenced groping to ascertain if the ledge offered any better screen from the dangerous shower, which promised to fall for some time longer.

Good! Hamersley felt his hand entering a hole that opened horizontally. It proved big enough to admit his body, as also the larger frame of his companion. Both were soon inside it. It was a sort of grotto they had discovered; and, crouching within it, they could laugh to scorn the storm that still came pouring from above; the stones, as they passed close to their faces, hissing and hurtling like aerolites.

The rocky rain at length ended. The Indians had evidently come to the conclusion that it was either barren in result, or must have effectually performed the purpose intended by it, and for a short time there was silence above and below.

They who were hidden in the shaft might have supposed that their persecutors, satisfied at what they had accomplished, were returning to the plain, and had retired from the spot.

Hamersley did think so; but Walt, an old prairie man, more skilled in the Indian character, could not console himself with such a fancy.

"Ne'er a bit o' it," he whisperingly said to his companion. "They ain't agoin' to leave us that easy—not if Horned Lizard be amongst 'em. They'll either stay thar till we climb out agin, or try to smoke us. Ye may take my word for it, Frank, thar's some'ut to come yet. Look up! Didn't I tell ye so?"

Wilder drew back out of the narrow aperture, through which he had been craning his neck and shoulders in order to get a view of what was passing above.

The hole leading into the grotto that held them was barely large enough to admit the body of a man. Hamersley took his place, and, turning his eyes upward, at once saw what his comrade referred to. It was the smoke of a fire, that appeared in the act of being kindled near the edge of the aperture above. The smoke was ascending towards the sky, diagonally drifting across the blue disc outlined by the rim of rock.

He had barely time to make the observation when a swishing sound admonished him to draw back his head; then there passed before his face a ruck of falling stalks and faggots. Some of them settled upon the ledge, the rest sweeping on to the bottom of the abyss.

In a moment after the shaft was filled with smoke, but not that of an ordinary wood fire. Even this would have been sufficient to stifle them where they were; but the fumes now entering their nostrils were of a kind to cause suffocation almost instantaneously.

The faggots set on fire were the stalks of the creosote plant— the *ideodondo* of the Mexican table lands, well known for its power to cause asphyxia. Walt Wilder recognised it at the first whiff.

"It's the stink-weed!" he exclaimed. "That darned stink-weed o' New Mexico! It'll kill us if we can't keep it out. Off wi' your coat, Frank; it are bigger than my hunting skirt. Let's spread it across the hole, an' see if that'll do."

His companion obeyed with alacrity, stripping off his coat as quickly as the circumscribed space would permit. Fortunately, it was a garment of the sack specialty, without any split in the tail, and when extended offered a good breadth of surface.

It proved sufficient for the purpose, and, before the little grotto had become so filled with smoke as to be absolutely untenable, its entrance was closed by a curtain of broadcloth, held so hermetically over the aperture that even the fumes of Assafoetida could not possibly have found their way inside.

Chapter Thirteen.
· Buried Alive.

For nearly half an hour they kept the coat spread, holding it close around the edges of the aperture with their heads, hands, knees, and elbows. Withal some of the bitter smoke found ingress, torturing their eyes, and half stifling them.

• They bore it with philosophic fortitude and in profound silence, using their utmost efforts to refrain from sneezing or coughing.

They knew that the least noise heard by the Indians above—anything to indicate their presence in the shaft—would ensure their destruction. The fumigation would be continued till the savages were certain of its having had a fatal effect. If they could hold out long enough, even Indian astuteness might be baffled.

From what Wilder had heard, their persecutors were in doubt about their having descended into the shaft; and this uncertainty promised to be their salvation. Unless sure that they were taking all this trouble to some purpose, the red men would not dally long over their work. Besides, there was the rich booty to be drawn from the captured waggons, which would attract the Indians back to them, each having an interest in being present at the distribution.

Thus reasoned Walt Wilder as they listened to detect a change in the performance, making use of all their ears.

Of course they could see nothing, no more than if they had been immured in the darkest cell of an Inquisitorial dungeon. Only by their ears might they make any guess at what was going on. These admonished them that more of the burning brush was being heaved into the hole. Every now and then they could hear it as it went swishing past the door of their curtained chamber, the stalks and sticks rasping against the rocks in their descent.

After a time these sounds ceased to be heard; the Indians no doubt thinking that sufficient of the inflammatory matter had been cast in to cause their complete destruction. If inside the cavern, they must by this time be stifled—asphyxiated—dead.

So must have reasoned the red-skinned fumigators; for after a while they desisted from their hellish task. But, as if to make assurance doubly sure, before taking departure from the spot, they performed another act indicative of an equally merciless intention.

During the short period of silence their victims could not tell what they were about. They only knew, by occasional sounds reaching them from above, that there was some change in the performance; but what it was they could not even shape a conjecture.

The interregnum at length ended with a loud rumbling noise, that was itself suddenly terminated by a grand crash, as if a portion of the impending cliff had become detached, and fallen down upon the platform.

Then succeeded a silence, unbroken by the slightest sound. No longer was heard either noise or voice—not the murmur of one.

It was a silence that resembled death; as if the vindictive savages had one and all met a deserved doom by being crushed under the falling cliff.

For some time after hearing this mysterious noise, which had caused the rock to tremble around them, the two men remained motionless within their place of concealment.

At length Wilder cautiously and deliberately pushed aside the curtain. At first only a small portion of it—a corner, so as to make sure about the smoke.

It still oozed in, but not so voluminously as at first. It had evidently become attenuated, and was growing thinner. It appeared also to be ascending with rapidity, as up the funnel of a chimney having a good draught. For this reason it was carried past the mouth of the grotto without much of it drifting in, and they saw that they could soon safely withdraw the curtain. It was a welcome relaxation from the irksome task that had been so long imposed upon them, and the coat was at length permitted to drop down upon the ledge.

Although there were no longer any sounds heard, or other signs to indicate the presence of the Indians, the fugitives did not feel sure of their having gone; and it was some time before they made any attempt to reascend the shaft. Some of the pursuers might still be lurking near, or straying within sight. They had so far escaped death, as if by a miracle, and they were cautious of again tempting fate. They determined that for some time yet they would not venture out upon the ledge, but keep inside the grotto that had given them such well-timed shelter. Some sulky savage, disappointed at not getting their scalps, might take it into his head to return and hurl down into the hole another shower of stones. Such a whim was probable to a prairie Indian.

Cautious against all like contingencies, the guide counselled his younger companion to patience, and for a considerable time they remained without stirring out of their obscure chamber.

At length, however, perceiving that the tranquillity continued, they no longer deemed it rash to make a reconnoissance; and for this purpose Walt Wilder crawled out upon the ledge and looked upward. A feeling of surprise, mingled with apprehension, at once seized upon him.

"Kin it be night?" he asked, whispering the words back into the grotto.

"Not yet, I should think?" answered Hamersley. "The fight was begun before daybreak. The day can't all have passed yet. But why do you ask, Walt?"

"Because thar's no light comin' from above. Whar's the bit o' blue sky we seed? Thar ain't the breadth o' a hand visible. It can't a be the smoke as hides it. That seems most cleared off. Darned if I can see a steim o' the sky. 'Bove as below, everything's as black as the ten o' spades. What kin it mean?"

Without waiting a reply, or staying for his companion to come out upon the ledge, Wilder rose to his feet, and, grasping the projecting points above his head, commenced swarming up the shaft, in a similar manner as that by which he had made the descent.

Hamersley, who by this time had crept out of the grotto, stood upon the ledge listening.

He could hear his comrade as he scrambled up; the rasping of his feet against the rocks, and his stentorian breathing.

At length Walt appeared to have reached the top, when Hamersley heard words that sent a thrill of horror throughout his whole frame.

"Oh!" cried the guide, in his surprise, forgetting to subdue the tone of his voice, "they've built us up! Thar's a stone over the mouth o' the hole— shettin' it like a pot lid. A stone—a rock that no mortal ked move. Frank Hamersley, it's all over wi' us; we're buried alive!"

Chapter Fourteen.
A Savage Saturnal.

Only for a short while had Wilder's trick held the pursuers in check. Habituated to such wiles, the Indians, at first suspecting it to be one, soon became certain. For, as they scattered to each side of the cleft, the steel tube no longer kept turning towards them, while the coonskin cap remained equally without motion.

At length, becoming convinced, and urged on by the Red Cross chief and the bearded savage by his side, they dashed boldly up, and, dismounting, entered the chine over the body of the butchered horse.

Only staying to take possession of the relinquished rifle, they continued on up the ravine fast as their feet could carry them. A moment's pause where the red kerchief lay on the rock, suspecting this also a ruse to mislead them as to the track taken by the fugitives. To make certain, they separated into two parties—one going up the gulch, that led left, the other proceeding by that which conducted to the place where the two men had concealed themselves.

Arriving upon the little platform, the pursuers at once discovered the cavity, at the same time conjecturing that the pursued had gone into it. Becoming sure of this, they who took the left-hand path rejoined them, these bringing the report that they had ascended to the summit of the cliff, and seen nothing of the two men who were chased.

Then the stones were cast in; after them the burning stalks of the *ideodondo*; when, finally, to make destruction sure, the rock was rolled over, closing up the shaft as securely as if the cliff itself had fallen face downward upon the spot.

The savages stayed no longer there. All were too eager to return to the waggons to make sure of their share in the captured spoils.

One alone remained—he with the bushed beard. After the others were gone he stepped up to the boulder, and, stooping down, placed his ear close to it. He appeared as if trying to catch some sound that might come from the cavity underneath.

None came—no noise, even the slightest. Within the shut shaft all was still as death. For death itself must be down there, if there ever was life.

For some time he crouched beside the rock, listening. Then rising to his feet, with a smile of satisfaction upon his grim, sinister features, he said, in soliloquy,—

"They're down there, no doubt of it; and dead long before this. One of the two must have been he. Who the other matters not *Carrai!* I'd like to have had a look at him too, and let him see who has given him his quietus. Bah! what does it signify? It's all over now, and I've had my revenge. *Vamos!* I must get back to the waggons, or my friend the Horned Lizard may be taking his pick of the plunder. Luckily these redskins don't know the different values of the goods; so I shall bestow the cotton prints with a liberal hand, keeping the better sorts to myself. And now to assist in the partition of spoils."

So saying, he strode away from the rock, and, gliding back down the gulch, climbed over the carcass of the dead horse. Then, finding his own outside, he mounted and rode off to rejoin his red-skinned comrades engaged in sacking the caravan.

On reaching it a spectacle was presented to his eyes—frightful, though not to him. For he was a man who had seen similar sights before—one with soul steeped in kindred crime.

The waggons had been drawn partially apart, disclosing the space between. The smoke had all ascended or drifted off, and clear sunlight once more shone upon the sand—over the ground lately barricaded by the bodies of those who had so bravely defended it. There were thirteen of them—the party of traders and hunters being in all but fifteen. Of those slain upon the spot there was not one now wearing his hair. Their heads were bare and bloody, the crown of each showing a circular disc of dark crimson colour. The scalping-knife had already completed its work, and the ghastly trophies were seen impaled upon the points of spears—some of them stuck upright in the sand, others borne triumphantly about by the exulting victors. Their triumph had cost them dear. On the plain outside at least thirty of their own lay extended, stone dead; while here and there a group bending over some recumbent form told of a warrior wounded.

By the orders of their chief, some had set about collecting the corpses of their slain comrades, with the intent of interring them. Others, acting without orders, still continued to wreak their savage spite upon the bodies of their white victims, submitting them to further mutilation. They chopped off their heads; then, poising these on the points of spears, tossed them to and fro, all the while shouting in savage glee, laughing with a cacchination that resembled the mirth of a madhouse.

Withal, there was stern vengeance in its tones. A resistance, they little expected, causing them such serious loss, had roused their passions to a pitch of the utmost exasperation; and they tried to allay their spiteful anger by expending it on the dead bodies of those who, while living, had so effectually chastised them. These were slashed and hacked with tomahawks, pierced with spears, and arrows, beaten with war clubs, then cut into pieces, to be tied to the tails of their horses, and dragged in gallop to and fro over the ground. For some time this tragical spectacle held play. Then ensued a scene savouring of the ludicrous and grotesque.

The waggons were emptied of their contents, while the rich freight, transported to a distance, was spread out upon the plain, and its partition entered upon—all crowding around to receive their share.

The distribution was superintended by the Horned Lizard, though he with the beard appeared to act with equal, or even greater, authority. Backed by the second personage, who wore hair on his cheeks, he dictated the apportionment.

And as he had said in soliloquy, the cotton prints of gaudy patterns satisfied the cupidity of his red-skinned companions, leaving to himself and his confidential friend the costlier fabrics of silken sheen. Among the traders' stock were knives of common sort—the cheapest cutlery of Sheffield; guns and pistols of the Brummagem brand, with beads, looking glasses, and such-like notions from the New England Boston. All these, delectable in the eyes of the Horned Lizard and his Tenawas, were left to them; while the bearded man, himself selecting, appropriated the silks and satins, the laces and real jewellery that had been designed to deck the rich *doncellas* of Santa Fé, El Paso, Chihuahua, and Durango.

The distribution over, the scene assumed a new aspect. It was now that the ludicrous came prominently into play. Though not much water had been found in the waggons, there was enough fluid of stronger spirit. A barrel of Monongahela whisky was part of the caravan stores left undestroyed. Knowing the white man's firewater but too well, the Indians tapped the cask, and quaffed of its contents.

In a short time two-thirds of the band became intoxicated. Some rolled over dead drunk, and lay a-stretch along the sand. Others tottered about, uttering maudlin speeches. Still others of stronger stomach and steader brain kept their feet, as also their senses; only that these became excited, increasing their cupidity. They wanted more than they had got, and would gamble to get it. One had a piece of cotton print, and so had another. Each wished to have both or none. How was it to be decided? By cards? By dice? No. There was a way more congenial to their tastes—more *à propos* to their habits. It should be done by their horses. They knew the sort of game, for it is not the first time they have played it. The piece of print is unrolled, and at each end tied to a horse's tail. The owners spring to the backs of the animals, then urge them in the opposite directions till the strain comes; at the pluck the web gives way, and he who holds the longer part becomes possessor of the whole.

Others, not gamblers, out of sheer devilry and diversion, similarly attach their stuffs, and gallop over the ground with the prints trailing fifty yards behind them. In the frenzied frolic that had seized hold of them they forgot their slain comrades, still unburied. They whoop, shout, and laugh till the cliffs, in wild, unwonted echo, send back the sound of their demoniac mirth. A riot rare as original—a true saturnal of savages.

Chapter Fifteen.
A Living Tomb.

Literally buried alive, as Walt Wilder had said, were he and his companion.

They now understood what had caused the strange noise that mystified them—the rumbling followed by a crash. No accidental *débâcle* or falling of a portion of the cliff, as they had been half supposing; but a deed of atrocious design—a huge rock rolled by the united strength of the savages, until it rested over the orifice of the shaft, completely coping and closing it.

It may have been done without any certain knowledge of their being inside—only to make things sure. It mattered not to the two men thus cruelly enclosed, for they knew that in any case there was no hope of their being rescued from what they believed to be a living tomb.

That it was such neither could doubt. The guide, gifted with herculean strength, had tried to move the stone on discovering how it lay. With his feet firmly planted in the projections below, and his shoulder to the rock above, he had given a heave that would have lifted a loaded waggon from its wheels.

The stone did not budge with all this exertion. There was not so much as motion. He might as successfully have made trial to move a mountain from its base. He did not try again. He remembered the rock itself. He had noticed it while they were searching for a place to conceal themselves, and had been struck with its immense size. No one man could have stirred it from its place. It must have taken at least twenty Indians. No matter how many, they had succeeded in their design, and their victims were now helplessly enclosed in the dark catacomb—slowly, despairingly to perish.

"All up wi' us, I reck'n," said the guide, as he once more let himself down upon the ledge to communicate the particulars to his companion.

Hamersley ascended to see for himself. They could only go one at a time. He examined the edge of the orifice where the rock rested upon it. He could only do so by the touch. Not a ray of light came in on any side, and groping round and round he could detect neither crevice nor void. There were weeds and grass, still warm and smouldering, the *débris* of what had been set on fire for their fumigation. The rock rested on a bedding of these; hence the exact fit, closing every crack and crevice.

On completing his exploration Hamersley returned to his companion below.

"Hopeless!" murmured Wilder, despondingly.

"No, Walt; I don't think so yet."

The Kentuckian, though young, was a man of remarkable intelligence as well as courage. It needed these qualities to be a prairie merchant—one who commanded a caravan. Wilder knew him to be possessed of them—in the last of them equalling himself, in the first far exceeding him.

"You think thar's a chance for us to get out o' hyar?" he said, interrogatively.

"I think there is, and a likely one."

"Good! What leads ye to think so, Frank?"

"Reach me my bowie. It's behind you there in the cave."

Wilder did as requested.

"It will depend a good deal upon what sort of rock this is around us. It isn't flint, anyhow. I take it to be either lime or sandstone. If so, we needn't stay here much longer than it would be safe to go out again among those bloodthirsty savages."

"How do you mean, Frank? Darn me if I yet understan ye."

"It's very simple, Walt. If this cliff rock be only sandstone, or some other substance equally soft, we may cut our way out—under the big stone."

"Ah! I didn't think o' thet. Thar's good sense in what ye say."

"It has a softish feel," said the Kentuckian, as he drew his hand across one of the projecting points. "I wish I only had two inches of a candle. However, I think I can make my exploration in the dark."

There was a short moment of silence, after which was heard a clinking sound, as of a knife blade being repeatedly struck against a stone. It was Hamersley, with his bowie, chipping off a piece from the rock that projected from the side of the shaft.

The sound was pleasant to the Kentuckian's ear, for it was not the hard metallic ring given out by quartz or granite. On the contrary, the steel struck against it with a dull, dead echo, and he could feel that the point of the knife easily impinged upon it.

"Sandstone," he said; "or something that'll serve our purpose equally as well. Yes, Walt, there's a good chance for us to get out of this ugly prison; so keep up your heart, comrade. It may cost us a couple of days' quarrying. Perhaps all the better for that; the Indians are pretty sure to keep about the waggons for a day or so. They'll find enough there to amuse them. Our work will depend a good deal on what sort of a stone they've rolled over the hole. You remember what size the boulder was?"

"'Twas a largish pebble; looked to me at least ten feet every way. It sort o' serprised me how the skunks ked a budged it. I reck'n 'twar on a coggle, an' rolled eezy. It must ha' tuk the hul clanjamfry o' them."

"If we only knew the right edge to begin at. For that we must go by guess-work. Well, we mustn't lose time, but set about our stone-cutting at once. Every hour will be taking the strength out of us. I only came down for the bowie to make a beginning. I'll make trial at it first, and then we can take turn and turn about."

Provided with his knife, the Kentuckian again climbed up; and soon after the guide heard a crinkling sound, succeeded by the rattling of pieces of rock, as they got detached and came showering down.

To save his crown, now uncovered by the loss of both kerchief and cap, he crept back into the alcove that had originally protected them from the stones cast in by the Indians. Along with the splinters something else came past Walt's face, making a soft, rustling sound; it had a smell also that told what it was—the "cussed stink-weed."

From the falling fragments, their size and number, he could tell that his comrade was making good way.

Walt longed to relieve him at his work, and called up a request to this end; but Hamersley returned a refusal, speaking in a cautious tone, lest his voice might be borne out to the ear of some savage still lingering near.

For over an hour Wilder waited below, now and then casting impatient glances upward. They were only mechanical; for, of course, he could see nothing. But they were anxious withal; for the success of his comrade's scheme was yet problematical.

With sufficient food and drink to sustain them, they might in time accomplish what they had set about; but wanting these, their strength would soon give way, and then—ah! then—

The guide was still standing on the ledge, pursuing this or a similar train of reflection, when all at once a sight came, not under but above his eyes, which caused him to utter an exclamation of joy.

It was the sight of his comrade's face—only that!

But this had in it a world of significance. He could hot have seen that face without light. Light had been let into their rock-bound abode, so late buried in the profoundest darkness.

It was but a feeble glimmer, that appeared to have found admission through a tiny crevice under the huge copestone; and Hamersley's face, close to it, was seen only in faint shadow—fainter from the film of smoke yet struggling up the shaft.

Still was it light—beautiful, cheering light—like some shore-beacon seen by the storm-tossed mariner amid the dangers of a night-shrouded sea.

Hamersley had not yet spoken a word to explain what had occurred to cause it. He had suddenly left off chipping the rock, and was at rest, apparently in contemplation of the soft silvery ray that was playing so benignly upon his features.

Was it the pleasure of once more beholding what he lately thought he might never see again—the light of day? Was it this alone that was keeping him still and speechless?

No, something else; as he told his comrade when he rejoined him soon after on the ledge.

"Walt," he said, "I've let daylight in, as you see; but I find it'll take a long time to cut a passage out. It's only the weeds I've been able to get clear of. The big rock runs over at least five feet, and the stone turns out harder than I thought of."

These were not cheering words to Walt Wilder.

"But," continued Hamersley, his speech changing to a more hopeful tone, "I've noticed something that may serve better still; perhaps save us all the quarrying. I don't know whether I'm right; but we shall soon see."

"What hev ye noticed?" was the question put by Wilder.

"You see there's still some smoke around us."

"Yes, Frank, my eyes tell me that plain enuf. I've nigh nibbed 'em out o' thar sockets."

"Well, as soon as I had scooped out the crack that let in the daylight. I noticed that the smoke rushed out as if blasted through a pair of bellows. That shows there's a draught coming up. It can only come from some aperture below, acting as a furnace or the funnel of a chimney. We must try to get down to the bottom, and see if there's such a thing. If there be, who knows but it may be big enough to let us out of our prison, without having to carve our way through the walls, which I feel certain would take us several days. We must try to get down to the bottom."

To accede to this request the guide needed no urging, and both—one after the other—at once commenced descending.

They found no great difficulty in getting down, any more than they had already experienced, for the shaft continued all the way down nearly the same width, and very similar to what it was above the ledge. Near the bottom, however, it became abruptly wider by the retrocession of the walls. They were now in a dilemma, for they had reached a point where they could go no further without dropping off. It might be ten feet, it might be a hundred—in any case enough to make the peril appalling.

Wilder had gone first, and soon bethought himself of a test. He unslung his powder-horn and permitted it to drop from his hand, listening attentively. It made scarce any noise; still he could hear it striking against something soft. It was the brush thrown in by the Indians. This did not seem far below; and the half-burnt stalks would be something to break their fall.

"I'll chance it," said Walt, and almost simultaneous with his words was heard the bump of his heavy body alighting on the litter below.

"You may jump without fear, Frank. 'Taint over six feet in the clar."

Hamersley obeyed, and soon both stood at the bottom of the chimney— on the hearthstone where the stalks of the creosote still smouldered.

Chapter Sixteen.
Off at Last!

On touching *terra firma*, and finding plenty of space around, they scrambled from off the pile of loose stones and stalks cast down by the Indians, and commenced groping their way about. Again touching the firm surrounding of rock, they groped searchingly along it.

They were not long engaged in their game of blind-man's buff, when the necessity of trusting to the touch came abruptly to an end—as if the handkerchief had been suddenly jerked from their eyes. The change was caused by a light streaming in through a side gallery into which they had strayed. It was at first dim and distant, but soon shone upon them with the brilliance of a flambeau.

Following the passage through which it guided them, they reached an aperture of irregular roundish shape, about the size, of the cloister window of a convent. They saw at once that it was big enough to allow the passage of their bodies. They saw, too, that it was admitting the sunbeams—admonishing them that it was still far from night.

They had brought all their traps down along with them—their knives and pistols, with Hamersley's gun still carefully kept. But they hesitated about going out. There could be no difficulty in their doing so, for there was a ledge less than three feet under the aperture, upon which they could find footing. It was not that which caused them to hesitate, but the fact of again falling into the hands of their implacable enemies.

That these were still upon the plain they had evidence. They could hear their yells and whooping, mingled with peals of wild demon-like laughter. It was at the time when the firewater was in the ascendant, and the savages were playing their merry game with the pieces of despoiled cotton goods.

There was danger in going out, but there might be more in staying in. The savages might return upon their search, and discover this other entrance to the vault. In that case they would take still greater pains to close it and besiege the two fugitives to the point of starvation.

Both were eager to escape from a place they had lately looked upon as a living tomb.

Still, they dared not venture out of it. They could not retreat by the plain so long as the Indians were upon it. At night, perhaps, in the darkness, they might. Hamersley suggested this.

"No," said Walt, "nor at night eyther. It's moontime, you know; an' them sharp-eyed Injuns niver all goes to sleep thegither. On that sand they'd see us in the moonlight 'most as plain as in the day. Ef we wait at all, we'll hev to stay till they go clar off."

Wilder, while speaking, stood close to the aperture, looking cautiously out. At that moment, craning his neck to a greater stretch, so as to command a better view of what lay below, his eye caught sight of an object that elicited an exclamation of surprise.

"Darn it," he said, "thar's my old clout lyin' down thar on the rocks."

It was the red kerchief he had plucked from his head to put the pursuers on the wrong track.

"It's jest where I flinged it," he continued; "I kin recognise the place. That gully, then, must be the one we didn't go up."

Walt spoke the truth. The decoy was still in the place where he had set it. The square of soiled and faded cotton had failed to tempt the cupidity of the savages, who knew that in the waggons they had captured were hundreds of such, clean and new, with far richer spoil besides.

"S'pose we still try that path, Frank. It may lead us to the top arter all. If they've bin up it they've long ago gone down agin; I kin tell by thar yelpin' around the waggons. They've got holt of our corn afore this; and won't be so sharp in lookin' arter us."

"Agreed," said Hamersley.

Without further delay the two scrambled out through the aperture, and, creeping along the ledge, once more stood in the hollow of the ravine, at the point of its separation into the forks that had perplexed them in their ascent. Perhaps, after all, they had chosen the right one. At the time of their first flight, had they succeeded in reaching the plain above, they would surely have been seen and pursued; though with superior swiftness of foot they might still have escaped.

Once more they faced upward, by the slope of the ravine yet untried.

On passing it, Walt laid hold of his "clout," as he called it, and replaced it, turban fashion, on his head.

"I can only weesh," he said, "I ked as convenient rekiver my rifle; an', darn me, but I would try, ef it war only thar still. It ain't, I know. Thet air piece is too precious for a Injun to pass by. It's gone back to the waggons."

They could now more distinctly hear the shouts of their despoilers; and, as they continued the ascent, the narrow chine in the cliff opened between them and the plain, giving them a glimpse of what was there going on.

They could see the savages—some on foot, others on horseback—the latter careering round as if engaged in a tournament.

They saw they were roystering, wild with triumph, and maddened with drink—the fire-water they had found in the waggons.

"Though they be drunk, we mustn't stay hyar so nigh 'em," muttered Walt. "I allers like to put space atween me and seech as them. They mout get some whimsey into their heads, an' come this ways. They'll take any amount o' trouble to raise ha'r; an' maybe grievin' that they hain't got ourn yit, an' mout think they'd hev another try for it. As the night's bound to be a mooner, we can't git too far from 'em. So let's out o' this quick's we kin."

"On, then!" said Hamersley, assenting; and the next moment the two were rapidly ascending the gorge, Wilder leading the way.

This time they were more fortunate. The ravine sloped on up to the summit of the cliff, debouching upon a level plain. They reached this without passing any point that could bring them under the eyes of the Indians.

They could still hear the shouts of triumph and wild revelry; but as they receded from the crest of the cliff these grew fainter and fainter, until they found themselves fleeing over an open table-land, bounded above by the sky, all round them silent as death—silent as the heart of a desert.

Chapter Seventeen.
Into the Desert.

The cliff, up which the young prairie merchant and his guide, after their series of hairbreadth escapes, have succeeded in climbing, is the scarped edge of a spur of the famous Llano Estacado, or "Staked Plain," and it is into this sterile tract they are now fleeing.

Neither have any definite knowledge of the country before them, or the direction they ought to take. Their only thought is to put space between themselves and the scene of their disaster—enough to secure them against being seen by the eye of any Indian coming after.

A glance is sufficient to satisfy them that only by distance can they obtain concealment. Far as the eye can reach the surface appears a perfect level, without shrub or tree. There is not cover enough to give hiding-place to a hare. Although now in full run, and with no appearance of being pursued, they are far from being confident of escaping. They are under an apprehension that some of the savages have ascended to the upper plain, and are still on it, searching for them. If so, these may be encountered at any moment, returning disappointed from the pursuit.

The fugitives draw some consolation from the knowledge that the pursuers could not have got their horses up the cliff; and, if there is to be another chapter to the chase, it will be on foot—a contest of pedestrian speed. In a trial of this kind Walt Wilder, at least, has nothing to fear. The Colossus, with his long strides, would be almost a match for the giant with the seven-leagued boots.

Their only uneasiness is that the savages may have gone out upon the track they are themselves taking, and, appearing in their front, may head them off, and so intercept their retreat. As there is yet no savage in sight—no sign either of man or animal—their confidence increases; and, after making a mile or so across the plain, they no longer look ahead, but backward.

At short intervals the great brown beard of the guide sweeps his left shoulder, as he casts anxious glances behind him. They are all the more anxious on observing—which he now does—that his fellow-fugitive flags in his pace, and shows signs of giving out.

With a quick comprehension, and without any questions asked, Wilder understands the reason. In the smoke-cloud that covered their retreat from the corralled waggons—afterwards in the sombre shadow of the chine, and the obscurity of the cave, he had not observed what now, in the bright glare of the sunlight, is too plainly apparent—that the nether garments of his comrade are saturated with blood.

Hamersley has scarce noticed it himself, and his attention is now called to it, less from perceiving any acute pain than that he begins to feel faint and feeble. Blood is oozing through the breast of his shirt, running down the legs of his trousers, and on into his boots. And the fountain from which it proceeds is fast disclosing itself by an aching pain in his side, which increases as he strides on.

A moment's pause to examine it. When the vest and shirt are opened it is seen that a bullet has passed through his left side, causing only a flesh wound, but cutting an artery in its course. Scratched and torn in several other places, for the time equally painful, he had not yet perceived this more serious injury.

It is not mortal, nor likely to prove so. The guide and hunter, like most of his calling, is a rough practical surgeon; and after giving the wound a hurried examination, pronounces it "only a scratch," then urges his companion onward.

Again starting, they proceed at the same quick pace; but before they have made another mile the wounded man feels his weakness sensibly overcoming him. Then the rapid run is succeeded by a slow dog-trot, soon decreasing to a walk, at length ending in a dead stop.

"I can go no farther, Walt; not if all the devils of hell were at my heels. I've done my best. If they come after you keep on, and leave me."

"Niver, Frank Hamersley, niver! Walt Wilder ain't the man to sep'rate from a kumrade, and leave him in a fix that way. If ye must pull up, so do this child. An' I see ye must; thar's no behelp for it."

"I cannot go a step farther."

"Enuf! But don't let's stan' to be seen miles off. Squat's the word. Down on yer belly, like a toad under a harrer. Thar's jest a resemblance o' kiver, hyar 'mong these tussocks o' buffler-grass; an' this child ain't the most inconspicerousest objeck on the plain. Let's squat on our breast-ribs, an' lay close as pancakes."

Whilst speaking he throws himself to the earth, flat on his face.

Hamersley, already tottering, drops down by his side; as he does so, leaving the plain, as far as the eye can reach, without salient object to intercept the vision—any more than might be seen on the surface of a sleeping ocean.

It is in favour of the fugitives that the day has now well declined. But they do not remain long in their recumbent position before the sun, sinking behind the western horizon, gives them an opportunity of once more getting upon their feet.

They do so, glad to escape from a posture whose restraint is exceedingly irksome. They have suffered from the hot atmosphere rising like caloric from the parched plain. But now that the sun had gone down, a cool breeze begins to play over its surface, fanning them to fresh energy. Besides, the night closing over them—the moon not yet up—has removed the necessity for keeping any longer in concealment, and they proceed onward without fear. Hamersley feels as if fresh blood had been infused into his veins; and he is ready to spring to his feet at the same time as his comrade.

"Frank! d'ye think ye kin go a little furrer now?" is the interrogatory put by the hunter.

"Yes, Walt; miles further," is the response. "I feel as if I could walk across the grandest spread of prairie."

"Good!" ejaculates the guide. "I'm glad to hear you talk that way. If we kin but git a wheen o' miles atween us an' them yelpin' savages, we may hev a chance o' salvation yit. The wust o' the thing air, that we don't know which way to go. It's a toss up 'tween 'em. If we turn back torst the Canadyen, we may meet 'em agin, an' right in the teeth. Westart lies the settlement o' the Del Nort; but we mout come on the same Injuns by goin' that direckshun. I'm not sartin they're Tenawas. Southart this Staked Plain hain't no endin' till ye git down to the Grand River below its big bend, an' that ain't to be thort o'. By strikin' east, a little southart, we mout reach the head sources o' the Loozyany Red; an' oncest on a stream o' runnin' water, this child kin generally navigate down it, provided he hev a rifle, powder, an' a bullet or two in his pouch. Thank the Almighty Lord, we've stuck to your gun through the thick an' the thin o't. Ef we hedn't we mout jest as well lie down agin' an' make a die at oncest."

"Go which way you please, Walt; you know best. I am ready to follow you; and I think I shall be able."

"Wal, at anyhow, we'd best be movin' off from hyar. If ye can't go a great ways under kiver o' the night, I reck'n we kin put enough o' parairia atween us an' these Injuns to make sure agin thar spyin' us in the mornin'.

So let's start south-eastart, an' try for the sources o' the Red. Thur's that ole beauty o' the North Star that's been my friend an' guide many's the good time. Thar it is, makin' the handle o' the Plough, or the Great Bar, as I've heern that colleckshin o' stars freekwently called. We've only to keep it on our left, a leetle torst the back o' the shoulder, an' then we're boun' to bring out on some o' the head-forks o' the Red—if we kin only last long enough to reach 'em. Darn it! thar's no danger; an' anyhow, thar's no help for't but try. Come along!"

So speaking, the guide started forward—not in full stride, but timing his pace to suit the feeble steps of his disabled comrade.

Chapter Eighteen.
A Lilliputian Forest.

Guiding their course by the stars the fugitives continue on—no longer going in a run, nor even in a very rapid walk. Despite the resolution with which he endeavours to nerve himself, the wounded man is still too weak to make much progress, and he advances but laggingly. His companion does not urge him to quicken his pace. The experienced prairie man knows it will be better to go slowly than get broken down by straining forward too eagerly. There is no sign or sound of Indian, either behind or before them. The stillness of the desert is around them—its silence only interrupted by the "whip-whip" of the night-hawk's wings, and at intervals its soft note answering to the shriller cry of the kid-deer plover that rises screaming before their feet. These, with the constant skirr of the ground-crickets and the prolonged whine of the coyote, are the only sounds that salute them as they glide on—none of which are of a kind to cause alarm.

There appears no great reason for making haste now. They have all the night before them, and, ere daylight can discover them, they will be sure to find some place of concealment.

The ground is favourable to pedestrianism in the darkness. The surface, hard-baked by the sun, is level as a set flagstone, and in most places so smooth that a carriage could run upon it as on the drive of a park. Well for them it is so. Had the path been a rugged one the wounded man would not go far before giving out. Even as it is, the toil soon begins to tell on his wasted strength. His veins are almost emptied of blood.

Nor do they proceed a very great distance before again coming to a halt; though far enough to feel sure that, standing erect, they cannot be descried by any one who may have ascended the cliff at the place where they took departure from it.

But they have also reached that which offers them a chance of concealment—in short, a forest. It is a forest not discernible at more than a mile's distance, for the trees that compose it are "shin oaks," the tallest rising to the height of only eighteen inches above the surface of the ground. Eighteen inches is enough to conceal the body of a man lying in a prostrate attitude; and as the Lilliputian trees grow thick as jimson weeds, the cover will be a secure one. Unless the pursuers should stray so close as to tread upon them, there will be no danger of their being seen. Further reflection has by this time satisfied them that the Indians are not upon the upper plain. It is not likely, after the pains they had taken to smoke them in the cave and afterwards shut them up. Besides, the distribution of the spoils would be an attraction sure to draw them back to the waggons, and speedily.

Becoming satisfied that there is no longer a likelihood of their being pursued across the plain, Wilder proposes that they again make stop; this time to obtain sleep, which in their anxiety during their previous spell of rest they did not attempt. He makes the proposal out of consideration for his comrade, who for some time, as he can see, has evidently been hard pressed to keep up with him.

"We kin lie by till sun-up," says Walt; "an' then, if we see any sign o' pursoot, kin stay hyar till the sun goes down agin. These shin oaks will gie us kiver enuf. Squatted, there'll be no chance o' thar diskiverin' us, unless they stumble right atop o' us." His companion is not in the mood to make objection, and the two lay themselves along the earth. The miniature forest not only gives them the protection of a screen but a soft bed, as the tiny trunks and leaf-laden branches become pressed down beneath their bodies.

They remain awake only long enough to give Hamersley's wound such dressing as the circumstances permit, and then both sink into slumber.

With the young prairie merchant it is neither deep nor profound. Horrid visions float before his rapt senses—scenes of red carnage—causing him ever and anon to awake with a start, once or twice with a cry that wakes his companion.

Otherwise Walt Wilder would have slept as soundly as if reposing on the couch of a log cabin a thousand miles removed from any scene of danger. It is no new thing for him to go to sleep with the yell of savages sounding in his ears. For a period of over twenty years he has daily, as nightly, stretched his huge form along mountain slope or level prairie, and often with far more danger of having his "hair raised" before rising erect again. For ten years he belonged to the "Texas Rangers"—that strange organisation that has existed ever since Stephen Austin first planted his colony in the land of the "Lone Star." If on this night the ex-Ranger is more than usually restless, it is from anxiety about his comrade, coupled with the state of his nervous system, stirred to feverish excitement by the terrible conflict through which they have just passed. Notwithstanding all, he slumbers in long spells, at times snoring like an alligator.

At no time does the ex-Ranger stand in need of much sleep, even after the most protracted toil. Six hours is his usual daily or nocturnal dose; and as the grey dawn begins to glimmer over the tops of the shin oaks, he springs to his feet, shakes the dew from his shoulders like a startled stag, and then stoops down to examine the condition of his wounded comrade.

"Don't ye git up yit, Frank," he says. "We mustn't start till we hev a clar view all roun', an' be sure there's neery redskin in sight. Then we kin take the sun a leetle on our left side, an' make tracks to the south-eastart. How is't wi' ye?"

"I feel weak as water. Still I fancy I can travel a little farther."

"Wall, we'll go slow. Ef there's none o' the skunks arter us, we kin take our time. Durn me! I'm still a wonderin' what Injuns they war; I'm a'most sartint thar the Tenawa Kimanch—a band o' the Buffler-eaters an' the wust lot on all the parairia. Many's the fight we rangers used to hev wi' 'em, and many's the one o' 'em this child hev rubbed out. Ef I only hed my rifle hyar—durn the luck hevin' to desart that gun—I ked show you nine nicks on her timmer as stan' for nine Tenawa Kimanch. Ef't be them, we've got to keep well to the southart. Thar range lays most in the Canadyen, or round the head o' Big Wichitu, an' they mout cross a corner o' the Staked Plain on thar way home. Tharfer we must go southart a good bit, and try for the north fork o' the Brazos. Ef we meet Indian thar, they'd be Southern Kimanch—not nigh sech feeroshus varmints as them. Do you know, Frank, I've been hevin' a dream 'bout them Injuns as attacked us?"

"A dream! So have I. It is not strange for either of us to dream of them. What was yours, Walt?"

"Kewrus enuf mine war, though it warn't all a dreem. I reck'n I war more 'n half awake when I tuk to thinkin' about 'em, an' 'twar somethin' I seed durin' the skrimmage. Didn't you observe nothin' queery?"

"Rather say, nothing that was not that way. It was all queer enough, and terrible, too."

"That this child will admit wi' full freedom. But I've f't redskin afore in all sorts an' shapes, yet niver seed redskin sech as them."

"In what did they differ from other savages? I saw nothing different."

"But I did; leastways, I suspeck I did. Didn't you spy 'mong the lot two or three that had ha'r on thar faces?"

"Yes; I noticed that. I thought nothing of it. It's common among the Comanches and other tribes of the Mexican territory, many of whom are of mixed breed—from the captive Mexican women they have among them."

"The ha'r I seed didn't look like it grew on the face o' a mixed blood."

"But there are pure white men among them—outlaws who have run away from civilisation and turned renegades—as also captives they have taken, who become Indianised, as the Mexicans call it. Doubtless it may have been some of these we saw."

"Wall, you may be right, Frank. Sartint thar war one I seed wi' a beard 'most as big as my own—only it war black. His hide war black, too, or nigh to it; but ef that skunk wan't white un'erneath a coatin' o' charcoal an' vermilion then Walt Wilder don't know a Kristyun from a heethun. I ain't no use spek'latin' on't now. White, black, yella-belly, or red, they've put us afoot on the parairia, an' kim darned nigh wipin' us out althegither. We've got a fair chance o' goin' un'er yet, eyther from thirst or the famishment o' empty stomaks. I'm hungry enuf already to eat a coyat. Thar's a heavy row afore us, Frank, an' we must strengthen our hearts to hoein' o' it. Wall, the sun's up; an' as thar don't appear to be any obstrukshun, I reck'n we'd best be makin' tracks."

Hamersley slowly and somewhat reluctantly rises to his feet. He still feels in poor condition for travelling. But to stay there is to die; and bracing himself to the effort, he steps out side by side with his colossal companion.

Chapter Nineteen.
The Departure of the Plunderers.

On the day after the capture of the caravan the Indians, having consumed all the whisky found in the waggons, and become comparatively sober, prepared to move off.

The captured goods, made up into convenient parcels, were placed upon mules and spare horses. Of both they had plenty, having come prepared for such a sequel to their onslaught upon the traders.

The warriors, having given interment to their dead comrades, leaving the scalped and mutilated corpses of the white men to the vultures and wolves, mounted and marched off.

Before leaving the scene of their sanguinary exploit, they had drawn the waggons into a close clump and set fire to them, partly from a wanton instinct of destruction, partly from the pleasure of beholding a great bonfire, but also with some thoughts that it might be as well thus to blot out all the traces of a tragedy for which the Americans—of whom even these freebooters felt dread—might some day call them to account.

They did not all go together, but separated into two parties on the spot where they had passed the night. They were parties, however, of very unequal size, one of them numbering only four individuals.

The other, which constituted the main body of the plunderers, was the band of the Tenawa Comanchey, under their chief, Horned Lizard. These last turned eastward, struck off towards the head waters of the Big Witches, upon which and its tributaries lie their customary roving grounds.

The lesser party went off in almost the opposite direction, south-westerly, leaving the Llano Estacado on their left, and journeying on, crossed the Rio Pecos at a point below and outside the farthest frontier settlement of New Mexico towards the prairies. Then, shaping their course nearly due south, they skirted the spurs of the Sierra Blanca, that in this latitude extend eastward almost to the Pecos.

On arriving near the place known as Gran Quivira—where once stood a prosperous Spanish town, devoted to gathering gold, now only a ruin, scarcely traceable, and altogether without record—they again changed their course, almost zigzagging back in a north-westerly direction. They were making towards a depression seen in the Sierra Blanca, as if with the intention to cross the mountains toward the valley of the Del Norte. They might have reached the valley without this circumstance, by a trail well known and often travelled. But it appeared as if this was just what they wanted to avoid.

One of the men composing this party was he already remarked upon as having a large beard and whiskers. A second was one of those spoken of as more slightly furnished with these appendages, while the other two were beardless.

All four were of deep bronze complexion, and to all appearance pure-blooded aboriginals. That the two with hirsute sign spoke to one another in Spanish was no sure evidence of their not being Indians. It was within the limits of New Mexican territory, where there are many Indians who converse in Castilian as an ordinary language.

He with the whiskered cheeks—the chief of the quartet, as well as the tallest of them—had not left behind the share of plunder that had been allotted to him. It was still in his train, borne on the backs of seven strong mules, heavily loaded. These formed an *atajo* or pack-train, guided and driven by the two beardless men of the party, who seemed to understand mule driving as thoroughly as if they had been trained to the calling of the *arriero*; and perhaps so had they been.

The other two took no trouble with the pack-animals, but rode on in front, conversing *sans souci*, and in a somewhat jocular vein.

The heavily-bearded man was astride a splendid black horse; not a Mexican mustang, like that of his companions, but a large sinewy animal, that showed the breed of Kentucky. And so should he—since he was the same steed Frank Hamersley had been compelled to leave behind in that rapid rush into the crevice of the cliff.

"This time, Roblez, we've made a pretty fair haul of it," remarked he who bestrode the black. "What with the silks and laces—to say nothing of this splendid mount between my legs—I think I may say that our time has not been thrown away."

"Yours hasn't, anyhow. My share won't be much."

"Come, come, *teniente!* don't talk in that way. You should be satisfied with a share proportioned to your rank. Besides, you must remember the man who puts down the stake has the right to draw the winnings. But for me there would have been no spoils to share. Isn't it so?"

This truth seeming to produce an impression on Roblez's mind, he made response in the affirmative.

"Well, I'm glad you acknowledge it," pursued the rider of the black. "Let there be no disputes between us; for you know, Roblez, we can't afford to quarrel. You shall have a liberal percentage on this lucky venture; I promise it. By the bye, how much do you think the plunder ought to realise?"

"Well," responded Roblez, restored to a cheerful humour, "if properly disposed of in El Paso or Chihuahua, the lot ought to fetch from fifteen to twenty thousand dollars. I see some silk-velvet among the stuff that would sell high, if you could get it shown to the rich damsels of Durango or Zacatecas. One thing sure, you've got a good third of the caravan stock."

"Ha! ha! More than half of it in value. The Horned lizard went in for bulk. I let him have it to his heart's content. He thinks more of those cheap cotton prints, with their red and green and yellow flowers, than all the silk ever spun since the days of Mother Eve. Ha! ha! ha!"

The laugh, in which Roblez heartily joined, was still echoing on the air as the two horsemen entered a pass leading through the mountains. It was the depression in the sierra, seen shortly after parting with the Horned Lizard and his band. It was a pass rugged with rock, and almost trackless, here and there winding about, and sometimes continued through canons or clefts barely wide enough to give way to the mules with the loads upon their backs.

For all this the animals of the travellers seemed to journey along it without difficulty, only the American horse showing signs of awkwardness. All the others went as if they had trodden it before.

For several hours they kept on through this series of canons and gorges—here and there crossing a transverse ridge that, cutting off a bend, shortened the distance.

Just before sunset the party came to a halt; not in the defile itself, but in one of still more rugged aspect, that led laterally into the side of the mountain. In this there was no trace or sign of travel—no appearance of its having been entered by man or animal.

Yet the horse ridden by Roblez, and the pack-mules coming after, entered with as free a step as if going into a well-known enclosure. True, the chief of the party, mounted on the Kentucky steed, had gone in before them; though this scarce accounted for their confidence.

Up this unknown gorge they rode until they had reached its end. There was no outlet, for it was a *cul-de-sac*—a natural court—such as are often found among the amygdaloidal mountains of Mexico.

At its extremity, where it narrowed to a width of about fifty feet, lay a huge boulder of granite that appeared to block up the path; though there was a clear space between it and the cliff rising vertically behind it.

The obstruction was only apparent, and did not cause the leading savage of the party to make even a temporary stop. At one side there was an opening large enough to admit the passage of a horse; and into this he rode, Roblez following, and also the mules in a string, one after the other.

Behind the boulder was an open space of a few square yards, of extent sufficient to allow room for turning a horse. The savage chief wheeled his steed, and headed him direct for the cliff; not with the design of dashing his brains against the rock, but to force him into a cavern, whose entrance showed its disc in the façade of the precipice, dark and dismal as the door of an Inquisitorial prison.

The horse snorted, and shied back; but the ponderous Mexican spur, with its long sharp rowel-points, soon drove him in; whither he was followed by the mustang of Roblez and the mules—the latter going in as unconcernedly as if entering a stable whose stalls were familiar to them.

Chapter Twenty.
A Transformation.

It was well on in the afternoon of the following day before the four spoil-laden savages who had sought shelter in the cave again showed themselves outside. Then came they filing forth, one after the other, in the same order as they had entered; but so changed in appearance that no one seeing them come out of the cavern could by any possibility have recognised them as the same men who had the night before gone into it. Even their animals had undergone some transformation. The horses were differently caparisoned; the flat American saddle having been removed from the back of the grand Kentucky steed, and replaced by the deep-tree Mexican *silla*, with its *corona* of stamped leather and wooden *estribos*. The mules, too, were rigged in a different manner, each having the regular *alpareja*, or pack-saddle, with the broad *apishamores* breeched upon its hips; while the spoils, no longer in loose, carelessly tied-up bundles, were made up into neat packs, as goods in regular transportation by an *atajo*.

The two men who conducted them had altogether a changed appearance. Their skins were still of the same colour—the pure bronze-black of the Indian—but, instead of the eagle's feathers late sticking up above their crowns, both had their heads now covered with simple straw hats; while sleeveless coats of coarse woollen stuff, with stripes running transversely—*tilmas*—shrouded their shoulders, their limbs having free play in white cotton drawers of ample width. A leathern belt, and apron of reddish-coloured sheepskin, tanned, completed the costume of an *arriero* of the humbler class—the *mozo*, or assistant.

But the change in the two other men—the chief and him addressed as Roblez—was of a far more striking kind. They had entered the cave as Indians, warriors of the first rank, plumed, painted, and adorned with all the devices and insignia of savage heraldry. They came out of it as white men, wearing the costume of well-to-do rancheros—or rather that of town traders—broad glazed hats upon their heads, cloth jackets and trousers— the latter having the seats and insides of the legs fended with a lining of stamped leather; boots with heavy spurs upon their feet, crape sashes around the waist, machetes strapped along the flaps of their saddles, and seraphs resting folded over the croup, gave the finishing touch to their travelling equipment. These, with the well appointed *atajo* of mules, made the party one of peaceful merchants transporting their merchandise from town to town.

On coming out of the cave, the leader, looking fresh and bright from his change of toilet and late purification of his skin, glanced up towards the sky, as if to consult the sun as to the hour. At the same time he drew a gold watch from his vest pocket, and looked also at that.

"We'll be just in the right time, Roblez," he said. "Six hours yet before sunset. That will get us out into the valley, and in the river road. We're not likely to meet any one after nightfall in these days of Indian alarms. Four more will bring us to Albuquerque, long after the sleepy townsfolk have gone to bed. We've let it go late enough, anyhow, and mustn't delay here any longer. Look well to your mules, *mozos! Vamonos!*"

At the word all started together down the gorge, the speaker, as before, leading the way, Roblez next, and the mozos with their laden mules stringing out in the rear.

Soon after, they re-entered the mountain defile, and, once more heading north-westward, silently continued on for the valley of the Rio del Norte. Their road, as before, led tortuously through canons and rugged ravines — no road at all, but a mere bridle path, faintly indicated by the previous passage of an occasional wayfarer or the tracks of straying cattle.

The sun was just sinking over the far western Cordilleras when the precipitous wall of the Sierra Blanca, opening wider on each side of the defile, disclosed to the spoil-laden party a view of the broad level plain known as the valley of the Del Norte.

Soon after, they had descended to it; and in the midst of night, with a starry sky overhead, were traversing the level road upon which the broad wheel-tracks of rude country carts — *carretas* — told of the proximity of settlements. It was a country road, leading out from the foot-hills of the sierra to a crossing of the river, near the village of Tomé, where it intersected with the main route of travel running from El Paso in the south through all the riverine towns of New Mexico.

Turning northward from Tomé, the white robbers, late disguised as Indians, pursued their course towards the town of Albuquerque. Any one meeting them on the road would have mistaken them for a party of traders *en route* from the Rio Abajo to the capital of Santa Fé.

But they went not so far. Albuquerque was the goal of their journey, though on arriving there — which they did a little after midnight — they made no stop in the town, nor any noise to disturb its inhabitants, at that hour asleep.

Passing silently through the unpaved streets, they kept on a little farther. A large house or hacienda, tree shaded, and standing outside the suburbs, was the stopping place they were aiming at; and towards this they directed their course. There was a *mirador* or belvidere upon the roof—the same beside which Colonel Miranda and his American guest, just twelve months before, had stood smoking cigars.

As then, there was a guard of soldiers within the covered entrance, with a sentry outside the gate. He was leaning against the postern, his form in the darkness just distinguishable against the grey-white of the wall.

"*Quien-viva?*" he hailed as the two horsemen rode up, the hoof-strokes startling him out of a half-drunken doze.

"*El Coronel-Commandante!*" responded the tall man in a tone that told of authority.

It proved to be countersign sufficient, the speaker's voice being instantly recognised.

The sentry, bringing his piece to the salute, permitted the horsemen to pass without further parley, as also the *atajo* in their train, all entering and disappearing within the dark doorway, just as they had made entrance into the mouth of the mountain cavern.

While listening to the hoof-strokes of the animals ringing on the pavement of the *patio* inside, the sentinel had his reflections and conjectures. He wondered where the colonel-commandant could have been to keep him so long absent from his command, and he had perhaps other conjectures of an equally perplexing nature. They did not much trouble him, however. What mattered it to him how the commandant employed his time, or where it was spent, so long as he got his *sueldo* and rations? He had them with due regularity, and with this consoling reflection he wrapped his yellow cloak around him, leaned against the wall, and soon after succumbed to the state of semi-watchfulness from which the unexpected event had aroused him.

"Carrambo!" exclaimed the Colonel to his subordinate, when, after looking to the stowage of the plunder, the two men sat together in a well-furnished apartment of the hacienda, with a table, decanters, and glasses between them. "It's been a long, tedious tramp, hasn't it? Well, we've not wasted our time, nor had our toil for nothing. Come, *teniente*, fill your glass again, and let us drink to our commercial adventure. Here's that in the disposal of our goods we may be as successful as in their purchase!"

Right merrily the lieutenant refilled his glass, and responded to the toast of his superior officer.

"I suspect, Roblez," continued the Colonel, "that you have been all the while wondering how I came to know about this caravan whose spoil is to enrich us—its route—the exact time of its arrival, the strength of its defenders—everything? You think our friend the Horned Lizard gave me all this information."

"No, I don't; since that could not well be. How was Horned Lizard to know himself—that is, in time to have sent word to you? In truth, *mio Coronel*, I am, as you say, in a quandary about all that. I cannot even guess at the explanation."

"This would give it to you, if you could read; but I know you cannot, *mio teniente*; your education has been sadly neglected. Never mind, I shall read it for you."

As the colonel was speaking he had taken from the drawer of a cabinet that stood close by a sheet of paper folded in the form of a letter. It was one, though it bore no postmark. For all that, it looked as if it had travelled far—perchance carried by hand. It had in truth come all the way across the prairies. Its superscription was:—

"El Coronel Miranda, Commandante del Distrito Militario de Albuquerque, Nuevo Mexico."

Its contents, also in Spanish, translated read thus:—

"My dear Colonel Miranda,—I am about to carry out the promise made to you at our parting. I have my mercantile enterprise in a forward state of readiness for a start over the plains. My caravan will not be a large one, about six or seven waggons with less than a score of men; but the goods I take are valuable in an inverse ratio to their bulk—designed for the 'ricos' of your country. I intend taking departure from the frontier town of Van Buren, in the State of Arkansas, and shall go by a new route lately discovered by one of our prairie traders, that leads part way along the Canadian river, by you called 'Rio de la Canada,' and skirting the great plain of the Llano Estacado at its upper end. This southern route makes us more independent of the season, so that I shall be able to travel in the fall. If nothing occur to delay me in the route, I shall reach New Mexico about the middle of November, when I anticipate renewing those relations of a pleasant friendship in which you have been all the giver and I all the receiver.

"I send this by one of the spring caravans starting from Independence for Santa Fé, in the hope that it will safely reach you.

"I subscribe myself, dear Colonel Miranda,—

"Your grateful friend,—

"Francis Hamersley."

"Well, *teniente*," said his Colonel, as he refolded the far-fetched epistle, and returned it to the drawer, "do you comprehend matters any clearer now?"

"Clear as the sun that shines over the Llano Estacado," was the reply of the lieutenant, whose admiration for the executive qualities of his superior officer, along with the bumpers he had imbibed, had now exalted his fancy to a poetical elevation. "*Carrai-i! Esta un golpe magnifico!* (It's a splendid stroke!) Worthy of Manuel Armilo himself. Or even the great Santa Anna!"

"A still greater stroke than you think it, for it is double—two birds killed with the same stone. Let us again drink to it!"

The glasses were once more filled, and once more did the associated bandits toast the nefarious enterprise they had so successfully accomplished.

Then Roblez rose to go to the *cuartel* or barracks, where he had his place of sleeping and abode, bidding *buena noche* to his colonel.

The latter also bethought him of bed, and, taking a lamp from the table, commenced moving towards his *cuarto de camara*.

On coming opposite a picture suspended against the *sala* wall—the portrait of a beautiful girl—he stopped in front, for a moment gazed upon it, and then into a mirror that stood close by.

As if there was something in the glass that reflected its shadow into his very soul, the expression of exultant triumph, so lately depicted upon his face, was all at once swept from it, giving place to a look of blank bitterness.

"One is gone," he said, in a half-muttered soliloquy; "one part of the stain wiped out—thanks to the Holy Virgin for that. But the other; and she—where, where?"

And with these words he staggered on towards his chamber.

Chapter Twenty One.
Struggling among the Sages.

It is the fourth day after forsaking the couch among the shin oaks, and the two fugitives are still travelling upon the Llano Estacado. They have made little more than sixty miles to the south-eastward, and have not yet struck any of the streams leading out to the lower level of the Texan plain.

Their progress has been slow; for the wounded man, instead of recovering strength, has grown feebler. His steps are now unequal and tottering. In addition to the loss of blood, something else has aided to disable him—the fierce cravings of hunger and the yet more insufferable agony of thirst.

His companion is similarly afflicted; if not in so great a degree, enough to make him also stagger in his steps. Neither has had any water since the last drop drank amid the waggons, before commencing the fight; and since then a fervent sun shining down upon them, with no food save crickets caught in the plain, an occasional horned frog, and some fruit of the *opuntia* cactus—the last obtained sparingly.

Hunger has made havoc with both, sad and quick. Already at the end of the fourth day their forms are wasted. They are more like spectres than men.

And the scene around them is in keeping. The plain, far as the eye can reach, is covered with *artemisia*, whose hoary foliage, in close contact at the tops, displays a continuation of surface like a vast winding-sheet spread over the world.

Across this fall the shadows of the two men, proportioned to their respective heights. That of the ex-Ranger extends nearly a mile before him; for the sun is low down, and they have its beams upon their backs.

They are facing eastward, in the hope of being able to reach the brow of the Llano where it abuts on the Texan prairies; though in the heart of one of them this hope is nearly dead. Frank Hamersley has but slight hopes that he will ever again see the homes of civilisation, or set foot upon its frontier. Even the ci-devant Ranger inclines to a similar way of thinking.

Not far off are other animated beings that seem to rejoice. The shadows of the two men are not the only ones that move over the sunlit face of the artemisia. There, too, are outlined the wings of birds—large birds with sable plumage and red naked necks, whose species both know well. They are *zopilotés*—the vultures of Mexico.

A score of such shadows are flitting over the sage—a score of the birds are wheeling in the air above.

It is a sight to pain the traveller, even when seen at a distance. Over his own head it may well inspire him with fear. He cannot fail to read in it a forecast of his own fate.

The birds are following the two men, as they would a wounded buffalo or stricken deer. They soar and circle above them, at times swooping portentously near. They do not believe them to be spectres. Wasted as their flesh may be, there will still be a banquet upon their bones.

Now and then Walt Wilder casts a glance up towards them. He is anxious, though he takes care to hide his anxiety from his comrade. He curses the foul creatures, not in speech—only in heart, and silently.

For a time the wearied wayfarers keep on without exchanging a word. Hitherto consolation has come from the side of the ex-Ranger; but he seems to have spent his last effort, and is himself now despairing.

In Hamersley's heart hope has been gradually dying out, as his strength gets further exhausted. At length the latter gives way, the former at the same time.

"No farther, Walt!" he exclaims, coming to a stop. "I can't go a step further. There is a fire in my throat that chokes me; something grips me within. It is dragging me to the ground."

The hunter stops too. He makes no attempt to urge his comrade on. He perceives it would be idle.

"Go on yourself," Hamersley adds, gasping out the words. "You have yet strength left, and may reach water. I cannot, but I can die, I'm not afraid to die. Leave me, Walt; leave me!"

"Niver!" is the response, in a hoarse, husky voice, but firm, as if it came from a speaking-trumpet.

"You will; you must. Why should two lives be sacrificed for one? Yours may still be saved. Take the gun along with you. You may find something. Go, comrade—friend—go!"

Again the same response, in a similar tone.

"I sayed, when we were in the fight," adds the hunter, "an' aterwards, when gallupin' through the smoke, that livin' or dyin' we'd got to stick thegither. Didn't I say that, Frank Hamersley? I repeat it now. Ef you go unner hyar in the middle o' this sage-brush, Walt Wilder air goin' to wrap his karkiss in a corner o' the same windin' sheet. There ain't much strength remainin' in my arms now, but enuf, I reck'n, to keep them buzzarts off for a good spell yit. They don't pick our bones till I've thinned thar count anyhow. Ef we air to be rubbed out, it'll be by the chokin' o' thirst, and not the gripin' o' hunger. What durned fools we've been, not to a-thinked o' 't afore! but who'd iver think o' eatin' turkey buzzart? Wall, it's die dog or swaller the hatchet; so onpalatable as thar flesh may be, hyar goes to make a meal o' it!"

While speaking, he has carried the gun to his shoulder.

Simultaneous with his last words comes the crack, quickly followed by the descent of a zopiloté among the sages.

"Now, Frank," he says, stooping to pick up the dead bird, while the scared flock flies farther away, "let's light a bit o' a fire, an' cook it. Thar's plenty o' sage for the stuffin', an' its own flavour'll do for seasonin' 'stead o' inyuns. I reck'n we kin git some o' it down, by holdin' our noses; an' at all events, it'll keep us alive a leetle longer. Wagh, ef we only hed water!"

As if a fresh hope has come suddenly across his mind, he once more raises himself erect to the full stretch of his gigantic stature, and standing thus, gazes eastwardly across the plain.

"Thar's a ridge o' hills out that way," he says. "I'd jest spied it when you spoke o' giein out. Whar thar's hills, thar's a likelihood o' streams. Sposin', Frank, you stay hyar, whiles I make tracks torst them. They look like they wa'n't mor'n ten miles off anyhow. I ked easy get back by the mornin'. D'ye think ye kin hold out thet long by swallerin' a bit o' the buzzart?"

"I think I could hold out that long as well without it. It's more the thirst that's killing me. I feel as if liquid fire was coursing through my veins. If you believe there be any chance of finding water, go, Walt."

"I'll do so; but don't you sturve in the meanwhile. Cook the critter afore lettin' it kim to thet. Ye've got punk, an' may make a fire o' the sage-brush. I don't intend to run the risk o' sturvin' myself; an' as I mayn't find any thin' on the way, I'll jest take one o' these sweet-smellin' chickens along wi' me."

He has already re-loaded the rifle; and, once more pointing its muzzle towards the sky, he brings down a second of the zopilotés.

"Now," he says, taking up the foul carcase, and slinging it to his belt, "keep up your heart till this chile return to ye. I'm sure o' gettin' back by the mornin'; an' to make sartint 'bout the place, jest you squat unner the shadder o' yon big palmetto—the which I can see far enuff off to find yur wharabouts 'thout any defeequelty."

The palmetto spoken of is, in truth, not a "palmetto," though a plant of kindred genus. It is a *yucca* of a species peculiar to the high table plains of Northern and Central Mexico, with long sword-shaped leaves springing aloe-like from a core in the centre, and radiating in all directions, so as to form a spherical chevaux-de-frize. Its top stands nearly six feet above the surface of the ground, and high over the artemisias; while its dark, rigid spikes, contrasted with the frosted foliage of the sage, render it a conspicuous landmark that can be seen far off over the level plain.

Staggering on till he has reached it, Hamersley drops down on its eastern side, where its friendly shadow gives him protection from the sun, fervid, though setting; while that of Walt Wilder is still projected to its full length upon the plain. Saying not another word, with the rifle across his shoulder and the turkey buzzard dangling down his thigh, he takes departure from the spot, striking eastward towards the high land dimly discernible on the horizon.

Chapter Twenty Two.
A Huntress.

"*Vamos*, Lolita! hold up, my pretty pet! Two leagues more, and you shall bury that velvet snout of yours in the soft *gramma* grass, and cool your heated hoof in a crystal stream. Ay, and you shall have a half peck of pinon nuts for your supper, I promise you. You have done well to-day, but don't let us get belated. At night, as you know, we might be lost on the Llano, and the wicked wolves eat us both up. That would be a sad thing, *mia yegua*. We must not let them have a chance to dispose of us in that manner. *Adelante!*"

Lolita is a mustang pony of clear chestnut colour, with white mane and tail; while the person thus apostrophising her is a young girl seated astride upon its back.

A beautiful girl, apparently under twenty of age, but with a certain commanding mien that gives her the appearance of being older. Her complexion, though white, has a tinge of that golden brown, or olive, oft observed in the Andalusian race; while scimitar shaped eyebrows, with hair of silken texture, black as the shadows of night, and a dark down on the upper lip, plainly proclaim the Moorish admixture.

It is a face of lovely cast and almost Grecian contour, with features of classic regularity; while the absence of obliquity in the orbs of the eye—despite the dusky hue of her akin—forbids the belief in Indian blood.

Although in a part of the world where such might be expected, there is, in truth, not a taint of it in her veins. The olivine tint is Hispano Moriscan—a complexion, if not more beautiful, certainly more picturesque than that of the Saxon blonde.

With the damask-red dancing out upon her cheeks, her eyes aglow from the equestrian exercise she has been taking, the young girl looks the picture of physical health; while the tranquil expression upon her features tells of mental contentment.

Somewhat singular is her costume, as the equipment. As already said, she bestrides her mustang man-fashion, the mode of Mexico; while a light fowling-piece, suspended *en bandoulière*, hangs down behind her back.

A woollen seraph of finest wool lies scarf-like across her left shoulder, half concealing a velveteen vest or spencer, close-buttoned over the rounded hemispheres of her bosom. Below, an embroidered skirt—the *enagua*—is continued by a pair of white *calzoncillas*, with fringe falling over her small feet, they are booted and spurred.

On her head is a hat of soft vicuna wool, with a band of bullion, a bordering of gold lace around the rim, and a plume of heron's feather curving above the crown.

This, with her attitude on horseback, might seem *outré* in the eyes of a stranger to the customs of her country. The gun and its concomitant accoutrements give her something of a masculine appearance, and at the first glance might cause her to be mistaken for a man—a beardless youth.

But the long silken tresses scattered loosely over her shoulders, the finely-cut features, the delicate texture of the skin, the petticoat skirt, the small hand, with slender tapering fingers stretched forward to caress the neck of the mustang mare, are signs of femininity not to be misunderstood.

A woman—a huntress; the character clearly proclaimed by a brace of hounds—large dogs of the mastiff bloodhound breed—following at the heels of the horse. And a huntress who has been successful in the chase—as proved by two prong-horn antelopes, with shanks tied together, lying like saddle-bags across the croup.

The mustang mare needs no spur beyond the sound of that sweet well-known voice. At the word *adelante* (forward) she pricks up her ears, gives a wave of her snow-white tail, and breaks into a gentle canter, the hounds loping after in long-stretching trot.

For about ten minutes is this pace continued; when a bird flying athwart the course, so close that its wings almost brush Lolita's muzzle, causes her rider to lean back in the saddle and check her suddenly up.

The bird is a black vulture—a zopiloté. It is not slowly soaring in the usual way, but shooting in a direct line, and swiftly as an arrow sent from the bow.

This it is that brings the huntress to a halt; and for a time she remained motionless, her eye following the vulture in its flight.

It is seen to join a flock of its fellows, so far off as to look like specks. The young girl can perceive that they are not flying in any particular direction, but swooping in circles, as if over some quarry that lies below. Whatever it is, they do not appear to have yet touched it. All keep aloft, none of them alighting on the ground, though at times stooping down, and skimming close to the tops of the sage-bushes with which the plain is thickly beset.

These last prevent the huntress from seeing what lies upon the ground; though she knows there must be something to have attracted the concourse of zopilotés. Evidently she has enough knowledge of the desert to understand its signs, and this is one of a significant character. It not only challenges curiosity, but calls for investigation.

"Something gone down yonder, and not yet dead?" she mutters, in interrogative soliloquy. "I wonder what it can be! I never look on those filthy birds without fear. *Santissima*! how they made me shudder that time when they flapped their black wings in my own face! I pity any poor creature threatened by them—even where it but a coyoté. It may be that, or an antelope. Nothing else likely to become their prey on this bare plain. Come, Lolita! let us go on and see what they're after. It will take us a little out of our way, and give you some extra work. You won't mind that, my pet? I know you won't."

The mare wheels round at a slight pressure upon the rein; and then commenced her canter in the direction of the soaring flock.

A mile is passed over, and the birds are brought near; but still the object attracting them cannot be seen. It may be down among the artemisias, or perhaps behind a large yucca, whose dark whorl rises several feet above the sage, and over which the vultures are wheeling.

As the rider of Lolita arrives within gun-shot distance of the yucca-tree she checks the mustang to a slower pace—to a walk in short. In the spectacle of death, in the throes and struggles of an expiring creature, even though it be but a dumb brute, there is something that never fails to excite commiseration, mingled with a feeling of awe. This last has come over the young girl, as she draws near the spot where the birds are seen circling.

It has not occurred to her that the cause of their presence may be a human being, though it is a remembrance of this kind that now prompts her to ride forward reflectively. For once in her life, with others around her who were near and dear, she has been herself an object of like eager solicitude to a flock of zopilotés.

But she has not the slightest suspicion of its being a human creature that causes their gathering now. There, upon the Llano Estacado, so rarely trodden by human feet, and even shunned by almost every species of animal, she could not.

As she draws still nearer, a black disc, dimly outlined against the dark green leaves of the yucca, upon scrutiny, betrays the form of a bird, itself a vulture. It is dead, impaled upon the sharp spikes of the plant, as it came there by falling from above.

A smile curls upon her lips as she sits regarding it.

"So, *yegua*!" she says, bringing the mare to a stand, and half-turning her. "I've been losing my time and you your labour. The abominable birds— it's only one of themselves that has dropped dead, and they're holding a *velorio* over it."

She continues, again facing towards the dead vulture.

"Now, I wonder if they are only waking it, or if the wakers are cannibals, and intend making a repast on one of their own kind. That would be a curious fact for our natural historian, Don Prospero. Suppose we stay awhile and see?"

For a moment she seems undecided as to staying or going. Only for a moment, when an incident occurs that changes the current of her thoughts from scientific curiosity to something of fear.

The bloodhounds that have lagged behind in the scurry across the plain, now close up; and, instead of stopping by the side of Lolita, rush on towards the yucca. It is not the odour of the dead buzzard—strong as that may be—that attracts them; but the scent of what is more congenial to their sanguinary instincts.

On arriving at the tree they run round to its opposite side; and then spring growling back, as if something they have encountered there has suddenly brought them to bay.

"A wounded bear or wolf!" is the muttered reflection of their mistress.

It has scarce passed her lips, when she is made aware of her mistake. Above the continued baying of the dogs she can distinguish the tones of a human voice; and at the same instant, a man's head and arm appear above the spikes of the plant—a hand clutching the hilt of a long-bladed knife!

Chapter Twenty Three.
"Down, Dogs!"

Notwithstanding her apparent *sang-froid*, and the presence of mind she surely possesses, the rider of Lolita is affrighted—far more than the vultures, that have soared higher at her approach.

And no wonder that she is affrighted at such a strange apparition—the head of a man, with a dark moustache on his lip, holding in his hand a blade that shows blood upon it! This, too, in such a solitary place!

Her first thought is to turn Lolita's head and hurry off from the spot. Then a reflection stays her. The man is evidently alone, and the expression on his countenance is neither that of villainy nor anger. The colour of his skin, with the moustache, bespeak him a white man, and not an Indian. Besides, there is pallor upon his cheeks—a wan, wasted look, that tells of suffering, not sin.

All this the quick eye of the huntress takes in at a glance, resolving her how to act. Instead of galloping away she urges the mustang on towards the yucca.

When close up to it she flings herself out of the saddle, and, whip in hand, rushes up to the hounds, that are still giving tongue and threatening to spring upon the stranger.

"*Abajo, perros! abajo, feos!*" (Down, dogs! down, you ugly brutes!)

"*A tierra!*" she continues to scold, giving each a sharp cut that at once reduces them to quiescence, causing them to cower at her feet. "Do you not see the mistake you have made?" she goes on addressing the dogs; "don't you see the caballero is not an Indio? It is well, sir!" she adds, turning to the caballero, "well that your skin is white. Had it been copper-coloured, I'm not certain I could have saved you from getting it torn. My pets are not partial to the American aboriginal."

During these somewhat bizarre speeches and the actions that accompany them, Frank Hamersley—for it is he—stands staring in silent wonder. What sees he before him? Two huge, fierce-looking dogs, a horse oddly caparisoned, a young girl, scarce a woman, strangely and picturesquely garbed. What has he heard? First, the loud baying of two bloodhounds, threatening to tear him to pieces; then a voice, sweet and musical as the warbling of a bird!

Is it all a dream?

Dreaming he had been, when aroused by the growling of the dogs. But that was a horrid vision. What he now sees is the very reverse. Demons had been assaulting him in his sleep. Now there is an angel before his eyes.

The young girl has ceased speaking; and as the vertigo, caused by his sudden uprising, has cleared away from his brain, he begins to believe in the reality of the objects around him.

The shock of surprise has imparted a momentary strength that soon passes; and his feebleness once more returning, he would fall back to the earth did he not clutch hold of the yucca, whose stiff blades sustain him.

"*Valga me Dios!*" exclaims the girl, now more clearly perceiving his condition. "*Ay de mi!*" she repeats in a compassionate tone, "you are suffering, sir? Is it hunger? Is it thirst? You have been lost upon the Llano Estacado?"

"Hunger, thirst—both, senorita," he answers, speaking for the first time. "For days I have not tasted either food or drink."

"*Virgen santissima!* is that so?"

As she says this she returns to her horse; and, jerking a little wallet from the saddle, along, with a suspended gourd, again advances towards him.

"Here, señor!" she says, plunging her hand into the bag and bringing forth some cold *tortillas*, "this is all I have; I've been the whole day from home, and the rest I've eaten. Take the water first; no doubt you need that most. I remember how I suffered myself. Mix some of this with it. Trust me, it will restore your strength."

While speaking she hands him the gourd, which, by its weight, contains over a pint; and then from another and smaller one she pours some liquid first into the water and then over the tortillas. It is vinegar, in which there is an infusion of *chile Colorado*.

"Am I not robbing you?" inquires Hamersley, as he casts a significant glance over the wide, sterile plain.

"No, no! I am not in need, besides I have no great way to go to where I can get a fresh supply. Drink, señor, drink it all."

In ten seconds after the calabash is empty.

"Now eat the tortillas. 'Tis but poor fare, but the *chili vinagre* will be sure to strengthen you. We who dwell in the desert know that."

Her words proved true, for after swallowing a few morsels of the bread she has besprinkled, the famished man feels as if some restorative medicine had been administered to him.

"Do you think you are able to ride?" she asks.

"I can walk—though, perhaps, not very far."

"If you can ride there is no need for your walking. You can mount my mare; I shall go afoot. It is not very far—only six miles."

"But," protests he, "I must not leave this spot."

"Indeed!" she exclaims, turning upon her *protégé* a look of surprise. "For what reason, señor? To stay here would be to perish. You have no companions to care for you?"

"I have companions—at least, one. That is why I must remain. Whether he may return to assist me I know not. He has gone off in search of water. In any case, he will be certain to seek for me."

"But why should you stay for him?"

"Need you ask, senorita? He is my comrade, true and faithful. He has been the sharer of my dangers—of late no common ones. If he were to come back and find me gone—"

"What need that signify, caballero? He will know where to come after you."

"How should he know?"

"Oh, that will be easy enough. Leave it to me. Are you sure he will find his way back to this place?"

"Quite sure. This tree will guide him. He arranged it so before leaving."

"In that case, there's not any reason for your remaining. On the contrary. I can see that you need a better bed than sleeping among these sage-plants. I know one who will give it. Come with me, caballero? By the time your comrade can get back there'll be one here to meet him. Lest he should arrive before the messenger I shall send, this will save him from going astray."

While speaking she draws forth a small slip of paper from a pouch carried *à la chatelaine*; along with it a pencil. She is about to write, when a thought restrains her.

"Does your comrade understand Spanish?" she asks.

"Only a word or two. He speaks English, or, as we call it, American."

"Can he read?"

"Indifferently. Enough, I suppose, for—"

"Señor," she says, interrupting him, "I need not ask if you can write. Take this, and put it in your own language. Say you are gone south, due south, to a distance of about six miles. Tell your friend to stay here till some one comes to meet and conduct him to where you'll be found."

Hamersley perceives the rationality of these instructions. There is no reason why he should not do as desired, and go at once with her who gives them. By staying some mischance might still happen, and he may never see his fair rescuer again. Who can tell what may arise in the midst of that mysterious desert? By going he will the sooner be able to send succour to his comrade.

He hesitates no longer, but writes upon the piece of paper—in large, carefully-inscribed letters, so that the *ci-devant* Ranger need have no difficulty in deciphering them:—

"Saved by an Angel.—Strike due south. Six miles from this you will find me. There is a horse, and you can take up his tracks. If you stay here for a time, one will come and guide you."

The huntress takes the paper from his hand, and glances at the writing, as if out of curiosity to read the script of a language unknown to her. But something like a smile playing around her lips might lead one to believe she has divined the meaning of at least the initial sentence.

She makes no remark, but stepping towards the yucca and reaching up, impales the piece of paper on one of its topmost spikes.

"Now, caballero," she says, "you mount my mare. See, she stands ready for you."

Hamersley again protests, saying he can walk well enough.

But his tottering steps contradict him, and he urges his objections in vain.

The young girl appealingly persists, until at length the gallantry of the Kentuckian gives way, and he climbs reluctantly into the saddle.

"Now, Lolita!" cries her mistress, "see that your step is sure, or you shan't have the pinons I promised you. *Adelante! Nos vamos, señor!*"

So saying, she strikes off through the sage, the mustang stepping by her side, and the two great hounds, like a rear guard, bringing up behind.

Chapter Twenty Four.
Foes or Friends?

Mounted on the mustang mare, Frank Hamersley pursues his way, wondering at his strange guide. So lovely a being encountered in such an out-of-the-way corner of the world—in the midst of a treeless, waterless desert, over a hundred miles from the nearest civilised settlement!

Who is she? Where has she come from? Whither is she conducting him?

To the last question he will soon have an answer; for as they advance she now and then speaks words of encouragement, telling him they are soon to reach a place of rest.

"Yonder!" she at length exclaims, pointing to two mound-shaped elevations that rise twin-like above the level of the plain. "Between those runs our road. Once there, we shall not have much farther to go; the rancho will be in sight."

The young prairie merchant makes no reply. He only thinks how strange it all is—the beautiful being by his side—her dash—her wonderful knowledge exhibited with such an air of *naïveté*—her generous behaviour— the picturesqueness of her dress—her hunter equipment—the great dogs trotting at her heels—the dead game on the croup behind—the animal he bestrides—all are before his mind and mingling in his thoughts like the unreal phantasmagoria of a dream.

And not any more like reality is the scene disclosed to his view when, after passing around the nearest of the twin mound-shaped hills, and entering a gate-like gorge that opens between them, he sees before him and below—hundreds of feet below—a valley of elliptical form like a vast basin scooped out of the plain. But for its oval shape he might deem it the crater of some extinct volcano. But then, where is the lava that should have been projected from it? With the exception of the two hillocks on each hand, all the country around, far as the eye can reach, is level as the bosom of a placid lake. And otherwise unlike a volcanic crater is the concavity itself. No gloom down there, no black scoriae, no returning streams of lava, nor *débris* of pumice-stone; but, on the contrary, a smiling vegetation—trees with foliage of different shades, among which can be distinguished the dark-green frondage of the live-oak and pecan, the more brilliant verdure of cottonwoods, and the flower-loaded branches of the wild China-tree. In their midst a glassy disc that speaks of standing water, with here and there a fleck of white, which tells of a stream with foaming cascades and cataracts. Near the lakelet, in the centre, a tiny column of blue smoke ascends over the tree-tops. This indicates the presence of a dwelling; and as they advance a little further into the gorge, the house itself can be descried.

In contrast with the dreary plain over which he has been so long toiling, to Hamersley the valley appears a paradise—worthy home of the Peri who is conducting him down to it. It resembles a landscape painted upon the concave sides of an immense oval-shaped dish, with the cloudless sky, like a vast cover of blue glass, arching over it.

The scene seems scarcely real, and once more the young prairie merchant begins to doubt the evidence of his senses. After all, is it only a vision of his brain, distempered by the long strain upon his intellect, and the agony he has been enduring? Or is it but the *mirage* of the desert, that has so oft already deceived him?

His doubts are dissipated by the sweet voice sounding once more in his ears.

"*Mira, caballero*! you see where you are going now? It is not far; you will need to keep a firm seat in the saddle for the next hundred yards or so. There is a steep descent and a narrow pathway. Take good hold with your knees, and trust yourself to the mare. She knows the way well, and will bear you in safety. Won't you, Lolita? You will, my pet!"

At this the mustang gives a soft whimper, as if answering the interrogatory.

"I shall myself go before," the girl continues. "So let loose the rein, and leave Lolita to take her own way."

After giving this injunction, she turns abruptly to the right, where a path almost perpendicular leads down a ledge, traversing the façade of the cliff. Close followed by the mustang, she advances fearlessly along it.

Certainly a most dangerous descent, even for one afoot; and if left to his own will, Hamersley might decline attempting it on horseback. But he has no choice now, for before he can make either expostulation or protest, Lolita has struck along the path, and continues with hind-quarters high in air and neck extended in the opposite direction, as though standing upon her head! To her rider there is no alternative but do as he has been directed—stick close to the saddle. This he manages by throwing his feet forward and laying his back flat along the croup, till his shoulders come between the crossed shanks of the prong-horns.

In this position he remains, without saying a word, or even daring to look below, till he at length finds himself moving forward with face upturned to the sky, thus discovering that the animal he bestrides is once more going along level ground.

Again he hears the voice of Lolita's mistress, saying, "Now, señor, you can sit upright; the danger is past. You have behaved well, *yegua—yeguita!*" she adds, patting the mare upon the neck; "you shall have the promised pinons—a whole *cuartilla* of them."

Once more stepping to the front, she strikes off among the trees, along a path which still inclines downward, though now in gentler slope.

Hamersley's brain is in a whirl. The strange scenes, things, thoughts, and fancies are weaving weird spells around him; and once more he begins to think that his senses have either forsaken or are forsaking him.

This time it is really so, for the long-protracted suffering—the waste of blood and loss of strength—only spasmodically resuscitated by the excitement of the strange encounter—is now being succeeded by a fever of the brain, that is gradually depriving him of his reason.

He has a consciousness of riding on for some distance farther—under trees, whose leafy boughs form an arcade over his head, shutting out the sun. Soon after, all becomes suddenly luminous, as the mustang bears him out into a clearing, with what appears a log-cabin in the centre. He sees or fancies the forms of several men standing by its door; and as the mare comes to a stop in their midst his fair conductor is heard excitedly exclaiming,—

"*Hermano!* take hold of him! *Alerte! Alerte!*"

At this one of the men springs towards him; whether to be kind, or. to kill, he cannot tell. For before a hand is laid on him the strange tableau fades from his sight; and death, with all its dark obliviousness, seems to take possession of his soul.

Chapter Twenty Five.
"Saved by an Angel!"

The shadow of Walt Wilder is again projected over the Staked Plain, as before, to a gigantic length. But this time westwardly, from a sun that is rising instead of setting.

It is the morning after he parted with his disabled companion; and he is now making back towards the spot where he had left the latter, the sun's disc just appearing above the horizon, and shining straight upon his back. Its rays illumine an object not seen before, which lends to Walt's shadow a shape weird and fantastic. It is that of a giant, with something sticking out on each side of his head that resembles a pair of horns, or as if his neck was embraced by an ox-yoke, the tines tending diagonally outwards.

On looking at Walt himself the singularity is at once understood. The carcase of a deer lies transversely across his back, the legs of the animal being fastened together so as to form a sling, through which he has thrust his head, leaving the long slender shanks, like the ends of the letter X, projecting at each side and high above his shoulders.

Despite the load thus borne by him, the step of the ex-Ranger is no longer that of a man either despairing or fatigued. On the contrary, it is light and elastic; while his countenance shows bright and joyous as the beams of the ascending sun. His very shadow seems to flit over the frosted foliage of the artemisias as lightly as the figure of a gossamer-robed belle gliding across the waxed floor of a ball-room.

Walt Wilder no longer hungers or thirsts. Though the carcase on his back is still unskinned, a huge collop cut out of one of its hind-quarters tells how he has satisfied the first craving; while the gurgle of water, heard inside the canteen slung under his arm, proclaims that the second has also been appeased.

He is now hastening on to the relief of his comrade, happy in the thought of being able soon to relieve him also from his sufferings.

Striding lightly among the sage-bushes, and looking ahead for the landmark that should guide him, he at length catches sight of it. The palmilla, standing like a huge porcupine upon the plain, cannot be mistaken; and he descries it at more than a mile's distance, the shadow of his own head already flickering among its bayonet-like blades.

Just then something else comes under his eyes, which at once changes the expression upon his countenance. From gay it grows grave, serious, apprehensive. A flock of buzzards, seemingly scared by his shadow, have suddenly flapped up from among the sage-plants, and are now soaring around, close to the spikes of the palmilla. They have evidently been down *upon the earth*. And what have they been doing there?

It is this question, mentally put by Walt Wilder, that has caused the quick change in his countenance—the result of a painful conjecture.

"Marciful heavens!" he exclaims, suddenly making halt, the gun almost dropping from his grasp. "Kin it be possyble? Frank Hamersley gone under! Them buzzards! They've been upon the groun' to a sartinty. Darnashin! what ked they a been doin' down thar? Right by the bunch o' palmetto, jest whar I left him. An' no sign o' himself to be seen? Marciful heavens! kin it be possyble they've been—?"

Interrupting himself, he remains motionless, apparently paralysed by apprehension, mechanically scanning the palmilla, as though from it he expected an answer to his interrogatory.

"It air possyble," he continues after a time, "too possyble—too likesome. He war well-nigh done up, poor young fellur; an' no wonder. Whar is he now? He must be down by the side o' the bush—down an' dead. Ef he war alive, he'd be lookin' out for me. He's gone under; an' this deer-meat, this water, purcured to no purpiss. I mout as well fling both away; they'll reach him too late."

Once more resuming his forward stride, he advanced towards the dark mass above which the vultures are soaring. His shadow, still by a long distance preceding him, has frightened the birds higher up into the air, but they show no signs of going altogether away. On the contrary, they keep circling around, as if they had already commenced a repast, and, driven off, intend returning to it.

On what have they been banqueting? On the body of his comrade? What else can be there?

Thus questioning himself, the ex-Ranger advances, his heart still aching with apprehension. Suddenly his eye alights on the piece of paper impaled upon the topmost spike of the palmilla. The sight gives him relief, but only for an instant; his conjectures again leading him astray.

"Poor young fellur!" is his half-spoken reflection; "he's wrote somethin' to tell how he died—mayhap somethin' for me to carry back to the dear 'uns he's left behind in ole Kaintuck. Wall, that thing shall sartinly be done ef ever this chile gets to the States agin. Darnashin! only to think how near I war to savin' him; a whole doe deer, an' water enough to a drownded him! It'll be useless venison now, I shan't care no more to put tooth into it myself. Frank Hamersley gone dead—the man o' all others I'd 'a died to keep alive. I'd jest as soon lie down an' stop breathin' by the side o' him."

While speaking he moves on towards the palmilla. A few strides bring him so near the tree that he can see the ground surface about its base. There is something black among the stems of the sage-bushes. It is not the dead body of a man, but a buzzard, which he knows to be that he had shot before starting off. The sight of it causes him again to make stop. It looks draggled and torn, as if partially dismembered.

"Kin he hev been eatin' it? Or war it themselves, the cussed kannybals? Poor Frank, I reck'n I'll find him on t'other side, his body mangled in the same way. Darn it, 't air kewrous, too. 'Twar on this side he laid down to git shade from the sun. I seed him squat whiles I war walkin' away. The sun ain't hot enuf yit to a druv him to westward o' the bush, though thar for sartin he must be. What's the use o' my stannin' shilly-shally hyar? I may as well face the sight at oncest, ugly as I know it'll prove. Hyar goes."

Steeling himself for the terrible spectacle, which he believes to be certainly awaiting him, he once more advances towards the tree.

A dozen strides bring him up, and less than half a dozen more carry him around it.

No body, living or dead—no remains of man, mutilated or otherwise!

For some time Wilder stands in speechless surprise, his glances going all around. But no human figure is seen, either by the palmilla or among the sage-bushes beside it. Can the wounded man have crawled away? But no; why should he? Still, to make sure, the ex-Ranger shouts out, calling Hamersley by name.

He gets no response. Alone he hears the echo of his own voice, mingling with the hoarse croaking of the vultures, scared by his shouts.

His hunter habits now counsel him to a different course of action. His comrade cannot be dead, else the corpse would be there. The vultures could not have eaten up both body and bones. There is no skeleton, no remains. His fellow fugitive has gone off or been taken. Whither? While asking the question Wilder sets about the right way to answer it. As a skilled tracker he begins by examining the signs that should put him on the trace of his missing companion. At a glance he perceives the prints of a horse's hoof, and sees they are those of one unshod. This bodes ill, for the naked-hoofed horse betokens a savage rider—an Indian. Still, it may not be; and he proceeds to a more careful scrutiny of the tracks. In a short time he is able to tell that but one horse has been there, and presumably but one rider, which promises better. And while shaping conjectures as to who it could have been his eye ascends to the piece of paper impaled upon the spike, which he has for a time forgotten. This promises still better. It may clear up everything.

Hoping it will, he strides towards and takes hold of it. Lifting it carefully from the leaf, he spreads it out. He sees some writing in pencil, which he prepares to read.

At first sight he supposed it might be a dying record. Now he believes it may be something else.

His hands tremble, and his huge frame is convulsed as he holds the paper to his eyes.

With a thrill of joy he recognises the handwriting of Hamersley, which he knows. He is not much of a scholar; still, he can read, and at a glance makes out the first four words, full of pleasant meaning:

"*Saved by an Angel!*"

He reads no farther, till after giving utterance to a "hurrah!" that might have been heard many miles over the Staked Plain. Then, more tranquillised, he continues deciphering the chirography of his companion to the end; when a second shout terminates the effort.

"Saved by a angel!" he says, muttering to himself. "A angel on the Staked Plain! Whar can the critter hev come from? No matter whar. Thar's been one hyar, for sartin. Darn me ef I don't smell the sweet o' her pettikotes now! This piece o' paper—'t ain't Frank's. I knows he hedn't a scrap about him. No. Thar's the scent o' a woman on it, sure; an' whar thar's a woman Frank Hamersley ain't likely to be let die o' sturvashun. He air too good-lookin' for that. Wall I reck'n it's all right an' thar ain't no more need for me to hurry. T'war rayther a scant breakfast I've hed, an' hain't gin this chile's in'ards saterfacshun. I'll jest chaw another griskin o' the deer-meat to strengthen me for this six-mile tramp southard."

In less than five minutes after, the smoke from a sage-stalk fire was seen ascending from beside the palmilla, and in its blaze, quickly kindled, a huge piece of venison, cut from the fat flanks of the doe, weighing at least four pounds, spitted upon one of the stiff blades of the plant, was rapidly turning from blood red to burnt brown.

As circumstances had ofttimes compelled the ex-Ranger to eat his deer-meat underdone, the habit had become his *goût*; and it was, therefore, not long before the griskin was removed from the spit. Nor much longer till it ceased to be a griskin—having altogether disappeared from his fingers, followed by a gurgling sound, as half the contents of the canteen went washing it down his throat.

"Now!" he said, springing to his feet, after he had completed his Homeric repast, "this chile feels strong enuf to face the devil hisself, an' tharfor he needn't be backward 'bout the encounterin' o' a angel. So hyar goes to find out Frank Hamersley, an' how *he's* farin'. Anyhow, I'll take the deer along in case thar mout be a scarcity o' eetables, though I reck'n thar's no fear o' that. Whar a angel makes dwelling-place thar oughter be a full crib, though it may be ambrosyer or mannar, or some o' them fixin's as a purairy man's stummick ain't used to. Anyways, a bit o' doe-deer meat won't do no harum. So, Walt Wilder, ole coon, let's you an' me set our faces southart, an' see what's to turn up at the tarminashun o' six miles' trampin'."

Once more shouldering the carcase, he strides off towards the south, guiding himself by the sun, but more by the hoof-marks of the mustang. These, though scarce distinguishable, under the over-shadowing sage-plants, are descried with little difficulty by the experienced eye of the Ranger.

On goes he, now and then muttering to himself conjectures as to what sort of a personage has appropriated and carried off his comrade. But, with all his jocular soliloquising, he feels certain the *angel* will turn out to be a *woman*.

Chapter Twenty Six.
Fallen among Friends.

If, before losing consciousness, Hamersley had a thought that he had fallen into the hands of enemies, never in all his life could he have been more mistaken, for those now around him, by their words and gestures, prove the very reverse. Six personages compose the group—four men and a girl; the sixth, she, the huntress, who has conducted him to the house. The girl is a brown-skinned Indian, evidently a domestic; and so also two of the four men. The other two are white, and of pronouncedly Spanish features. One is an oldish man, greyheaded, thin-faced, and wearing spectacles. In a great city he would be taken for a *savant*, though difficult to tell what he may be, seen in the Llano Estacado surrounded by a desert. In the same place, the other and younger man is equally an enigma, for his bearing proclaims him both gentleman and soldier, while the coat on his back shows the undress uniform of an officer of more than medium rank.

It is he who answers to the apostrophe, "Hermano!" springing forward at the word, and obeying the command of his sister—for such is she whom Hamersley has accompanied to the spot.

Throwing out his arms, and receiving the wounded man as he falls insensible from the saddle, the obedient brother for a moment stands aghast, for in the face of him unconscious he recognises an old friend—one he might no more expect to see there than to behold him falling from the sky.

He can have no explanation from the man held in his arms. The latter has fainted—is dying—perhaps already dead. He does not seek it, only turns to him who wears the spectacles, saying,—

"Doctor, is he, indeed, dead? See if it be so. Let everything be done to save him."

He thus addressed takes hold of Hamersley's pulse, and, after a moment or two, pronounces upon it. It beats; it indicates extreme weakness, but not absolute danger of death.

Then the wounded man is carried inside—tenderly borne, as if he, too, were a brother—laid upon a couch, and looked after with all the skill the grey-haired *medico* can command, with all the assiduity of her who has brought him to the house, and him she calls "Hermano."

As soon as the stranger has been disposed of, between these two there is a dialogue—the brother seeking explanations from the sister, though first imparting information to her. He knows the man she has saved; telling her how and where their acquaintance was made. Few words suffice, for already is the story known to her. In return, she too gives relation of what has happened—how, after her chase upon the plain, coming back successful, she saw the zopilotés, and was by them attracted out of her way; narrating all the rest already told.

And now nothing more can be known. The man still lives—thank Heaven for that!—but lies on the couch unconscious of all around him. Not quiet, for he is turning about, with quick-beating pulse, and brain in a condition of delirium.

For a night and a part of a day they keep by his bedside—all three, sister, brother, and doctor, grouped there, or going and coming. They know who the wounded man is, though ignorant of how he came by his wounds, or what strange chance left him stranded on the Staked Plain.

They have no hope of knowing until he may regain consciousness and recover. And of this the doctor has some doubt; when asked, shaking his head ominously, till the spectacles get loosened upon his nose.

But, though the prognosis remain uncertain, the diagnosis is learnt in a manner unexpected. Before noon of the next day the hounds are heard baying outside; and the watchers by the sick-bed, summoned forth, see one approaching—a personage whose appearance causes them surprise. Any one seen there would do the same, since for months no stranger had come near them. Strange, indeed, if one had, for they are more than a hundred miles from any civilised settlement, in the very heart and centre of a desert.

What they see now is a man of colossal form and gigantic stature, with bearded face and formidable aspect, rendered somewhat grotesque by a deer's carcase carried over his shoulders, the shanks of the animal rising crossways over his crown.

They are not dismayed by the uncouth apparition. She who has brought Hamersley to the house guesses it to be the comrade of whom he spoke— describing him as "true and faithful."

And, without reflecting further, she glides out, grasps the great hunter by the hand, and conducts him to the bedside of his unconscious companion.

Looking at her as she leads him, Walt Wilder mutters to himself,—

"Saved by a *angel*! I knowed it would turn out a *woman*, and this is one for sartin."

Chapter Twenty Seven.
The Lone Ranche.

A singular habitation was that into which Frank Hamersley, and after him Walt Wilder, had found their way. Architecturally of the rudest description—a kind among Mexicans especially styled *jacal*, or more generally *rancho*, the latter designation Anglicised or Americanised into ranche. The *rancho*, when of limited dimensions, is termed *ranchito*, and may be seen with walls of different materials, according to the district or country. In the hot low lands (*tierras calientes*) it is usually built of bamboos, with a thatching of palm-leaf; higher up, on the table lands (*tierras templadas*) it is a structure of mud bricks unburnt (adobe's); while still higher, upon the slopes of the forest-clad sierras, it assumes the orthodox shape of a log cabin, though in many respects differing from that of the States.

The one which gave shelter to the fugitives differed from all these, having walls of split slabs, set stockade fashion, and thatched with a sedge of *tulé*, taken from a little lake that lay near. It had three rooms and a kitchen, with some sheds at the back—one a stable appropriated to the mustang mare, another to some mules, and a third occupied by two men of the class of "peons"—the male domestics of the establishment.

All, with the house itself, structures of the rudest kind, unlike as possible to the dwelling-place of a lady, to say nought of an *angel*.

This thought occurs to Wilder as he enters under its roof. But he has no time to dwell upon it. His wounded comrade is inside, to whom he is conducted. He finds the latter still alive—thank God for that!—but unconscious of all that is passing around. To the kindly words spoken in apostrophe he makes no reply, or only in speeches incoherent. His skin is hot, his lips parched, his pulse throbbing at ninety to the minute. He is in the throes of a raging fever, which affects his brain as his blood.

The stalwart hunter sits down by his side, and stays there, tenderly nursing him. It glads him to observe there are others solicitous as himself— to find that he and Hamersley have fallen among friends. Though also surprising him, as does the sort of people he sees around. First, there is a lady, easily recognised as the *angel*; then a man of military aspect, who addresses her as "Hermanita," unquestionably a gentleman with a second and older man wearing spectacles, by both spoken of as "el medico." Strange inhabitants for a hovel, as that this should be in such an odd situation— hundreds of miles beyond the borders of civilisation, as Walt well knows.

No wonder at his wondering, above all when he discovers that his comrade is already known to them—to the younger of the two men, who is their host. This, however, is soon explained. Walt was already aware that the young prairie trader had made a former trip to New Mexico, when and where, as he is now told, the acquaintance commenced, along with some other particulars, to satisfy him for the time.

In return for this confidence he gives a detailed account of the caravan and its mischances—of the great final misfortune, which explains to them why its owner and himself had been forced to take to the Staked Plain, and were there wandering about, helpless fugitives.

To his narrative all three eagerly listen. But when he enlarges on the bravery of his young comrade, lying unconscious beside them, one bends upon the latter eyes that express an interest amounting to admiration. It is the "angel."

In the days that succeed she becomes Walt's fellow-watcher by the bedside of the sufferer; and often again does he observe similar glances given to their common patient. Rough backwoodsman though he be, he can tell them to be looks of love.

He thinks less about them because he has himself found something of like kind stealing over his thoughts. All his cares are not given to his invalided comrade; for in the hut is a fourth individual, whose habitual place is the *cocina*, coming and going, as occasion calls.

A little brown-skinned beauty, half Spanish, half Pueblo Indian, whose black eyes have burnt a hole through his buckskin hunting-shirt, and set fire to his heart. Though but little more than half his height, in less than a week after making her acquaintance she has become his master, as much as if their stature were reversed.

Walt does not want her for his mistress. No; the hunter is too noble, too honourable, for that His glance following her as she flits about the room, taking in her dainty shape, and the expression of her pretty face, always wreathed in smiles, he has but one single-hearted desire, to which he gives muttered expression, saying,—

"Thet's jest the kind o' gurl a fellow ked freeze to. I ne'er seed a apple dumplin' as looked sweeter or more temptin'; an' if she's agreeable, we two air born to be bone o' one bone, and flesh o' one flesh!"

Chapter Twenty Eight.
A Sweet Awakening.

For many days the young Kentuckian remains unconscious of all that is passing around. Fortunately for him, he has fallen into the right hands; for the old gentleman in spectacles is in reality a medical man—a skilled surgeon as well as a physician, and devotes all his time and skill to restoring his patient to health.

Soon the wound shows signs of healing, and, along with it, the fever begins gradually to abate. The brain at length relieved, reason resumes its sway.

Hamersley becomes conscious that he still lives, on hearing voices. They are of men. Two are engaged in a dialogue, which appears to be carried on with some difficulty, as one is speaking English, which the other but slightly understands. Neither is the English of the first speaker of a very correct kind, nor is his voice at all euphonious. For all that, it sounds in Hamersley's ears sweet as the most seraphic music, since in its tones he recognises the voice of Walt Wilder.

A joyous throb thrills through his heart on discovering that his comrade has rejoined him. After their parting upon the plain he had his fears they might never come together again.

Walt is not within sight, for the conversation is carried on outside the room. The invalid sees that he is in a room, a small one, of which the walls are wood, roughly-hewn slabs, with furniture fashioned in a style corresponding. He is lying upon a *catré*, or camp bedstead, rendered soft by a mattress of bearskins, while a *serapé* of bright-coloured pattern is spread over him, serving both for blanket and counterpane. In the apartment is a table of the rudest construction, with two or three chairs, evidently from the hand of the same unskilful workman, their seats being simply hides with the hair on. On the table is a cup with a spoon in it, and two or three small bottles, that have the look of containing medicines.

All these objects come under his eyes at the first dim glance; but as his vision grows clearer, and he feels strength enough to raise his head from the pillow, other articles are disclosed to view, in strange contrast with the chattels first observed. Against the wall hang several articles of female apparel—all of a costly kind. They are of silk and silk-velvet, richly brocaded; while on a second table, slab like the first, he can distinguish bijouterie, with other trifles usually belonging to a lady's toilet.

These lie in front of a small mirror set in a frame which appears to be silver; while above is suspended a guitar, of the kind known as *bandolon*.

The sick man sees all these things with a half-bewildered gaze, for his senses are still far from clear. The costly articles of apparel and adornment would be appropriate in a lady's boudoir or bed chamber. But they appear strange, even grotesque, in juxtaposition with the roughly-hewn timbers of what is evidently a humble cottage—a log cabin!

Of course he connects them with her, that singular being who has succoured, and perhaps saved his life. He can have no other conjecture. He remembers seeing a house as they approached its outside. It must be that he is now in; though, from the last conscious thought, as he felt himself swooning in the saddle, all has been as blank as if he had been lying lifeless in a tomb. Even yet it might appear as a dream but for the voice of Walt Wilder, who, outside, seems labouring hard to make himself intelligible to some personage with whom he is conversing.

Hamersley is about to utter a cry that will summon his comrade to his side, when he perceives that the voices are becoming fainter, as if the two speakers had gone outside the house and were walking away from it. Feeling too weak even for the slightest exertion, he remains silent, taking it for granted they will soon return.

It is broad daylight, the sun glancing in through an aperture in the wall that serves for a window. It has neither frame nor glass, and along with the bright beams there drifts in a cool breeze laden with the delicious fragrance of flowers, among which he can distinguish the aromatic perfume of the wild China tree. There are voices of birds mingling their music with the sough of falling water—sounds very different from those of the desert through which he has of late been straying.

He lies thinking of the beautiful being who brought him thither, shaping conjectures in regard to the strangeness of the situation. He has no idea how long he may have been unconscious; nor has the whole time been like death—unless death have its dreams. For he has had dreams, all with a fair form and lovely face flitting and figuring in them. It is the wild huntress.

He has a fancy that the face seemed familiar to him; or, if not familiar, one he has looked upon before. He endeavours to recall all those he had met in Mexico during his sojourn there; for if encountered anywhere, it must have been there. His female acquaintances had been but few in that foreign land. He can remember every one of them. She is not of their number. If he has ever seen her before their encounter on the Staked Plain, it must have been while passing along the street of some Mexican city.

And this could scarcely be, in his silent reflection; for such a woman once seen—even but for a moment—could never be forgotten.

He lies pondering on all that has passed—on all he can now recall. Walt had got back, then, to the place where they parted. He must have found food and water, though it matters now no more. Enough that he has got back, and both are in an asylum of safety, under friendly protection. This is evident from the surroundings.

Still feeble as a child, the effort of thought very soon fatigues him; and this, with the narcotic influence of the flower perfume, the songs of the birds, and the soothing monotone of the waters, produces a drowsiness that terminates in a profound slumber. This time he sleeps without dreaming.

How long he cannot tell; but once more he is awakened by voices. As before, two persons are engaged in conversation. But far different from those already heard. The bird-music still swelling in through the window is less sweet than the tones that now salute his ear.

As before, the speakers are invisible, outside the room. But he can perceive that they are close to the door, and the first words heard admonish him of their design to enter.

"Now, Conchita! Go get the wine, and bring it along with you. The doctor left directions for it to be given him at this hour."

"I have it here, senorita."

"*Vaya*! you have forgotten the glass. You would not have him drink out of the bottle?"

"*Ay Dios*! and so I have," responds Conchita, apparently gliding off to possess herself of the required article, with which she soon returns.

"Ish!" cautions the other voice; "if he be still asleep, we must not wake him. Don Prospero said that. Step lightly, *muchacha*!"

Hamersley is awake, with eyes wide open, and consciousness quite restored. But at this moment something—an instinct of dissembling— causes him to counterfeit sleep; and he lies still, with shut eyelids. He can hear the door turning upon its hinges of raw hide, then the soft rustle of robes, while he is sensible of that inexpressible something that denotes the gentle presence of woman.

"Yes, he is asleep," says the first speaker, "and for the world we may not disturb him. The doctor was particular about that, and we must do exactly as he said. You know, Conchita, this gentleman has been in great danger. Thanks to the good Virgin, he'll get over it. Don Prospero assures us he will."

"What a pity if he should not! Oh, senorita, isn't he—"

"Isn't he what?"

"Handsome—beautiful! He looks like a picture I've seen in the church; an angel—only that the angel had wings, and no mustachios."

"Pif, girl; don't speak in that silly way, or I shall be angry with you. *Vayate!* you may take away the wine. We can come again when he awakes. *Guardate!* Tread lightly."

Again there is the rustling of a dress; but this time as if only one of the two were moving off. The other seems still to linger by the side of the couch.

The invalid queries which of the two it is. There is an electricity that tells him; and, for an instant, he thinks of opening his eyes, and proclaiming consciousness of what has been passing.

A thought restrains him—delicacy. The lady will know that he has been awake all the while, and overheard the conversation. It has been in Spanish, but she is aware that he understands this, for he has no doubt that the "señorita" is she who has saved him.

He remains without moving, without unclosing his eyelids. But his ears are open, and he hears a speech pleasanter than any yet spoken.

It is in the shape of a soliloquy—a few words softly murmured. They are, "*Ay de mil* 'Tis true what Conchita says, and as Valerian told me. *He is, indeed, handsome—beautiful!*"

More than ever Hamersley endeavours to counterfeit sleep, but he can resist no longer. Involuntarily his eyes fly open, and, with head upraised, he turns towards the speaker.

He sees what he has been expecting, what he beheld in fancy throughout his long, delirious dream—the fair form and beautiful face that so much interested him, even in that hour when life seemed to be forsaking him. It is the angel of the desert, no longer in huntress garb, but dressed as a lady.

There is a red tinge upon her cheek, that appears to have flushed up suddenly, as if suspecting her soliloquy has been heard. The words have but parted from her lips, and the thought is yet thrilling in her heart.

Can he have heard it? He shows no sign.

She approaches the couch with a look of solicitude, mingled with interrogation. A hand is held out to her, and a word or two spoken to say she is recognised. Her eyes sparkle with joy, as she perceives in those of the invalid that reason is once more seated on its throne.

"I am so happy," she murmurs, "we are all so happy, to know you are out of danger. Don Prospero says so. You will now get well in a short time. But I forget; we were to give you something as soon as you should awake. It is only some wine. Conchita, come hither!"

A young girl is seen stepping into the chamber. A glance would tell her to be the maid, if the overheard conversation had not already declared it. A little brown-skinned damsel, scarce five feet in height, with raven hair hanging in double plait down her back, and black eyes that sparkle like those of a basilisk.

Provident Conchila has brought the bottle and glass with her, and a portion of the famed grape juice of El Paso is administered to the invalid.

"How good and kind you've all been!" he says, as his head once more settles down upon the pillow. "And you especially, senorita. If I mistake not, I'm indebted to you for the saving of my life."

"Do not speak of that," she rejoins; "I've shown you no kindness in particular. You would not have one leave a fellow creature to perish?"

"Ah! but for you I should now have been in another world."

"No, indeed. There you are mistaken. If I had never come near you, you'd have been saved all the same. I have good news for you. Your comrade is safe, and here. He returned to your trysting-place, with both food and drink; so, as you see, I have no merit in having rescued you. But I must not talk longer. Don Prospero has given instructions for you to be kept quiet. I shall bring the doctor at once. Now that you are awake it is necessary he should see you."

Without waiting for a reply, she glides out of the room, Conchita having gone before.

Chapter Twenty Nine.
Don Valerian.

Hamersley lies pondering on what he has seen and heard, more especially on what he has overheard—that sweet soliloquy. Few men are insensible to flattery. And flattery from fair lips! He must be indeed near death whose heart-pulsations it does not affect.

But Don Prospero! Who is he? Is he the owner of the voice heard in dialogue with Walt Wilder? May he be the owner of all? This thought troubles the Kentuckian.

Approaching footsteps put a stop to his conjectures. There are voices outside, one of them the same late sounding so sweetly in his ears. The other is a man's, but not his who was conversing with Wilder. Nor is it that of the ex-Ranger himself. It is Don Prospero, who soon after enters the room, the lady leading the way.

A man of nigh sixty years of age, spare form and face, hair grizzled, cheeks wrinkled; withal hale and hearty, as can be told by the pleasant sparkle of his eye. Dressed in a semi-military suit, of a subdued tint, and facings that tell of the medical staff.

At a glance there is no danger in Don Prospero. The invalid feels easier, and breathes freely.

"Glad to see you looking so well," says Don Prospero, taking hold of his patient's wrist and trying the pulse. "Ah! much more regular; it will be all right now. Keep quiet, and we shall soon get you on your feet again. Come, señor! A little more of this grape-juice will do you no harm. Nothing like our New Mexican wine for bringing back a sick man to his appetite. After that, we shall give you some wild-turkey broth and a bone to pick. In a day or two you'll be able to eat anything."

Other personages are now approaching the chamber. The lady glides out, calling,—

"Valerian!"

"Who is Valerian?" feebly interrogates the invalid. Once more the name of a man is making him unhappy.

"Don Valerian!" responds the doctor, in a tone that tells of respect for the individual so designated; "you shall see, señor. You are about to make his acquaintance. No; I am wrong about that. I forgot. You cannot now."

"Cannot! Why?"

"Because you have made it already. *Mira*! He is there!"

This as a tall, elegant man, under thirty years of age, steps inside the chamber, while a still taller form appears in the doorway, almost filling up the space between the posts.

The latter is Walt Wilder, but the former—who is he? Don Valerian, of course!

"Colonel Miranda!" exclaims Hamersley, starting up on his couch. He has already dismissed all suspicious fears of Don Prospero; and now he no longer dreads Valerian.

"Colonel Miranda, is it you?"

"It is, *mio amigo*, myself, as you see. And I need not tell you how glad I am to meet you again. So unexpected in this queer quarter, where I little hoped to have the pleasure of entertaining an old friend. Our worthy doctor here informs us you will soon get strong again, and become more of a tax on my hospitality than you have yet been. No doubt, after your illness, you'll have the appetite of an ostrich. Well, in one way, that will be fortunate, since we are living, as you may see, in a somewhat Homeric fashion. *Carrambo*! you will be deeming my manners quite as rude as the roughest of Homer's heroes. I am forgetting to introduce you to one of whom you've heard me speak. Though it don't so much signify, since the lady has made your acquaintance already. Permit me to present my dear Adela."

It is the beautiful huntress who steps forward to be introduced, now looking more beautiful than ever.

To Hamersley all is explained by her presence. He remembers the portrait upon the wall, which accounts for his fancy of having seen her face before.

He sees it now; his wonder giving way to an intense, ardent admiration.

Soon, the young lady retiring, his curiosity comes back, and he asks his host for an explanation. How came Colonel Miranda there, and why? By what sinister combination of circumstances has the military commandant of Albuquerque made his home in the midst of a howling wilderness, for such is the Llano Estacado?

Despite the smiling oasis immediately surrounding it, it cannot have been choice. No. Chance, or rather mischance, must have led to this change in the affairs of his New Mexican acquaintance. More than an acquaintance—a friend who stood by him in the hour of danger, first courageously protecting, then nobly volunteering to act as his second in a duel; afterwards taking him on to his home and showing him hospitality, kind as was ever extended to a stranger in a strange land.

No wonder Frank Hamersley holds him dear. Dearer now, after seeing his sister *in propriâ personâ*—she whose portrait had so much impressed nis fancy—the impression now deepened by the thought that to her he has been indebted for his life.

Naturally enough, the young Kentuckian is desirous of knowing all, and is anxious about the fortunes of his Mexican friend, that for the time seem adverse.

"No," is Colonel Miranda's response to his appeal. "Not now, Señor Don Francisco. Our good doctor here places an embargo on any further conversation for the present. The tale I have to tell might too much excite you. Therefore let it rest untold till you are stronger and more able to hear it rehearsed. Now, *amigo*, we must leave you alone, or rather, I should say, in the best of good company, for such has your worthy comrade, the Señor Wilder, proved himself to be. No doubt you'll be anxious to have a word with one who, while your life was in danger, would have sacrificed his own to save it. Don Prospero permits him to remain with you and give such explanations as you may need. The rest of us are to retire. *Hasta luega.*" So saying, Miranda steps out of the room. "Keep perfectly quiet," adds the ex-army surgeon, preparing to follow. "Don't excite yourself by any act or thought that may cause a return of the fever. For in that lies your greatest danger. Feel confident, *caballero*, that you're in the company of friends. Don Gaulterio here will be able to convince you of that. Ah! señor, you've a nurse who feels a great interest in seeing you restored to health."

Pronouncing these last words in undertone and with an accent of innuendo, accompanied by a smile which the invalid pleasantly interprets, Don Prospero also retires, leaving his patient alone with his old caravan guide.

Drawing one of the chairs up to the side of the bed, the ex-Ranger sits down upon it, saying,—

"Wal, Frank, ain't it wonderful? That we shed both be hyar, neested snug an' comfortable as two doons in the heart of a hollow tree, arter all the dangersome scrapes we've been passin' through. Gheehorum! To think o' thar bein' sech a sweet furtile place lyin' plum centre in the innermost recesses o' the Staked Plain, whar we purairey men allers believed thar wun't nothin' 'ceptin' dry desert an' stinkin' sage-bush. Instead, hyar's a sort o' puradise aroun' us, sech as I used read o' when I war a youngster in the big Book. Thar's the difference, that in the Gardin o' Eeden thar's but one woman spoken of; hyar thar's two, one o' which you yurself hev called a angel, an' ye hain't sayed anythin' beyont the downright truth. She air a angel, if iver thar was sech on airth. Now, not detractin' anythin' from her merits, thar's another near hand—somewhat of a smaller sort, though jest as much, an' a little bit more, to my likin'. Ye won't mind my declarin' things that way. As they say in Mexican Spanish, *cadder uner a soo gooster* (cada una a su gusto), every one to his own way o' thinkin', so my belief air that in this. Gardin o' Eeden thar air two Eves, one o' which, not countin' to be the mother o' all men, will yit, supposin' this chile to hev his way, be the mother o' a large family o' young Wilders."

While Hamersley is still smiling at the grotesque prognostication, the ex-Ranger, seizing hold of his hand, continues,—

"I'm so glad you're a goin' to rekiver. Leavin' out the angels we love, ther'll be some chance to git square wi' the devils we've sech reezun to hate. We may yit make them pay dear for the bloody deed they've done in the murderin' o' our innercent companyuns."

"Amen to that," mutters Hamersley, returning the squeeze of his comrade's hand with like determined pressure. "Sure as I live, it shall be so."

Chapter Thirty.
The Raiders Returning.

An Indian bivouac. It is upon a creek called "Pecan," a confluent of the Little Witchita river, which heads about a hundred miles from the eastern edge of the Llano Estacado.

There are no tents in the encampment; only here and there a blanket or buffalo robe extended horizontally upon upright poles—branches cut from the surrounding trees. The umbrageous canopy of the pecans protects the encamped warriors from the fervid rays of a noonday sun, striking vertically down.

That they are on the maraud is evidenced by the absence of tents. A peaceful party, in its ordinary nomadic passage across the prairies, would have lodges along with it—grand conical structures of painted buffalo skins—with squaws to set them up, and dogs or ponies to transport them when struck for another move.

In this encampment on the Pecan are neither squaws, dogs, nor ponies; only men, naked to the breech clout, their bodies brightly painted from hip to head, chequered like a hatchment, or the jacket of a stage harlequin, with its fantastic devices, some ludicrous, others grotesque; still others of aspect terrible—showing a death's-head and cross-bones.

A prairie man on seeing them would at once say, "Indians on the war trail!"

It does not need prairie experience to tell they are returning upon it. If there are no ponies or dogs beside them, there are other animals in abundance—horses, mules, and horned cattle. Horses and mules of American breed, and cattle whose ancestral stock has come from Tennessee or Kentucky along with the early colonists of Texas.

And though there are no squaws or papooses in the encampment, there are women and children that are white. A group comprising both can be seen near its centre. It does not need the dishevelled hair and torn dresses to show they are captives; nor yet the half-dozen savages, spear-armed, keeping guard over them. Their drooping heads, woeful and wan countenances, are too sure signs of their melancholy situation.

What are these captives, and who their captors? Two questions easily answered. In a general way, the picture explains itself. The captives are the wives and children, with sisters and grown-up daughters among them, of Texan colonists. They are from a settlement too near the frontier to secure itself against Indian attack. The captors are a party of Comanches, with whom the reader has already made acquaintance; for they are no other than the sub-tribe of Tenawas, of whom the Horned Lizard is leader.

The time is two weeks subsequent to the attack on Hamersley's train; and, judging by the spectacle now presented, we may conclude that the Tenawa chief has not spent the interval in idleness. Nearly three hundred miles lie between the place where the caravan was destroyed and the site of the plundered settlement, whose spoils are now seen in the possession of the savages.

Such quick work requires explanation. It is at variance with the customs and inclinations of the prairie freebooter, who, having acquired a booty, rarely strikes for another till the proceeds of the first be squandered. He resembles the anaconda, which, having gorged itself, lies torpid till the craving of a fresh appetite stirs it to renewed activity.

Thus would it have been with the Tenawa chief and his band, but for a circumstance of a somewhat unusual kind. As is known, the attack on the prairie traders was not so much an affair of the Horned Lizard as his confederate, the military commandant of Albuquerque. The summons had come to him unexpected, and after he had planned his descent on the Texas settlement. Sanguinary as the first affair was, it had been short, leaving him time to carry out his original design, almost equally tragical in its execution. Here and there, a spear standing up, with a tuft of light-coloured hair, blood-clotted upon its blade, is proof of this. Quite as successful, too. The large drove of horses and horned cattle, to say nothing of that crowd of despairing captives, proves the proceeds of the later maraud worth as much, or perhaps more, than what had been taken from the traders' waggons.

Horned Lizard is jubilant; so, also, every warrior of his band. In loss their late foray has cost them comparatively little—only one or two of their number, killed by the settlers while defending themselves. It makes up for the severe chastisement sustained in their onslaught upon the caravan. And, since the number of their tribe is reduced, there are now the fewer to share with, so that the calicoes of Lowell, the gaudy prints of Manchester, with stripes, shroudings, and scarlet cloth to bedeck their bodies, hand mirrors in which to admire themselves, horses to ride upon, mules to carry their tents, and cattle to eat—with white women to be their concubines, and white children their attendants—all these fine things in full possession have put the savages in high spirits—almost maddened them with delight.

A new era has dawned upon the tribe of which Horned Lizard is head. Hitherto it has been a somewhat starving community, its range lying amid sterile tracts, on the upper tributaries of the Red River and Canadian. Now, before it is a plentiful future—a time of feasting and revelry, such as rarely occurs to a robber band, whether amidst the forest-clad mountains of Italy, or on the treeless steppes of America.

The Tenawa chief is both joyous and triumphant. So, too, his second in command, whose skin, with the paint cleansed from it, would show nearly white. For he is a Mexican by birth; when a boy made prisoner by the Comanches, and long since matriculated into the mysteries of the redman's life—its cunning, as its cruelties.

Now a man, he is one of the chiefs of the tribe, in authority only less than the Horned Lizard himself, but equal to the latter in all the cruel instincts that distinguish the savage. "El Barbato" he is called, from having a beard, though this he keeps clean shaven, the better to assimilate himself to his beardless companions; while, with painted face and hair black as their own, he looks as Indian as any of them. But he has not forgotten his native tongue, and this makes him useful to those who have adopted him, especially when raiding in the Republic of Mexico. It was through him the Tenawa chief was first brought to communicate with the military robber, Uraga.

The Indian bivouac is down in the creek bottom in a little valley, on both sides flanked by precipitous cliffs. Above and below these approach each other, so near as to leave only a narrow path along the edge of the stream.

The savages are resting after a long, rapid march, encumbered with their spoils and captives. Some have lain down to sleep, their nude bodies stretched along the sward, resembling bronze statues tumbled from their pedestals. Others squat around fires, roasting collops from cattle they have killed, or eating them half raw.

A few stand or saunter by the side of the captives, upon these casting covetous glances, as if they only waited for the opportunity to appropriate them. The women are all young; some of them scarce grown girls, and some very beautiful.

A heart-harrowing sight it would be for their fathers, brothers, husbands and sweethearts, could they but witness it. These may not be far off.

Some suspicion of this has carried the Horned Lizard and El Barbato up to the crest of the cliff. They have been summoned thither by a sign, which the traveller on the prairies of Texas or the table plains of Mexico never sees without stopping to scrutinise and shape conjecture about its cause. Before entering the canon through which runs Pecan Creek, the Tenawa chief had observed a flock of turkey-buzzards circling about in the air. Not the one accompanying him and his marauders on their march, as is the wont of these predatory birds. But another quite separate gang, seen at a distance behind, apparently above the path along which he and his freebooters had lately passed.

As the Comanche well knows, a sign too significant to be treated lightly or with negligence. And so, too, his second in command. Therefore have they climbed the cliff to obtain a better view of the birds—those flying afar—and, if possible, draw a correct conclusion as to the cause of their being there.

On reaching the summit they again see them, though so far off as to be barely visible—black specks against the blue canopy of the sky. Still near enough to show a large number circling about over some object that appears stationary.

This last observation seems satisfactory to the Tenawa chief, who, turning to his fellow-freebooter, shouts out,—

"Nothing to fear. Don't you remember, Barbato, one of our horses gave out there, and was left? It's over him the zopilotés are swooping. He's not dead yet; that's why they don't go down."

"It may be," rejoins the renegade. "Still I don't like the look of it. Over a dead horse they'd hardly soar so high. True, they keep in one place. If it were Texans pursuing us they'd be moving onward—coming nearer and nearer. They're not. It must be, as you say, the horse. I don't think the people of the settlement we struck would be strong enough to come after us—at least not so soon. They may in time, after they've got up a gathering of their Rangers. That isn't likely to be till we've got safe beyond their reach. They won't gain much by a march to the Witchita mountains. *Por cierte!* the zopilotés out yonder are over something; but, as they're not moving on, most likely it's the horse."

Again the Horned Lizard gives a grunt, expressing satisfaction; after which the two scramble back down the cliff, to seek that repose which fighting and forced marching make necessary to man, be he savage or civilised.

Chapter Thirty One.
Pursuers on the Path.

Despite common belief, the instinct of the Indian is not always sure, nor his intellect unerring. An instance of the contrary is afforded by the behaviour of the Tenawa chief and his subordinate Barbato.

About the buzzards both have been mistaken. The second flock seen by them is not hovering over a horse, but above an encampment of horsemen. Not correctly an encampment, but a halt *en bivouac*—where men have thrown themselves from their saddles, to snatch a hurried repast, and take quick consultation about continuing on.

They are all men, not a woman or child among them, bearded men with white skins, and wearing the garb of civilisation. This not of the most fashionable kind or cut, nor are they all in the exact drew of civilised life. For many of them wear buckskin hunting shirts, fringed leggings, and moccasins; more a costume peculiar to the savage. Besides these there are some in blanket-coats of red, green, and blue; all sweat-stained and dust-tarnished, till the colours nearly correspond. Others in Kentucky jeans, or copper-coloured homespun. Still others in sky-blue *cottonade*, product of the hand-mills of Attakapas. Boots, shoes, and brogans fabricated out of all kinds of leather; even that from the corrugated skin of the illigator. Hats of every shape, fashion, size, and material—straw, chip, Panama, wool, felt, silk, and beaver.

In one respect they are all nearly alike—in their armour and accoutrements. All are belted, pouched, and powder-horned. Each carries a bowie-knife and a revolving pistol—some two—and none are without a rifle. Besides this uniformity there are other points of resemblance—extending to a certain number. It is noticeable in their guns, which are jägers of the US army-brand. Equally apparent is the caparison of their horses; these carrying cavalry saddles, with peaks and cantles brass mounted. Among the men to whom these appertain there is a sort of half-military discipline, indicated by some slight deference shown to two or three, who appear to act with the authority of officers. It is, in fact, a troop—or, as by themselves styled, a "company"—of Texan Rangers.

About one-half the band belongs to this organisation. The others are the people of the plundered settlement—the fathers, brothers, and husbands, whom the Horned Lizard and his red robbers have bereft of daughters, sisters, and wives.

They are in pursuit of the despoilers; a chase commenced as soon as they could collect sufficient force to give it a chance of success. Luckily, a troop of Rangers, scouting in the neighbourhood, came opportunely along, just in time to join them. Soldiers and settlers united, they are now on the trail of the Tenawas, and have only halted to breathe and water their horses, eat some food themselves, and then on.

Not strange their hot haste—men whose homes have been made desolate, their kindred carried into captivity. Each has his own painful reflections. In that hour, at that very moment, his beloved wife, his delicate daughter, his fair sister, or sweetheart, may be struggling in the embrace of a brawny savage. No wonder that to them every hour seems a day, every minute an hour.

Though with a different motive, not much less impatient are their associates in the pursuit—the Rangers. It chances to be a company especially rabid for defence against the incursions of the Tenawa tribe; and more than once baffled by these cunning red-skins, they are anxious to make up for past disappointment. Twice before have they followed the retreating trail of these same savages, on both occasions returning foiled and empty-handed. And, now that they are again on it, with surer signs to guide them, the young men of the corps are mad to come up with the red marauders, while the elder ones are almost equally excited. Both resemble hounds in a hunt where the scent is hot—the young dogs dashing forward without check, the old ones alike eager, but moving with more circumspection.

Between them and the settlers there is the same earnestness of purpose, though stimulated by resentment altogether different. The latter only think of rescuing their dear ones, while the former are stirred by soldier pride and the instinctive antagonism which a Texan Ranger feels for a Tenawa. Many of them have old scores to settle with the Horned Lizard, and more than one longs to send a bullet through his heart.

But, despite the general reckless impatience to proceed, there are some who counsel caution. Chief among those is a man named Cully, a thin wiry sexagenarian, who looks as if he had been at least half a century upon the prairies. All over buckskin, fitting tight to his body, without tag or tail, he is not one of the enrolled Rangers, though engaged to act as their guide. In this capacity he exercises an influence over the pursuers almost equalling that of their leader, the Ranger captain, who, with a group gathered around, is now questioning the guide as to the next move to be made.

"They can't be very far off now," replies Cully, in answer to the captain's interrogatory. "All the signs show they passed this hyar point a good hour arter sun-up. The dew war off the grass as they druv over it, else the blades 'ud a been pressed flatter down. Besides, there's the dead hoss they've left ahint. Ye see some o' 'em's cut out his tongue an' tuk it along for a tit-bit at thar next campin' place. Now, as the blood that kim out o' the animal's mouth ain't been long cruddled up, thet shows to a sartinty they can't be far forrad. I reck'n I know the adzact spot whar they're squatted."

"Where?"

"Peecawn creek. There they'll get good water for thar stock, an' the shade o' trees to rest unner; the which last they'll take to in this hottish spell o' sun."

"If they're upon the Pecan," puts in a third speaker, a tall, lathy individual, in a green blanket coat, badly faded, "and anywhere near its mouth, we can't be more than five miles from them. I know this part of the country well. I passed through it last year along with the Santa Fé expedition."

"Only five miles!" exclaims another man, whose dress bespeaks a planter of respectability, while his woe-begone countenance proclaims him to be one of the bereaved. "Oh, gentlemen I surely our horses are now rested enough. Let us ride forward and fall upon them at once!"

"We'd be durned foolish to do so," responded Cully. "Thet, Mr Wilton, 'ud be jest the way to defeet all our plans an' purpisses. They'd see us long afore we ked git sight o' them, an' maybe in time to run off all the stolen hosses an' cattle, but sartinly the keptyves."

"What's your way, Cully?" interrogates a lieutenant of the Rangers.

"My way air to wait till the sun go down, then steal torst 'm. Thar boun' to hev fires, an' thet'll guide us right into thar camp. Ef it's in the Peecawn bottom, as I'm pretty sure it air, we kin surround 'em eesy. Thar's bluffs a-both sides, an' we kin divide inter two lots—one slippin' roun' an' comin' from up the creek, while t'other approaches 'em from below. In thet way we'll make sure o' keepin' 'em from runnin' off the weemen; beside it'll gie us the more likelier chance to make a good count o' the redskin sculps."

"What do you say, boys?" asks the Ranger captain, addressing himself more especially to the men composing his command.

"Cully's right," is the response from a majority of voices.

"Then we must stay here till night. If we go forward now, they may see us before we get within shooting distance. So you think, Cully, you can take up the trail at night, supposing it to be a dark one?"

"Pish!" retorts the old prairie-man, with a disdainful toss of his head.

"Take up the trail o' a Tenawa Injun? I'd do that in the darkest night as iver shet down over a prairie. The skunks! I ked smell the place they'd passed over."

There is no further discussion. Cully's opinion is all-powerful, and determines the course to be pursued. The halt intended to be temporary, is to continue till near sunset, despite expostulations, almost prayerful appeals, from those who have left desolate homes behind, and who burn with impatience to ride forward and rescue their captive kindred.

Chapter Thirty Two.
The Savages Surprised.

Throughout the afternoon hours both parties remained stationary; the pursued indulging in a siesta, which days of rough riding and raiding, with nights of watchfulness, have made necessary; the pursuers, on their part, wearied as well, but unable to sleep so long as their vengeance remains unappeased, and such dread danger hangs over the heads of those near and dear to them.

Above the bivouacs the black vultures spread their shadowy wings, soaring and circling, each "gang" over the cohort it has been all day accompanying.

Every now and then between the two "gangs" one is seen coming and going, like so many mutual messengers passing between; for, although the flocks are far apart, they can see one another, and each is aware, by instinct clearer than human ken, what the other is after. It is not the first time for them to follow two such parties travelling across the Texan prairie. Nor will it be the first for them to unite in the air as the two troops come into collision on the earth. Often have these birds, poised in the blue ether, looked down upon red carnage like that now impending. Their instincts—let us call them so, for the sake of keeping peace with the naturalists of the closet— then admonish them what is likely to ensue. For if not reason, they have at least recollection; and as their eyes rest upon men with dusky skins, and others dimly white, they know that between such is a terrible antagonism, oft accruing to their own interest. Many a time has it given them a meal. Strange if they should not remember it!

They do. Though tranquilly soaring on high—each bird with outstretched neck and eye bent, in hungry concupiscence, looks below on the forms moving or at rest, saying to itself, "Ere long these vermin will furnish a rich repast." So sure are they of this—the birds of both flocks— that, although the sun is nigh setting, instead of betaking themselves to their roosts, as is their wont, they stay, each by its own pet party. Those accompanying the pursuers still fly about in the air. They can tell that these do not intend to remain much longer on that spot. For they have kindled no fires, nor taken other steps that indicate an encampment for the night.

Different with those that soar over the halting-place of the pursued. As night approaches they draw in their spread wings and settle down to roost; some upon trees, others on the ledges of rock, still others on the summits of the cliffs that overhang the camping place of the Indians.

The blazing fires, with meat on spits sputtering over them; the arms abandoned, spears stuck in the ground, with shields suspended; the noise and revelry around—all proclaim the resolve of the savages to stay there till morning.

An intention which, despite their apparent stolidity—in contradiction to the ideas of the closet naturalist and his theory of animal instinct—the vultures clearly comprehend.

About the behaviour of the birds the marauders take no note. They are used to seeing turkey-buzzards around—better known to them by the name "zopilotés."

For long ere the Anglo-American colonists came in contact with the Comanche Indians a Spano-Mexican vocabulary had penetrated to the remotest of these tribes.

No new thing for the Tenawas to see the predatory birds swooping above them all day and staying near them all night. Not stranger than a wolf keeping close to the sheepfold, or a hungry dog skulking around shambles.

As night draws near, and the purple twilight steals over the great Texan plain, the party of chasing pursuers is relieved from a stay by all deemed so irksome. Remounting their horses, they leave the scene of their reluctant halt, and continue the pursuit silently, as if moving in funeral march.

The only sounds heard are the dull thumping of their horses' hoofs upon the soft prairie turf; now and then a clink, as one strikes against a stone; the occasional tinkle of a canteen as it comes in contact with saddle mounting or pistol butt; the champing of bits, with the breathing of horses and men.

These last talk in low tones, in mutterings not much louder than whispers. In pursuit of their savage foe, the well-trained Rangers habitually proceed thus, and have cautioned the settlers to the same. Though these need no compulsion to keep silent; their hearts are too sore for speech; their anguish, in its terrible intensity, seeks for no expression, till they stand face to face with the red ruffians who have caused, and are still causing, it. The night darkens down, becoming so obscure that each horseman can barely distinguish the form of him riding ahead. Some regret this, thinking they may get strayed. Not so Cully. On the contrary, the guide is glad, for he feels confident in his conjecture that the pursued will be found in Pecan Creek, and a dark night will favour the scheme of attack he has conceived and spoken of. Counselled by him, the Ranger captain shares his confidence, and they proceed direct towards the point where the tributary stream unites with the main river—the little Witchita, along whose banks they have been all that day tracking. Not but that Cully could take up the Indian trail. Despite the obscurity he could do that, though not, as he jestingly declared, by the smell. There are other indices that would enable him, known but to men who have spent a lifetime upon the prairies. He does not need them now, sure he will find the savages, as he said, "squatted on the Peecawn."

And, sure enough, when the pursuers, at length at the creek's mouth, enter the canon through which it disembogues its crystal water into the grander and more turbid stream, they discovered certain traces of the pursued having passed along its banks.

Another mile of travelling, the same silence observed, with caution increased, and there is no longer a doubt about the truth of Cully's conjecture. Noises are heard ahead, sounds disturbing the stillness of the night air that are not those of the uninhabited prairie. There is the lowing of cattle, in long monotonous moans, like when being driven to slaughter, with, at intervals, the shriller neigh of a horse, as if uneasy at being away from his stable.

On hearing these sounds, the Ranger captain, acting by the advice of the guide, orders a halt. Then the pursuing party is separated into two distinct troops. One, led by Cully, ascends the cliff by a lateral ravine, and pursues its way along the upper table-land. The other, under the command of the captain, is to remain below until a certain time has elapsed, its length stipulated between the two leaders before parting.

When it has passed, the second division moves forward up the creek, again halting as a light shines through the trees, which, from its reddish colour, they know to be the glare of log fires.

They need not this to tell them they are close to an encampment—that of the savages they have been pursuing. They can hear their barbarous jargon, mingled with shouts and laughter like that of demons in the midst of some fiendish frolic.

They only stay for a signal the guide arranged to give as soon as he has got round to attack on the opposite side. The first shot heard, and they will dash forward to the fires.

Seated in their saddles, with reins tight drawn, and heels ready to drive home the spur—with glances bent greedily at the gleaming lights, and ears keenly alert to catch every sound—the hearts of some trembling with fear, others throbbing with hope, still others thrilling with the thought of vengeance—they wait for the crack that is to be the signal—wait and listen, with difficulty restraining themselves.

It comes at length. Up the glen peals a loud report, quickly followed by another, both from a double-barrelled gun.

This was the signal for attack, arranged by Cully.

Soon as hearing it, the reins are slackened, the spurs sent home, and, with a shout making the rocks ring, and the trees reverberate its echoes, they gallop straight towards the Indian encampment, and in a moment are in its midst.

They meet little resistance—scarce any. Too far from the settlements to fear pursuit—in full confidence they have not been followed, the red robbers have been abandoning themselves to pleasure, spending the night in a grand gluttonous feast, furnished by the captured kine.

Engrossed with sensual joys, they have neglected guard; and, in the midst of their festivities, they are suddenly set upon from all sides; the sharp cracking of rifles, with the quick detonation of repeating pistols, soon silences their cacchinations, scattering them like chaff.

After the first fusillade, there is but little left of them. Those not instantly shot down retreat in the darkness, skulking of! among the pecan trees. It is altogether an affair of firearms: and for once the bowie—the Texan's trusted weapon—has no part in the fray.

The first rays of next morning's sun throw light upon a sanguinary scene—a tableau terrible, though not regrettable. On the contrary, it discloses a sight which, but for the red surroundings, might give gladness. Fathers, half frantic with joy, are kissing children they never expected to see again; brothers clasping the hands of sisters late deemed lost for ever; husbands, nigh broken-hearted, once more happy, holding their wives in fond, affectionate embrace.

Near by, things strangely contrasting—corpses strewn over the ground, stark and bleeding, but not yet stiff, all of coppery complexion, but bedaubed with paint of many diverse colours. All surely savages.

A fearful spectacle, but one too often witnessed on the far frontier land of Texas.

Chapter Thirty Three.
A Forced Confession.

The party of Texans has made what prairie men call a "coup." On counting the corpses of their slain enemies they find that at least one-half of the Tenawa warriors have fallen, including their chief. They can make an approximate estimate of the number that was opposed to them by the signs visible around the camp, as also upon the trail they have been for several days following. Those who escaped have got off, some on their horses, hastily caught and mounted; others afoot, by taking to the timber. They were not pursued, as it was still dark night when the action ended, and by daylight these wild centaurs, well acquainted with the country, will have scattered far and wide, beyond all likelihood of being again encountered.

The settlers are satisfied at having recovered their relatives, as also their stolen stock. As to the Rangers, enough has been accomplished to slake their revengeful thirst—for the time. These last, however, have not come off unscathed; for the Comanches, well armed with guns, bows, and lances, did not die unresistingly. In Texas Indians rarely do, and never when they engage in a fight with Rangers. Between them and these border *guerrilleros*—in one sense almost as much savages as themselves—war is an understood game—to the bitter end, with no quarter either asked or given.

The Rangers count three of their number killed and about twice as many wounded—enough, considering the advantage they had in their unwarned attack upon enemies who for once proved unwatchful.

When the conflict has finally come to a close, and daylight makes manifest the result, the victors take possession of the spoil—most of it their own property. The horses that strayed or stampeded during the fight are again collected into a drove—those of the Indians being united to it. This done, only a short stay is intended—just long enough to bury the bodies of the three Rangers who have been killed, get stretchers prepared for such of the wounded as are unable to sit in the saddle, and make other preparations for return towards the settlements.

They do not hasten their departure through any apprehension of a counter-attack on the side of the Comanches. Fifty Texan Rangers—and there are this number of them—have no fear on any part of the plains, so long as they are mounted on good horses, carry rifles in their hands, bowie-knives and pistols in their belts, with a sufficient supply of powder in their flasks, and bullets in their pouches. With all these items they are amply provided; and were there now any necessity for continuing the pursuit, or the prospect of striking another coup, they would go on, even though the chase should conduct them into the defiles of the Rocky Mountains. To pursue and slay the savage is their vocation, their duty, their pastime and pleasure.

But the settlers are desirous of a speedy return to their homes, that they may relieve the anxiety of other dear ones, who there await them. They long to impart the glad tidings they will take with them.

While the preparations for departure are going on, Cully—who, with several others, has been collecting the arms and accoutrements of their slain enemies—gives utterance to a cry that brings a crowd of his comrades around him.

"What is it, Nat?" inquires the Ranger captain.

"Look hyar, cap! D'ye see this gun?"

"Yes; a hunter's rifle. Whose is it?"

"That's jess the questyin; though thar ain't no questyin about it. Boys, do any o' ye recognise this hyar shootin' iron?"

One after another the Rangers step up, and look at the rifle.

"I do," says one.

"And I," adds another.

And a third, and fourth, make the same affirmation, all speaking in tones of surprise.

"Walt Wilder's gun," continues Cully, "sure an' sartin. I know it, an oughter know it. See them two letters in the stock thar—'WW.' Old Nat Cully hez good reezun to recconise them, since 'twas hisself that cut 'em. I did it for Walt two yeern ago, when we war scoutin' on the Collyrado. It's his weepun, an' no mistake."

"Where did you find it?" inquires the captain.

"I've jess tuk it out o' the claws o' the ugliest Injun as ever made trail on a puraira—that beauty thar, whose karkidge the buzzards won't be likely to tech."

While speaking Cully points to a corpse. It is that of the Tenawa chief, already identified among the slain.

"He must a' hed it in his clutch when suddenly shot down," pursues the guide. "An' whar did he git it? Boys, our ole kummerade's wiped out for sartin. I know how Walt loved that thar piece. He w'udn't a parted wi' it unless along wi' his life."

This is the conviction of several others acquainted with Wilder. It is the company of Rangers to which he formerly belonged.

"Thar's been foul play somewhar," continues Cully. "Walt went back to the States—to Kaintuck, ef this chile ain't mistook. But 'tain't likely he stayed thar; he kedn't keep long off o' the purairas. I tell ye, boys, these hyar Injens hev been makin' mischief somewhar'. Look thar, look at them leggin's! Thar's no eend o' white sculps on' 'em, an' fresh tuk, too!"

The eyes of all turned towards these terrible trophies that in gory garniture fringe the buck-skin leg-wear of the savages. Cully, with several others who knew Wilder well, proceed to examine them, in full expectation of finding among them the skin of their old comrade's head. There are twelve scalps, all of white men, with others that are Indian, and not a few that exhibit the equally black, but shorter crop of the Mexican. Those that are indubitably of white men show signs of having been recently taken, but none of them can be identified as the scalp of Walt Wilder.

There is some relief in this, for his old comrades love. Walt. Still, there is the damning evidence of the gun, which Cully declares could only have been taken from him along with his life. How has it got into the hands of the Horned Lizard?

"I reckon we can settle that," says the Captain of the Rangers. "The renegade ought to know something about it."

This speech refers to Barbato, who has been taken prisoner, and about whose disposal they have already commenced to deliberate. His beard betrayed him as a renegade; and, the paint having been partially wiped from his skin, all perceive that he is a white man—a Mexican. Some are for shooting him on the spot, others propose hanging, while only a few of the more humane advocate taking him on to the settlements and there giving him a trial. He will have to die anyhow—that is pretty sure; for not only as a Mexican is he their enemy, but now doubly so from being found in league with their most detested foes, the Tenawa Comanches.

The wretch is lying on the ground near by, shaking with fear, in spite of the fastenings in which he is tightly held. He knows he is in dire danger, and has only so far escaped through having surrendered to a settler instead of to one of the Rangers.

"Let's gie him a chance o' his life; ef he'll tell all about it," counsels Cully. "What d'ye say, cap?"

"I agree to that," responds the Ranger captain. "He don't appear to be worth shooting; though it may be as well to take him on to the settlements, and shut him up in prison. The promise of pardon may get out of him all he knows; if not, the other will. He's not an Indian, and a bit of rope looped round his neck will, no doubt, loosen his tongue. Suppose we try boys?"

The "boys" are unanimous in their assent, and the renegade is at once brought up for examination. The man in the green blanket coat, who, as a Santa Fé expeditioner, has spent over twelve months in Mexican prisons, is appointed examiner. He has been long enough among the "yellerbellies" to have learnt their language.

The renegade is for a time reticent, and his statements are contradictory. No wonder he declines to tell what has occurred, so compromising to himself! But when the *lariat* is at length noosed around his neck, the loose end of it thrown over the limb of a pecan tree—the other conditions being clearly expounded to him—he sees that things can be no worse; and, seeing this, makes confession—full, if not free. He discloses everything—the attack and capture of the caravan, with the slaughter of the white men who accompanied it; he tells of the retreat of two of them to the cliff, one of whom, by the description, can be none other than Walt Wilder. When he at length comes to describe the horrible mode in which their old comrade has perished, the Rangers are almost frenzied with rage, and it is with difficulty some of them can be withheld from breaking their given word, and tearing him limb from limb.

He makes appeal to them for mercy, stating that he himself had no part in that transaction; that, although they have found him among the Indians, he was only as their prisoner; and forced to fight along with them.

This is evidently untrue; but, false or true, it has the effect of pacifying his judges, so far, that the *lariat* is left loose around his neck.

Further examination, and cross-examination, elicit other facts about the captured caravan—in short, everything, except the secret alliance between the Mexican officer and the Tenawa chief. Not thinking of this—in truth, having no suspicion of it—his examiners do not put any questions about it; and, for himself, the wretch sees no reason to declare it, but the contrary. He indulges in the hope of one day returning to the Del Norte, and renewing his relations with Colonel Gil Uraga.

"Comrades!" cries the Ranger captain, addressing himself to his men, as soon as the examination is concluded, "you all of you loved Walt Wilder— all who knew him?"

"We did! we did!" is the response feelingly spoken. "So did I. Well, he's dead, beyond a doubt. It's nearly a month ago, and he could not last so long, shut up in that cave. His bones will be there, with those of the other poor fellow, whoever he was, that went in with him. It's dreadful to think of it! Now, from what this scoundrel says, it can't be so very far from here. And, as we can make him guide us to the place, I propose we go there, get the remains of our old comrade, and give them Christian burial."

With the Texan Rangers obedience to duty is less a thing of command than request; and this is a request of such nature as to receive instant and unanimous assent "Let us go!" is the universal response. "We needn't all make this journey," continues the captain. "There's no need for any more than our own boys, the Rangers, and such of the settlers as may choose to go with us. The rest, who have to look after the women, and some for driving back the stock, can make their way home at once. I reckon we've left the track pretty clear of Indians, and they'll be in no further danger from them."

Without further discussion, this arrangement is decided upon; and the two parties commence making the preparations suitable to their respective plans.

In less than half an hour after they separate; the settlers, with the women, children, and cattle, wending their way eastward; while the Rangers, guided by the renegade, ride off in the opposite direction—toward the Llano Estacado.

Chapter Thirty Four.
A Proposal by Proxy.

Day by day Hamersley grows stronger, and is able to be abroad.

Soon after Wilder, plucking him by the sleeve, makes request to have his company at some distance from the dwelling.

Hamersley accedes to the request, though not without some surprise. In the demeanour of his comrade there is an air of mystery. As this is unusual with the ex-Ranger, he has evidently something of importance to communicate.

Not until they have got well out of sight of the house, and beyond the earshot of anyone inside or around it, does Walt say a word. And then only after they have come to a stop in the heart of a cotton-wood copse, where a prostrate trunk offers them the accommodation of a seat.

Sitting down upon it, and making sign to Hamersley, still with the same mysterious air, to do likewise, the backwoodsman at length begins to unburden himself.

"Frank," says he, "I've brought ye out hyar to hev a little spell o' talk, on a subjeck as consarns this coon consid'able."

"What subject, Walt?"

"Wal, it's about a wumman."

"A woman! Why, Walt Wilder, I should have supposed that would be the farthest thing from your thoughts, especially a such a time and in such a place as this."

"True it shed, as ye say. For all that, ef this chile don't misunnerstan' the sign, a wumman ain't the furrest thing from yur thoughts, at the same time an' place."

The significance of the observation causes the colour to start to the cheeks of the young prairie merchant, late so pale. He stammers out an evasive rejoinder,—

"Well, Walt; you wish to have a talk with me. I'm ready to hear what you have to say. Go on! I'm listening."

"Wal, Frank, I'm in a sort o' a quandary wi' a critter as wears pettikotes, an' I want a word o' advice from ye. You're more practised in thar ways than me. Though a good score o' year older than yurself, I hain't hed much to do wi' weemen, 'ceptin' Injun squaws an' now an' agin a yeller gurl down by San Antone. But them scrapes wan't nothin' like thet Walt Wilder heve got inter now."

"A scrape! What sort of a scrape? I hope you haven't—"

"Ye needn't talk o' hope, Frank Hamersley. The thing air past hopin', an' past prayin' for. Ef this chile know anythin' o' the signs o' love, he has goed a good ways along its trail. Yis, sir-ee; too fur to think o' takin' the backtrack."

"On that trail, indeed?"

"Thet same; whar Cyubit sots his little feet, 'ithout neer a moccasin on 'em. Yis, kummerade, Walt Wilder, for oncest in in his kureer, air in a difeequelty; an' thet difeequelty air bein' fool enuf to fall in love—the which he hez dun, sure, sartin."

Hamersley gives a shrug of surprise, accompanied with a slight glance of indignation. Walt Wilder in love! With whom can it be? As he can himself think of only one woman worth falling in love with, either in that solitary spot, or elsewhere on earth, it is but natural his thoughts should turn to her.

Only for an instant, however. The idea of having the rough Ranger for a rival is preposterous. Walt, pursuing the theme, soon convinces him he has no such lofty aspirations.

"Beyond a doubt, she's been an' goed an' dud it—that air garl Concheeter. Them shining eyes o' her'n hev shot clar through this chile's huntin' shirt, till thar's no peace left inside o' it. I hain't slep a soun' wink for mor'en a week o' nights; all the time dreemin' o' the gurl, as ef she war a angel a hoverin' 'bout my head. Now, Frank, what am I ter do? That's why I've axed ye to kum out hyar, and enter into this confaberlation."

"Well, Walt, you shall be welcome to my advice. As to what you should do, that's clear enough; but what you may or can do will depend a good deal on what Miss Conchita says. Have you spoken to her upon the subject?"

"Thar hain't yit been much talk atween us—i'deed not any, I mout say. Ye know I can't parley thar lingo. But I've approached her wi' as much skill as I iver did bear or buffler. An', if signs signerfy anythin', she ain't bad skeeart about it. Contrarywise, Frank. If I ain't terribly mistuk, she shows as ef she'd be powerful willin' to hev me."

"If she be so disposed there can't be much difficulty in the matter. You mean to marry her, I presume?"

"In coorse I duz—that for sartin'. The feelin's I hev torst that gurl air diffrent to them as one hez for Injun squaws, or the queeries I've danced wi' in the fandangoes o' San Antone. Ef she'll agree to be myen, I meen nothin' short o' the hon'rable saramony o' marridge—same as atween man an' wife. What do ye think o't?"

"I think, Walt, you might do worse than get married. You're old enough to become a Benedict, and Conchita appears to be just the sort of girl that would suit you. I've heard it said that these Mexican women make the best of wives—when married to Americans."

Hamersley smiles, as though this thought were pleasant to him.

"There are several things," he continues, "that it will be necessary for you to arrange before you can bring about the event you're aiming at. First, you must get the girl's consent: and, I should think, also that of her master and mistress. They are, as it were, her guardians, and, to a certain extent, responsible for her being properly bestowed. Last of all, you'll require the sanction of the Church. This, indeed, may be your greatest difficulty. To make you and your sweetheart one, a priest, or Protestant clergyman, will be needed; and neither can be had very conveniently here, in the centre of the Staked Plain."

"Durn both sorts!" exclaims the ex-Ranger in a tone of chagrin. "Ef't warn't for the need o' 'em jest now, I say the Staked Plain air better 'ithout 'em, as wu'd anywars else. Why can't she an' me be tied thegither 'ithout any sech senseless saramony? Walt Wilder wants no mumblin' o' prayers at splicin' him to the gurl he's choosed for his partner. An' why shed thar be, supposin' we both gie our mutooal promises one to the tother?"

"True. But that would not be marriage such as would lawfully and legally make you man and wife."

"Doggone the lawfulness or legullity o' it! Priest or no priest, I want Concheteter for my squaw; an' I've made up my mind to hev her. Say, Frank! Don't ye think the old doc ked do it? He air a sort o' professional."

"No, no; the doctor would be of no use in that capacity. It's his business to unite broken bones, not hands and hearts. But, Walt, if you are really resolved on the thing, there will, no doubt, be an opportunity to carry out your intention in a correct and legitimate manner. You must be patient, however, and wait till you come across either a priest or a Protestant clergyman."

"Doggoned ef I care which," is the rejoinder of the giant. "Eyther'll do; an' one o' 'em 'ud be more nor surficient, ef 't war left ter Walt Wilder. But, hark'ee, Frank!" he continues, his face assuming an astute expression, "I'd like to be sure 'bout the thing now—that is, to get the gurl's way o' thinking on 't. Fact is, I've made up my mind to be sure, so as thar may be no slips or back kicks."

"Sure, how?"

"By procurin' her promise; getting betrothed, as they call it."

"There can be no harm in that. Certainly not."

"Wal, I'm gled you think so; for I've sot my traps for the thing, an' baited 'em too. Thet air's part o' my reezun for askin' ye out hyar. She's gin me the promise o' a meetin' 'mong these cotton woods, an' may kum at any minnit. Soon's she does, I'm agoin' to perpose to her; an' I want to do it in reg'lar, straightforrard way. As I can't palaver Spanish, an' you kin, I know'd ye wudn't mind transleetin' atween us. Ye won't, will ye?"

"I shall do that with the greatest pleasure, if you wish it. But don't you think, Walt, you might learn what you want to know without any interpreter? Conchita may not like my interference in an affair of such a delicate nature. Love's language is said to be universal, and by it you should understand one another."

"So fur's thet's consarned, I reck'n we do. But she, bein' a Mexikin, may hev queery ideas about it; an' I want her promise guv in tarms from which thar'll be no takin' the back track; same's I meen to give myen."

"All right, old fellow. I'll see you get such a promise, or none."

"Thet's satisfactory, Frank. Now, as this chile air agoin' to put the thing stiff an' strong, do you transleet it in the same sort."

"Trust me, it shall be done—*verbatim et literatim*."

"Thet's the way!" joyfully exclaims Walt; thinking that the *verbatim et literatim*—of the meaning of which he has not the slightest conception—will be just the thing to clinch his bargain with Conchita.

The singular contract between the prairie merchant and his *ci-devant* guide has just reached conclusion as a rustling is heard among the branches of the cottonwoods, accompanied by a soft footstep.

Looking around, they see Conchita threading her way through the grove. Her steps, cautious and stealthy, would tell of an "appointment," even were this not already known to them. Her whole bearing is that of one on the way to meet a lover; and the sight of Walt Wilder, who now rises erect to receive her, proclaims him to be the man.

It might appear strange that she does not shy back, on seeing him in company with another man. She neither starts nor shows any shyness; evidence that the presence of the third party is a thing understood and pre-arranged.

She advances without show of timidity; and, curtseying to the "Señor Francisco," as she styles Hamersley, takes seat upon the log from which he has arisen; Walt laying hold of her hand and gallantly conducting her to it.

There is a short interregnum of silence. This Conchita's sweetheart endeavours to fill up with a series of gestures that might appear uncouth but for the solemnity of the occasion. So considered, they may be deemed graceful, even dignified.

Perhaps not thinking them so himself, Walt soon seeks relief by turning to his interpreter, and making appeal to him as follows—

"Doggone it, Frank! Ye see I don't know how to talk to her, so you do the palaverin. Tell her right off, what I want. Say I hain't got much money, but a pair o' arems strong enuf to purtect her, thro' thick an' thro' thin, agin the dangers o' the mountain an' the puraira, grizzly bars, Injuns, an' all. She sees this chile hev got a big body; ye kin say to her thet his heart ain't no great ways out o' correspondence wi' his karkidge. Then tell her in the eend, thet his body an' his hands an' heart—all air offered to her; an' if she'll except 'em they shall be hern, now, evermore, an' to the death—so help me God!"

As the hunter completes his proposal thus ludicrously, though emphatically pronounced, he brings his huge hand down upon his brawny breast with a slap like the crack of a cricket bat.

Whatever meaning the girl may make out of his words, she can have had no doubt about their earnestness or sincerity, judging by the gestures that accompany them.

Hamersley can scarce restrain his inclination to laugh; but with an effort he subdues it, and faithfully, though not very literally, translates the proposal into Spanish.

When, as Walt supposes, he has finished, the ex-Ranger rises to his feet and stands awaiting the answer, his huge frame trembling like the leaf of an aspen. He continues to shake all the while Conchita's response is being delivered; though her first words would assure, and set his nerves at rest, could he but understand them. But he knows not his fate, till it has passed through the tedious transference from one language to another—from Spanish to his own native tongue.

"Tell him," is the response of Conchita, given without sign of insincerity, "tell him that I love him as much as he can me. That I loved him from the first moment of our meeting, and shall love him to the end of my life. In reply to his honourable proposal, say to him yes. I am willing to become his wife."

When the answer is translated to Walt, he bounds at least three feet into the air, with a shout of triumph such as he might give over the fall of an Indian foe.

Then, advancing towards the girl, he flings his great arms around her, lifts her from the ground as if she were a child's doll; presses her to his broad, throbbing breast, and imprints a kiss upon her lips—the concussion of which can be heard far beyond the borders of the cottonwood copse.

Chapter Thirty Five.
A Dangerous Eavesdropper.

However successful in his suit with Conchita, Walt Wilder is not without a rival. Hamersley has reason to suspect this soon after separating from the lovers, which he does, leaving them to themselves. It has occurred to him, that the presence of more than two on that spot can be no longer desirable. His part has been performed, and he withdraws without saying a word.

There is a third man, notwithstanding—a spectator—whose breast is stirred with terrible emotion.

As the Kentuckian passes out through the copse, he catches sight of a figure crouching behind the trunk of a tree—apparently that of a man. Twilight is now on, and beneath the leafy branches reigns an obscurity almost equalling night. What he sees may be some straying animal, or perhaps it is only fancy. His thoughts are engrossed with that which carries him on towards the house. There one will be awaiting him, in whose refined presence he will soon forget the uncouth spectacle of courtship at which he has been assisting.

But the form he has observed cowering under the shadow of the cottonwoods was no fancy, nor four-footed creature, but a human being, a man—in short, Manuel the Indian.

Manuel is mad in love with the little mestiza, who, with Spanish blood in her veins, is, nevertheless, maternally of his own race—that of the *Indios mansos*, or "tame Indians," of New Mexico—so called in contradistinction to the *Indios bravos*, the savages who, from the conquest till this day, have never submitted themselves to Spanish rule. Though Christianised, after a fashion, by the Franciscans, with others of the missionary fathers—living in walled towns, each with its *capilla* or church, and cultivating the lands around, many of these so-called Christian Indians still continue to practice Pagan rites, more or less openly. In some of their villages, it is said, the *estafa*, or sacred fire, is kept burning, and has never been permitted to go out since the time of Montezuma, from whom and his people they believe themselves descended. They are undoubtedly of Aztec race, and sun-worshippers, as were the subjects of the unfortunate Emperor of Tenochtitlas.

Travellers who have visited their more remote "pueblos" have witnessed something of this sun-worship, seeing them ascend to the flat roofs of their singularly constructed houses, and there stand in fixed attitude, devoutly gazing at the sun as it ascends over the eastern horizon.

Notwithstanding the epithet "tame," which their Spanish conquerors have applied to them, they are still more than half wild; and, upon occasions, the savage instinct shows itself in deeds of cruelty and blood.

This very instinct has been kindled in the heart of Manuel. It was not devotion to Don Valerian Miranda that moved him to follow the fortunes of his master into exile; his love for Conchita accounts for his presence there. And he loves her with an ardour and singleness of passion such as often burns in the breasts of his people.

The girl has given him no encouragement, rather the reverse. For all that, he has pursued her with zealous solicitation, regardless of rebuffs and apparently unconscious of her scorn.

Hitherto he has had no rival, which has hindered him from despairing. Conchita is still young, in her earliest teens, having just turned twelve. But even at this age a New Mexican maiden is deemed old enough for matrimony; and Manuel, to do justice to him, has eyes upon her with this honest intent. For months he had made up his mind to have her for his wife—long before their forced flight into the Llano Estacado. And now that they are in the desert, with no competitor near—for Chico does not count as one—he has fancied the time come for the consummation of his hopes.

But just when the fair fruit seems ripe for plucking, like the fox in the fable, he discovers it is beyond his reach. What is worse still, another, taller than he, and who can reach higher, is likely to gather it.

Ever since the arrival of Walt Wilder in the valley he has been watching the movements of the latter.

Not without observing that between the great Texan hunter and the little Mexican *muchacha* there has sprung up an attachment of a suspicious nature.

He has not heard them express it in speech, for in this way they cannot communicate with one another; but certain looks and gestures exchanged, unintelligible to others, have been easily interpreted by the Indian as the signs of a secret and mutual understanding between them.

They have driven the poor peon well nigh distracted with jealousy—felt all the keener from its being his first experience of it, all the angrier from consciousness of his own honest love—while he believes that of the intruder to have a different intent.

As the days and hours pass he observes new incidents to sharpen his suspicions and strengthen his jealous ire.

In fine, he arrives at the conclusion that Conchita—long loved by him, long vainly solicited—has surrendered her heart to the gigantic Texan, who like a sinister shadow, a ghoul, a very ogre, has chanced across the sunlight of his path.

Under the circumstances, what is he to do? He is powerful in passion, but weak in physical strength. Compared with his rival, he is nought. In a conflict the Texan would crush him, squeeze the breath out of his body, as a grizzly bear would that of a prairie squirrel or ground gopher.

He does not show open antagonism—does not think of it. He knows it would but end in his ruin—his utter annihilation.

Still, he is not despairing.

With the instincts peculiar to his race, he contemplates revenge. All his idle hours are spent brooding over plans to frustrate the designs of his rival—in short, to put him out of the way altogether.

More than once has a thought of poison passed through his mind as the surest way of effecting his fiendish purpose, as also the safest; and upon this mode of killing the Texan he has at length determined.

That very day he has been engaged in making ready for the deed—preparing the potion. Certain plants he has found growing in the valley, well known among his people as poisonous, will furnish him with the means of death—a slow, lingering death, therefore all the surer to avert suspicion from the hand that has dealt it.

To all appearance, Walt Wilder is doomed. He has escaped the spears, arrows, and tomahawks of the Tenawa savages to fall a victim to a destroyer, stealthy, subtle, unseen.

And is the noble Texan—guide, ranger, and hunter—thus sadly to succumb? No. Fate has not decreed his death by such insidious means. A circumstance, apparently accidental, steps in to save him. On this very day, when the poison it being prepared for him, the poisoner receives a summons that for the time at least, will frustrate his foul plans. His master commands him to make ready for a journey. It is an errand similar to that he has been several times sent upon before. He is to proceed to the settlements on the Rio Grande, where Don Valerian has friends with whom, in his exile, he keeps up secret correspondence, Manuel acting as messenger. Thence the trusted peon is to bring back, as oft before, despatches, news, provisions — the last now more than ever needed, on account of the stranger guests so unexpectedly thrown upon his hospitality.

Manuel is to commence his journey on the following day at the earliest hour of dawn. There will be no chance for him now to carry out his nefarious design. It must remain uncompleted till his return.

While chafing at the disappointment, he sees Conchita stealing out from the house and entering the cotton-wood grove. He follows her with a caution equalling her own, but from a far different cause. Crouching on through the trees, he takes stand behind a trunk, and, concealed by it, becomes spectator of all that passes. He is at first surprised at seeing three where he expected only two. Pleased also; for it gives him hope the girl's errand may not be the keeping of a love appointment. But as the triangular conference proceeds; above all, when it arrives at its conclusion, and he sees the Texan raise Conchita in his arms, giving her that kiss, the echo of which is distinctly audible to him, his blood boils, and with difficulty does he restrain himself from rushing up to the spot, and taking the lives of all three, or ending his own if he fail.

For a time he stands erect, with his *machete* drawn from its sheath, his eyes flashing with the fires of jealous vengeance. Fortunately for those upon whom they are bent, an instinct of self-preservation stays him. His hand is ready, but his heart fails him. Terrible as is his anger, it is yet controlled by fear. He will wait for a more favourable time and surer opportunity. A safer means, too — this more than aught else restraining him. While still in intense agitation, he sees Hamersley depart, leaving the other two to themselves. And now, as other kisses are exchanged between the lovers, his jealous fury becomes freshly excited, and for the second time he is half resolved to rush forward and kill — kill.

But again his fears gain the ascendency, and his hand refuses to obey the dictates of his angry heart. With the bare blade held tremblingly, he continues spectator of that scene which fills his breast with blackest, bitterest emotion. He has not the courage to interrupt it. Calculating the chances, he perceives they are against him. Should he succeed in killing the Texan, with Conchita standing by and bearing witness to the deed, would be to forfeit his own life. He could find it in his heart to kill her too; but that would lead to the same result. Failing in his first blow, the great hunter would have him under his heel, to be crushed as a crawling reptile.

Thus cogitating, he sticks to his place of concealment, and overlooks the love scene to its termination; then permits the lovers to depart in peace — the woman he so wildly loves, the man he so madly hates.

After they have gone out of the grove, he advances towards the log upon which they were seated. Himself taking seat on it, he there ponders upon a plan of vengeance surer and safer than the assassin's steel.

It is no longer his intent to employ poison. A new idea has entered his brain—has been in it ever since receiving notice of the journey on which he is about to set forth; in truth, suggested by this. A scheme quite as efficient as poisoning, but also having a purpose far more comprehensive, for it includes others besides his rival the Ranger. Of late neglectful of his duties, Colonel Miranda has severely chided him, thus kindling the hereditary antipathy of his race towards the white man.

His master is to be among the victims—in short, all of them, his fellow-servant, Chico, excepted. Should the diabolical plan prove a success, not one of them can escape ruin, and most of them may meet death.

Chapter Thirty Six.
A Tale of Peril.

Thanks to the skill of Don Prospero, exerted with kind assiduity, Hamersley's wounds are soon healed, his strength completely restored. Doubtless the tender nursing of the "angel" has something to do with his rapid recovery, while her presence, cheerful as gentle, does much to remove the gloom from his spirits, caused by the terrible disaster he had sustained. Long before reaching convalescence he has ceased to lament the loss of his property, and only sorrows as he reflects on the fate of his brave followers, whose lives were sacrificed in the effort to preserve it.

Happily, however, as time passes the retrospect of the red carnage loses something of its sanguinary hue, its too vivid tints becoming gradually obscured in the oblivion of the past with the singular surroundings of the present. Amid these his spirit yields itself to pleasanter reflections. How could it be otherwise?

Still, with restored strength, his curiosity has been increasing, till it has reached a point of keenness requiring to be satisfied. He wonders at all around him, especially the strange circumstance of finding his old friend and duelling second in such an out-of-the-way place. As yet, Miranda has only given him a hint, though one pretty much explaining all. There has been a revolution; and they are refugees.

But the young Kentuckian is curious to learn the details, about which, for some reason, the Mexican has hitherto preserved silence. His reticence has been due to an injunction of the doctor, who, still under some anxiety about the recovery of his patient, forbade imparting to him particulars that might have an injurious effect on his nervous system, sadly debilitated by the shock it has received.

Don Prospero is an acute observer. He perceives the growing interest which Hamersley takes in the sister of his host. He knows the story of the Chihuahua duel; and thinks that the other story—that of the disastrous revolution—told in detail, might retard the convalescence of his patient. Counselled by him, Colonel Miranda has refrained from communicating it.

Ignorant of the cause, Hamersley is all the more eager to learn it. Still, his curiosity does not impel him to importunate inquiry. In the companionship of such kind friends he can afford to be patient.

Walt Wilder has no curiosity of any kind. His thoughts have become centred, his whole soul wrapped up in Conchita. The heart of the colossal hunter has received a shock such as it never had before; for, as he declared himself, he is in love for the first time in his life.

Not but that he has made love before, after a fashion. For he has shared his tent with more than one Indian squaw, drank and danced with those nondescript damsels who now and then find their way to the forts of the fur-traders scattered among the Rocky Mountains and along the border-land of the prairies. To all this he has confessed.

But these have been only interludes, "trifling love scrapes." His present affair with the little mestiza is different. Her sparkling black eyes pierced deeper and more direct—"straight plum-centre to his heart," as, in professional jargon, he described it.

The invalid is at length convalescent; the doctor removes the seal of injunction placed upon the lips of Colonel Miranda, and the latter fulfils his promise made to give a narrative of the events which have led to their residence in that remote and solitary spot.

The two seated together sipping Paseno wine and smoking cigars, the Mexican commences his tale.

"We are refugees, as I've already stated, and came here to save our heads. At least, there was danger of my losing mine—or, rather, the certainty of it—had we not succeeded in making our escape from Albuquerque. The word *pronunciamento* explains all. A revolt of the troops under my command, with a name, that of the leader, will give you a key to the whole affair."

"Uraga!" exclaims Hamersley, the word coming mechanically from his red lips; while a cloud passes over his brow, and a red flush flecks the pallor on his cheeks. "Captain Uraga! 'Twas he?"

"It was."

"The scoundrel! I thought so."

"Not Captain Uraga now, but Colonel; for the reward of his treason reached him simultaneously with its success, and the traitor is now in command of the district from which I have been, deposed. Not only that, but, as I have heard, he has appropriated my house—the same where, twelve months ago, I had the pleasure of showing you some hospitality. Contrasting it with our present humble abode, you will see, señor, that my family affairs have not prospered, any more than my political fortunes. But to the narration.

"Not long after you left us I made application to the Government for an increase to the mounted force at my disposal. This had become necessary for due protection of the district from our warlike neighbours in the west— the Navajoes. They had made several raids upon the river settlements, and carried off goods, cattle, and a number of captives. The force I had made requisition for was obtained; but not the right men, or at least the officers I should have chosen to command it. A troop of light cavalry was sent me—Lancers. You may imagine my chagrin, not to say disgust, when I saw Captain Gil Uraga at its head. Marching into the town of Albuquerque, he reported himself for duty.

"I need not tell you how unpleasant it was for me to have such a fellow for subordinate. In addition to our Chihuahua duel, there were many reasons for my having an aversion to him—one, and not the least, that which I have already hinted to you—his pretensions to be the suitor of my sister."

Hamersley writhes as he listens, the red spot on his cheek spreading and flushing redder.

Miranda proceeds—

"He continued his ill-received attentions whenever chance gave him an opportunity. It was not often. I took care of that; though, but for precautions and my authority as his superior officer, his advances would, no doubt, have been bolder—in short, persecutions. I knew that to my sister, as to myself, his presence was disagreeable, but there was no help for it. I could not have him removed. In all matters of military duty he took care to act so that there should be no pretext for a charge against him. Besides, I soon found that he was in favour with one of the Government dignitaries. Though I did not then know why, I learnt it afterwards; and why he, of all others, had been sent to Albuquerque. The *sap* had commenced for a new revolution, and he was one of its secret fomenters. He had been chosen by the *parti prêtre* as a fitting agent to act in that district, of which, like myself, he was a native.

"Having no suspicion of this, I only thought of him in regard to his impertinent solicitation of my sister; and against this I could restrain him. He was polite; obsequiously so, and cautiously guarded in his gallantries; so that I had no cause for resorting to the *desafio*. I could only wait and watch.

"The vigil was not a protracted one; though, alas! it ended differently from what I expected. About two months after his coming under my command, the late *grito* was proclaimed all over Mexico. One morning as I went down to the military quarters I found confusion and disturbance. The

The Lone Ranche | 159

soldiers were under arms, many of them drunk, and vociferating *'Viva Santa Anna! Viva el Coronel Uraga!'* Hearing this, I at once comprehended all. It was a *pronunciamento*. I drew my sword, thinking to stem the tide of treason; and called around me such of my followers as were still faithful. It was too late. The poison had spread throughout the whole command. My adherents were soon overpowered, several of them killed; myself wounded, dragged to the *carcel*, and there locked up. The wonder is that I was not executed on the spot; since I know Gil Uraga thirsted for my life. He was only restrained, however, by a bit of caution; for, although I was not put to death on that day, he intended I should never see the sun rise upon another. In this he was disappointed, and I escaped.

"I know you will be impatient to learn how," resumes the refugee, after rolling and igniting a fresh cigarrito. "It is somewhat of an incident, and might serve the writer of a romance. I owe my life, my liberty, and, what is more, my sister's safety, to our good friend Don Prospero. In his capacity of military surgeon he was not compromised like the rest of us; and after the revolt in the cuartel he was left free to follow his vocation. While seeking permission to dress the wound I had received, chance conducted him to a place where he could overhear a conversation that was being carried on between Uraga and one of his lieutenants—a ruffian named Roblez, fit associate for his superior. They were in high glee over what had happened, carousing, and in their cups not very cautious of what they said. Don Prospero heard enough to make him acquainted with their scheme, so diabolical you will scarcely give credence to it. I was to be made away with in the night—carried up to the mountains, and there murdered! With no traces left, it would be supposed that I had made my escape from the prison. And the good doctor heard other designs equally atrocious. What the demons afterwards intended doing when my sister should be left unprotected—"

Something like a groan escapes from the listener's lips, while his fingers move nervously, as if clutching at a weapon.

"Devoted to me, Don Prospero at once resolved upon a course of action. There was not a moment to be lost. He obtained permission to attend me professionally in the prison. It was a cheap grace on Uraga's part, considering his ulterior design. An attendant, a sort of hospital assistant, was allowed to accompany the doctor to the cell, carrying his lints, drugs, and instruments. Fortunately, I had not been quite stripped by the ruffians who had imprisoned me, and in my own purse, along with that of Don Prospero, was a considerable sum of gold—enough for tempting the attendant to change clothes and places with me. He was the more ready to do so, relying upon a story he intended to tell—that we had overpowered and compelled him. Poor fellow! As we afterwards learnt, it did not save him. He was shot the next morning to appease the chagrin of Uraga, furious at our escape. We cannot help feeling regret for his fate; but, under the circumstances, what else could have been done?

"We stepped forth from the *carcel*, the doctor leading the way, and I, his assistant, bearing the paraphernalia after him. We passed out of the barracks unchallenged. Fortunately, the night was a dark one, and the guards were given to carousing. The sentries were all intoxicated.

"By stealth, and in silence, we hastened on to my house, where I found Adela, as you may suppose, in a state of agonised distress. But there was no time for words—not even of explanation. With two of my servants whom I could trust, we hastily collected some of our animals—horses and pack-mules. The latter we loaded with such things as we could think of as being requisite for a journey. We intended it to be a long one—all the way across the great prairies. I knew there would be no safety for us within the limits of New Mexico; and I remembered what you had said but a few months before—your kind proffer of hospitality, should it ever be my fate to seek refuge in your country. And to seek it we set forth, leaving my house untenanted, or only in charge of the remaining domestics, from whom gold had gained a promise not to betray us. The doctor, Adela and myself, the two peons who had volunteered to accompany us, with the girl, Conchita, composed our travelling party. I knew we dared not take the route usually travelled. We should be followed by hostile pursuers and forced back, perhaps slain upon the spot. I at least would have had a short shrift. Knowing this, we made direct for the mountains, with whose passes I was familiar, having traversed them in pursuit of the savages.

"We passed safely through the Sierra, and kept on towards the Rio Pecos. Beyond this river all was unknown to us. We only knew that there lay the Llano Estacado, invested with mysterious terrors—the theme of our childhood's fears—a vast stretch of desert, uninhabited, or only by savages seeking scalps, by wild beasts ravening for blood, by hideous reptiles—serpents breathing poison. But what were all these dangers to that we were leaving behind? Nothing, and this thought inspired us to proceed.

"We crossed the Pecos and entered upon the sterile plain. We knew not how far it extended; only that on the other side lay a fertile country through which we might penetrate to the frontier settlements of your great free nation. This was the beacon of our hopes, the goal of safety.

"We travelled in an easterly course; but there were days when the sun was obscured by clouds; and then, unguided, we had either to remain at rest or run the chance of getting strayed.

"We toiled on, growing weak for want of food, and suffering terribly from thirst. No water was to be found anywhere—not a drop.

"Our animals suffered as ourselves. Staggering under the weight of their loads, one by one they gave out, dropping down upon the desert plain. Only one held out bravely to the last—the mustang mare that brought you to our present abode. Yes, Lolita survived to carry my dear sister, as if she understood the value we all placed upon her precious burden. The others gave out—first the horses ridden by Don Prospero and myself, then the pack-mules. Fortunately, these fell near the spot where we at length found relief—near enough for their loads, and two of themselves, to be afterwards recovered.

"One day, as we toiled on afoot, in the hourly expectation of death, we came in sight of this fair spot. It appeared to us a Paradise, as you say it did to yourself. Under our eyes were green trees and the gleam of crystal streams; in our ears the songs of birds we had never expected to hear again. Chance had brought us direct to the path, the only one by which the valley can be reached from the upper plain. Inspirited by the fair spectacle below, we gained strength enough to descend. We drank of the sweet water, and procured food from the branches of the trees that shaded it. It was the season when fruits and berries were abundant. Afterwards we discovered game, and were successful in capturing it.

"Soon with restored strength we were able to go back, and recover the paraphernalia we had left upon the plain, along with two of the mules that, after resting, had regained their feet, and could stagger on a little farther.

"At first we only thought of making this a temporary resting-place; though there seemed but slight hope of being able to continue our journey. But as the days passed, and we were left undisturbed, we began to realise the fact that we had found an asylum, safe as pleasant.

"It was not likely that anyone would discover the track we had taken in our flight. Even the resentment of Uraga would scarce pursue us across the Staked Plain. In any case, there was no help for it but to remain in the valley, as we had not animals enough to carry us on. Our only alternative was to go back to the Del Norte—a thing not to be thought of. We resolved, therefore, on staying, at least for a time. I had conceived a plan for communicating with my friends in New Mexico, and am not without hope that sooner or later we may get tidings that will make it safe for as to return. In our country, as you know, there is nothing permanent; and we have hopes ere long to see the Liberal party once more in the ascendant.

"Our resolution to remain here becoming fixed we sot about making our situation as comfortable as circumstances would permit. We erected this humble tenement whose roof now shelters us. We turned fishermen and hunters; in the last my sister proving more accomplished than any of us—a real huntress, as you have seen. We have enjoyed the life amazingly; more especially our worthy *medico*, who is an enthusiastic naturalist, and here finds a rare opportunity of gratifying his scientific tastes. For subsistence we have not had to depend altogether upon the chase. Manuel, one of our peons, an old muleteer, makes an occasional trip to Albuquerque, the route of which he has good reason to remember. I send him with messages, and to purchase provisions. He is cautious to make his approaches under cover of night, and do his marketing with circumspection. With our gold, not yet all gone, he is enabled to bring back such commodities as we stand in need of; while a friend, entrusted with the secret of our hiding-place, keeps us informed of the *novedades*. Now you know all."

Chapter Thirty Seven.
The Intercepted Letter.

Colonel Miranda, having told the tale of his perilous escape, for a time remains silent and reflective. So does his listener. Both are thinking on the same subject—the villainy of Gil Uraga.

Hamersley first breaks silence, asking the question,—

"Did you get my letter?"

"What letter?"

"I wrote you only one. Now I think of it, you could not have received it. No. By the time it would reach Albuquerque, you must have been gone from there."

"I got no letter from you, Don Francisco. You say you sent one. What was the nature of its contents?"

"Nothing of any importance. Merely to say that I was coming back to New Mexico, and hoped to find you in good health."

"Did it particularise the time you expected to reach Albuquerque?"

"Yes; as far as I could fix that, if I remember rightly, it did."

"And the route you were to take?"

"That too. When I wrote the letter I intended to make trial of a new trail lately discovered—up the Canadian, and touching the northern end of the Staked Plain. I did make trial of it, alas! with lamentable result. But why do you ask these questions, Colonel Miranda?"

The colonel does not make immediate answer. He appears more meditative than ever, as though some question has come before his mind calling for deliberate examination.

While he is thus occupied the ex-Ranger enters the room and sits down beside them. Walt is welcome. Indeed, Don Valerian had already designed calling him into their counsel. For an idea has occurred to the Mexican Colonel requiring the joint consideration of all three. Turning to the other two, he says,—

"I've been thinking a good deal about the attack on your caravan. The more I reflect on it the more I am led to believe that some of the Indians who plundered you were painted."

"They were all painted," is the reply of the young prairie merchant.

"True, Don Francisco; but that isn't what I mean."

"I reckon I knows what ye mean," interposes the ex-Ranger, rising excitedly from his chair on hearing the Mexican's remark. "It's been my own suspeeshun all along. You know what I tolt ye, Frank?"

Hamersley looks interrogatively at his old comrade.

"Did I not say," continues Wilder, "that I seed two men 'mong the Injuns wi' ha'r upon thar faces? They wa'n't Injuns; they war whites. A'n't that what ye mean, Kurnel Meoranda?"

"*Precisamente!*" is the colonel's reply.

The other two wait for him to continue on with the explanation Wilder has already surmised. Even the young prairie merchant—less experienced in Mexican ways and wickedness, in infamy so incredible—begins to have a glimmering of the truth.

Seemingly weighing his words, Miranda proceeds,—

"No doubt it was a band of Comanche Indians that destroyed your caravan and killed your comrades. But I have as little doubt of there being white men among them—one at least, and that one he who planned and instigated the deed."

"Who, Colonel Miranda?" is the quick interrogatory of the Kentuckian, while with flashing eyes and lips apart he breathlessly awaits the answer. For all, he does not much need it; the name to be pronounced is on the tip of his own tongue.

It is again "Gil Uraga!"

"Yes," replies the Mexican, with added emphasis. "He is, undoubtedly, the robber who despoiled you. Though done in the guise of an Indian onslaught, with real Indians as his assistants, he has been their instructor—their leader. I see it all now clear as sunlight. He got your letter, which you say was addressed to me as colonel commanding at Albuquerque. As a matter of course, he opened it. It told him when and where to meet you; your strength, and the value of your cargo. The last has not been needed as an incentive for him to assail you, Don Francisco. The mark you made upon his cheek was sufficient. Didn't I tell you at the time he would move heaven and earth to have revenge on you—on both of us? He has succeeded; behold his success. I a refugee, robbed of everything; you plundered the same; both ruined men!"

"Not yet!" cries the Kentuckian, starting to his feet. "Not ruined yet, Colonel Miranda. If the thing be as you say, I shall seek a second interview with this scoundrel—this fiend; seek till I obtain it. And then—"

"Hyur's one," interrupts the ex-Ranger, unfolding his gigantic form with unusual rapidity, "who'll take part in that sarch. Yis, Frank, this chile's willin' to go wi' ye to the heart o' Mexiko, plum centre; to the halls o' the Montyzoomas; reddy to start this minnit."

"If," resumes Hamersley, his coolness contrasting with the excited air of his comrade, now roused to a terrible indignation, "if, Colonel Miranda, it turns out as you conjecture, that Gil Uraga has taken part in the destruction of my waggon-train, or even been instrumental in causing it, I shall leave no stone unturned to obtain justice."

"Justice!" exclaims the ex-Ranger, with a deprecatory toss of the head. "In case o' this kind we want somethin' beside. To think o' thirteen innercent men attacked without word o' warnin', shot down, stabbed, slaughtered, and sculped! Think o' that; an' don't talk tamely o' justice; let's shout loudly for revenge!"

Chapter Thirty Eight.
The Land of the "Lex Talionis."

During the quarter of a century preceding the annexation of New Mexico to the United States, that distant province of the Mexican Republic, like all the rest of the country, was the scene of constantly recurring revolutions. Every discontented captain, colonel, or general who chanced to be in command of a district, there held sway as a dictator; so demeaning himself that martial and military rule had become established as the living law of the land. The civic authorities rarely possessed more than the semblance of power; and where they did it was wielded in the most flagitious manner. Arbitrary arts were constantly committed, under the pretext of patriotism or duty. No man's life was safe who fell under the displeasure of the ruling military chieftain; and woman's honour was held in equally slight respect.

In the northern frontier provinces of the republic this irresponsible power of the soldiery was peculiarly despotic and harassing. There, two causes contributed to establish and keep it in the ascendency. One of these was the revolutionary condition of the country, which, as elsewhere, had become chronic. The contest between the party of the priests and that of the true patriots, begun in the first days of Mexico's independence, has been continued ever since; now one, now the other, in the ascendant. The monstrous usurpation of Maximilian, supported by Napoleon the Third, and backed by a soldier whom all Mexicans term the "Bandit Bazaine," was solely due to the hierarchy; while Mexico owes its existing Republican government to the patriot party—happily, for the time, triumphant.

The province of New Mexico, notwithstanding its remoteness from the nation's capital, was always affected by, and followed, its political fortunes. When the *parti prêtre* was in power at the capital, its adherents became the rulers in the distant States for the time being; and when the Patriots, or Liberals, gained the upper hand this *rôle* was reversed.

It is but just to say that, whenever the latter were the "ins," things for the time went well. Corruption, though not cured, was to some extent checked; and good government would begin to extend itself over the land. But such could only last for a brief period. The monarchical, dictatorial, or imperial party—by whatever name it may be known—was always the party of the Church; and this, owning three-fourths of the real estate, both in town and country, backed by ancient ecclesiastical privileges, and armed with another powerful engine—the gross superstition it had been instrumental in fostering—was always able to control events; so that no Government, not despotic, could stand against it for any great length of time. For all, freedom at intervals triumphed, and the priests became the "outs;" but ever potent, and always active, they would soon get up a new "grito" to bring about a revolutionary change in the Government. Sanguinary scenes would be enacted—hangings, shooting, garrottings—all the horrors of civil war that accompany the bitterest of all spite, the ecclesiastical.

In such an uncertain state of things it was but natural that the *militarios* should feel themselves masters of the situation, and act accordingly.

In the northern districts they had yet another pretext for their unrestrained exercise of power—in none more than New Mexico. This remote province, lying like an oasis in the midst of uninhabited wilds, was surrounded on all sides by tribes of hostile Indians. There were the Navajoes and Apaches on its west, the Comanche and other Apache bands on the south and east, the Utahs on its north, and various smaller tribes distributed around it. They were all more or less hostile at one time or another: now on terms of an intermittent peace, secured by a "palaver" and treaty; this anon to be broken by some act of bad faith, leaving their "braves" at liberty once more to betake themselves to the war-path.

Of course this condition of things gave the soldiery a fine opportunity to maintain their ascendency over the peaceful citizens. Rabble as these soldiers were, and poltroons as they generally proved themselves in every encounter with the Indians, they were accustomed to boast of being the country's protectors, for this "protection" assumed a sort of right to despoil it at their pleasure.

Some few years preceding the American-Mexican war—which, as well known, gave New Mexico to the United States—these belligerent swaggerers were in the zenith of their arbitrary rule. Their special pet and protector, Santa Anna, was in for a new spell of power, making him absolute dictator of Mexico and disposer of the destinies of its people. At the same time, one of his most servile tools and successful imitators was at the head of the Provincial Government, having Santa Fé for its capital. This man was Manuel Armijo, whose character may be ascertained, by those curious to study it, from reading the chronicles of the times, especially the records of the prairie merchants, known as the "Santa Fé traders." It will there be learnt that this provincial despot was guilty of every act that could disgrace humanity; and that not only did he oppress his fellow-citizens with the soldiery placed at his disposal to protect them from Indian enemies, but was actually in secret league with the savages themselves to aid him in his mulcts and murders! Whatever his eye coveted he was sure to obtain, by fair means or foul—by open pillage or secret theft—not unfrequently accompanied by assassination. And as with the despot himself, so with his subordinates—each in his own town or district wielding irresponsible power; all leading lives in imitation of the provincial chieftain, as he of him—the great prototype and patron of all—who held dictatorial sway in the capital of the country, Don Antonio Lopez de Santa Anna.

A knowledge of this abnormal and changeable condition of Mexican affairs will, in some measure, explain why Colonel Miranda so suddenly ceased to be commandant of Albuquerque. Santa Anna's new accession to power brought in the *Padres*, turning out the *Patriotas*, many of the latter suffering death for their patriotism, while the adherents of the former received promotion for their support.

Staunchest among these was the captain of Lancers, Gil Uraga, promoted to be colonel as also commandant of the district from which its deposed chief so narrowly escaped with his life.

And now this revolutionary usurper is in full authority, his acts imitating his master, Armijo, like him in secret league with the savages, even consorting with the red pirates of the plains, taking part in their murderous marauds, and sharing their plunder.

Chapter Thirty Nine.
Prosperous, but not Happy.

Despite his rapid military promotion and the ill-gotten wealth he has acquired, Colonel Gil Uraga is anything but a happy man. Only at such times as he is engaged in some stirring affair of duty or devilry, or when under the influence of drink, is he otherwise than wretched. To drinking he has taken habitually, almost continually. It is not to drown conscience; he has none. The canker-worm that consumes him is not remorse, but disappointment in a love affair, coupled with a thirst for vengeance.

There are moments when he is truly miserable, his misery reaching its keenest whenever he either looks into his mirror or stands before a portrait that hangs against the wall of the *sala*. It is a likeness of Adela Miranda; for he has taken possession of the house of his predecessor, with all its furniture and pictures, left in their hasty retreat, the young lady's portrait as the rest.

The Lancer colonel loves Adela Miranda; and though his love be of a coarse, brutal nature, it is strong and intense as that the noblest man may feel.

In earlier days he believed there was a chance of his obtaining her hand. Humble birth is no bar in Mexico—land of revolutions—where the sergeant or common soldier of to-day may be a lieutenant, captain, or colonel to-morrow. His hopes had been a stimulant to his military aspirations; perchance one of the causes that first led him into crime. He believed that wealth might bridge over the social distinction between himself and her, and in this belief he cared not how it should be acquired. For the rest he was not ill-looking, rather handsome, and fairly accomplished. Like most Mexican *militarios*, he could boast of his *bonnes fortunes*, which he often did.

These have become more rare since receiving the sword-thrust from his American adversary in the duel at Chihuahua, which not only cost him three front teeth, but a hideous scar across the cheek. The teeth have been replaced, but the scar cannot be effaced; it remains a frightful cicatrix. Even his whiskers, let grow to their extremest outcrop, will not all conceal it; it is too far forward upon the face.

It was after this unfortunate affair that he made proposal to Adela Miranda. And now he cannot help thinking it had something to do with her abrupt and disdainful rejection of him, though the young lady's little concealed disgust, coupled with her brother's indignation, had no reference to the physical deformity. But for his blind passion he might have perceived this. Fancying it so, however, it is not strange that he goes half frantic, and can be heard giving utterance to fearful oaths every time he glances in his looking-glass.

After returning from his secret expedition of murder and pillage, he can gaze with more equanimity into the glass. From the man who caused the disfiguration of his visage he has exacted a terrible retribution. His adversary in the Chihuahua duel is now no more. He has met with a fate sufficient to satisfy the most implacable vengeance; and often, both sober and in his cups, does Gil Uraga break out into peals of laughter, like the glee of a demon, as he reflects on the torture, prolonged and horrible, his hated enemy must have endured before life became extinct!

But even all this does not appease his malevolent spirit. A portion of his vengeance is yet unappeased—that due to him who was second in the duel. And if it could be satisfied by the death of Miranda himself, then there would still be the other thought to torture him—his thwarted love scheme. The chagrin he suffers from this is stronger than his thirst for vengeance.

He is seated in the sala of Miranda's house, which he occupies as his official headquarters. He is alone, his only companion being the bottle that stands upon a table beside him—this and a cigar burning between his lips. It is not wine he is drinking, but the whisky of Tequila, distilled from the wild maguey. Wine is too weak to calm his perturbed spirit, as he sits surveying the portrait upon the wall.

His eyes have been on it several times; each time, as he takes them off, drinking a fresh glass of the mezcal and igniting another cigar. What signifies all his success in villainy? What is life worth without her? He would plunder a church to obtain possession of her—murder his dearest friend to get from Adela Miranda one approving smile.

Such are his coarse thoughts as he sits soliloquising, shaping conjectures about the banished commandant and his sister.

Where can they have gone to? In all probability to the United States—that asylum of rebels and refugees. In the territory of New Mexico they cannot have stayed. His spies have searched every nook and corner of it, their zeal secured by the promise of large rewards. He has dispatched secret emissaries to the Rio Abajo, and on to the *Provincias Internas*. But no word of Miranda anywhere—no trace can be found either of him or his sister. "*Chingara!*"

As if this exclamatory phrase, sent hissing through his teeth—too foul to bear translation—were the name of a man, one at this moment appears in the doorway, who, after a gesture of permission to enter, steps inside the room.

He is an officer in full uniform—one whom we have met before, though not in military costume. It is Lieutenant Roblez, Uraga's adjutant, as also his confederate in crime.

"I'm glad you've come, *ayudante*," says the Colonel, motioning the new-comer to a seat. "I'm feeling a little bit lonely, and I want some one to cheer me. You, Roblez, are just the man for that; you've got such a faculty for conversation."

This is ironical; for Roblez is as silent as an owl.

"Sit down and give me your cheerful company," the Colonel adds. "Have a cigar and a *copita* of this capital stuff; it's the best that Tequila produces."

"I've brought other company that may be more cheerful than mine," returns the adjutant, still keeping his feet.

"Ah! some of our fellows from the cuartel? Bring them in."

"It is not any of the officers, Colonel. There's only one man, and he's a civilian.

"Civilian or soldier, you're free to introduce him. I hope," he adds, in an undertone, "it's one of the *ricos* of the neighbourhood, who won't mind taking an *albur* at *montè* or a throw of the dice. I'm just in the vein for a bit of play."

"He I'm going to introduce don't look much like a *rico*. From what I can see of him in the darkness, I should say that the blanket upon his shoulders and his sheepskin smallclothes—somewhat dilapidated by the way—are about all the property he possesses."

"He's a stranger to you, then?"

"As much as to yourself, as you'll say after seeing him—perhaps more."

"What sort of man is he?"

"For that matter, he can hardly be described as a man. At least, he's not one of the *gent-de-razon*. He's only an Indian."

"Ha! Comanche?"

As he utters this interrogatory, Colonel Gil Uraga gives a slight start, and looks a little uneasy. His relations with men of the Indian race are of a delicate nature; and, although keen to cultivate their acquaintance whenever occasion requires it, he prefers keeping all Indians at a distance— more especially Comanches, when he has no particular need of their services. The thought has flashed across his mind that the man waiting to be ushered into his presence may be a messenger from the Horned Lizard; and with the Tenawa chief he desires no further dealings—at least for a time. Therefore, the belief of its being an emissary from his red-skinned confederate somewhat discomposes him.

The reply of his subordinate, however, reassures him.

"No, colonel, he's not a Comanche; bears no resemblance to one, only in the colour of his skin. He appears to be a Pueblo; and from his tattered costume, I take him to be some poor labourer."

"But what does he want with me?"

"That, colonel, I cannot say; only that he has expressed a very urgent desire to speak with you. I fancy he has something to communicate, which might be important for you to hear; else I should not have taken the liberty to bring him here."

"You have him at hand?"

"I have. He is outside in the *patio*. Shall I usher him in?"

"By all means; there can be no harm in hearing what the fellow has to say. It may be about some threatened invasion of the savages; and as protectors of the people, you, ayudante, know it's our duty to do whatever we can for warding off such a catastrophe."

The colonel laughs at his sorry jest; the adjutant expressing his appreciation of it in a shrug of the shoulders, accompanied by a grim smile.

"Bring the brute in!" is the command that followed, succeeded by the injunction.

"Stay outside in the court till I send for or call you. The fellow may have something to say intended for only one pair of ears. Take a glass of the *mezcal*, light cigarrito, and amuse yourself as you best may."

The adjutant obeys the first two of these directions; then, stepping out of the *sala*, leaves his superior officer alone.

Uraga glances around to assure himself that there are weapons within reach. With a conscience like his, a soul charged with crime, no wonder.

His sabre rests against the wall close to his hand, while a pair of dragoon pistols, both loaded, lie upon the table.

Satisfied with the proximity of these weapons, he sits upright in his chair and tranquilly awaits the entrance of the Indian.

Chapter Forty.
A Confidence Well Rewarded.

Only a short interval, a score of seconds elapses, when the door, once more opening, admits the expected visitor. The adjutant, after ushering him into the room, withdraws, and commences pacing to and fro in the patio.

Colonel Gil Uraga feels very much inclined to laugh as he contemplates the new-comer, and reflects on the precautions he has taken. A poor devil of an Indian *peon*, in coarse woollen *tilma*, tanned sheepskin trousers reaching only to the knee, bare legs below, *guaraches* upon his feet, and a straw hat upon his head; his long black hail hanging unkempt over his shoulders; his mien humble and looks downcast, like all of his tribe. Yet it might be seen that, on occasion, his eyes could flash forth a light, indicative of danger—a fierce, fiery light, such as may have shone in the orbs of his ancestors when they rallied around Guatimozin, and with clubs and stakes beat back the spears and swords of their Spanish invaders.

At the entrance of this humble personage, into the splendidly furnished apartment, his first act is to pull off his tattered straw hat, and make lowly obeisance to the gorgeously attired officer he sees sitting behind the table.

Up to this time Uraga has presumed him to be a perfect stranger, but when the broad brim of the sombrero no longer casts its shade over his face, and his eyelids become elevated through increasing confidence, the colonel starts to his feet with an exclamatory speech that tells of recognition.

"*Carrambo*! You are Manuel—mule driver for Don Valerian Miranda?"

"*Si, Señor; a servido de V* (Yes, Sir; at your Excellency's service)," is the reply meekly spoken, and accompanied with a second sweep of the straw hat—as gracefully as if given by a Chesterfield.

At sight of this old acquaintance, a world of thought rushes crowding through the brain of Gil Uraga—conjectures, mingled with pleasant anticipations.

For it comes back to his memory, that at the time of Colonel Miranda's escape, some of his domestics went off with him, and he remembers that Manuel was one of them. In the Indian bending so respectfully before him he sees, or fancies, the first link of a chain that may enable him to trace the fugitives. Manuel should know something about their whereabouts? And the *ci devant* mule driver is now in his power for any purpose—be it life or death.

There is that in the air and attitude of the Indian which tells him there will be no need to resort to compulsory measures. The information he desires can be obtained without, and he determines to seek it by adopting the opposite course.

"My poor fellow," he says, "you look distressed—as if you had just come from off a toilsome journey. Here, take a taste of something to recuperate your strength; then you can let me know what you've got to say. I presume you've some communication to make to me, as the military commandant of the district. Night or day, I am always ready to give a hearing to those who bring information that concerns the welfare of the State."

While speaking the colonel has poured out a glass of the distilled mezcal juice. This the peon takes from his hand, and, nothing loth, spills the liquor between his two rows of white glittering teeth.

Upon his stomach, late unused to it, the fiery spirit produce! an effect almost instantaneous; and the moment after he becomes freely communicative—if not so disposed before. But he has been; therefore the disclosures that follow are less due to the alcohol than to a passion every whit as inflammatory. He is acting under the stimulus of a revenge, terrible and long restrained.

"I've missed you from about here, Manuel," says the colonel, in kindly tones, making his approaches with skill. "Where have you been all this while, my good man?"

"With my master," is the peon's reply.

"Ah, indeed! I thought your master had gone clear out of the country?"

"Out of the settled part of it only, señor."

"Oh! he is still, then, within Mexican territory! I am glad to hear that. I was very sorry to think we'd lost such a good citizen and patriot as Don Valerian Miranda. True, he and I differ in our views as regards government; but that's nothing, you know, Manuel. Men may be bitter political enemies, yet very good friends. By-the-way, where is the colonel now?"

Despite his apparent stolidity, the Indian is not so stupid as to be misled by talk like this. With a full knowledge of the situation—forced upon him by various events—the badinage of the brilliant *militario* does not for a moment blind him. Circumstances have given him enough insight into Uraga's character and position to know that the tatter's motives should somewhat resemble his own. He has long been aware that the Lancer colonel is in love with his young mistress, as much as he himself with her maid. Without this knowledge he might not have been there—at least, not with so confident an expectation of success in the design that has brought him hither. For design he has, deep, deadly, and traitorous.

Despite the influence of the aguardiente, fast loosening his tongue, he is yet somewhat cautious in his communications; and not until Uraga repeats the question does he make answer to it. Then comes the response, slowly and reluctantly, as if from one of his long-suffering race, who has discovered a mine of precious metal, and is being put to the torture to "denounce" it.

"Señor coronel," he says, "how much will your excellency give to know where my master now is? I have heard that there's a large bounty offered for Don Valerian's head."

"That is an affair that concerns the State. For myself, I've nothing personally to do with it. Still, as an officer of the Government, it is my duty to take what steps I can towards making your master a prisoner. I think I may promise a good reward to anyone who, by giving information, would enable me to arrest a fugitive rebel and bring him before the bar of justice. Can you do that?"

"Well, your excellency, that will depend. I'm only a poor man, and need money to live upon. Don Valerian is my master, and if anything were to happen to him I should lose my situation. What am I to do?"

"Oh, you'd easily get another, and better. A man of your strength— By the way, talking of strength, my good Manuel, you don't seem to have quite recovered from your journey, which must have been long and fatiguing. Take another *copita*; you're in need of it; 'twill do you good."

Pressure of this sort put upon an Indian, be he *bravo* or *manso*, is rarely resisted. Nor is it in Manuel's case. He readily yields to it, and tosses off another glass of the aguardiente.

Before the strong alcohol can have fairly filtered down into his stomach its fumes ascend to his skull.

The cowed, cautious manner—a marked characteristic of his race—now forsakes him; the check-strings of his tongue become relaxed, and, with nothing before his mind save his scheme of vengeance, and that of securing Conchita, he betrays the whole secret of Colonel Miranda's escape—the story of his retreat across the Staked Plain, and his residence in the lone valley.

When he further informs Uraga about the two guests who have strayed to this solitary spot, and, despite his maudlin talk, minutely describes the men, his listener utters a loud cry, accompanied by a gesture of such violence as to overturn the table, sending bottle and glasses over the floor.

He does not stay to see the damage righted, but with a shout that reverberates throughout the whole house, summons his adjutant, and also the corporal of his guard.

"*Cabo!*" he cries, addressing himself to the latter in a tone at once vociferous and commanding; "take this man to the guard-house! And see you keep him there, so that he may be forthcoming when wanted. Take heed to hold him safe. If he be missing, you shall be shot ten minutes after I receive the report of it. You have the word of Gil Uraga for that."

From the way the corporal makes prisoner the surprised peon, almost throttling him, it is evident he does not intend running any risk of being shot for letting the latter escape. The Indian appears suddenly sobered by the rough treatment he is receiving. But he is too much astonished to find speech for protest. Mute, and without offering the slightest resistance, he is dragged out through the open doorway, to all appearance more dead than alive.

"Come, Roblez!" hails his superior officer, as soon as the door has closed behind the guard corporal and his captive, "Drink with me! Drink! First to revenge! I haven't had it yet, as I'd thought; that has all to be gone over again. But it's sure now—surer than ever. After, we shall drink to success in love. Mine is not hopeless, yet. Lost! she is found again—found! Ah, my darling Adela!" he exclaims, staggering towards the portrait, and in tipsy glee contemplating it, "you thought to escape me; but no. No one can get away from Gil Uraga—friend, sweetheart, or enemy. You shall yet be enfolded in these arms; if not as my wife, my—*margarita!*"

Chapter Forty One.
An Earthly Paradise.

"Oh that the desert were my dwelling-place,
    With one fair spirit for my monitor!
That I might all forget the human race,
    And, hating no one, love but only her.
Ye elements, in whose ennobling stir
    I feel myself exalted, can ye not
Accord me such a being? Do I err
    In deeming such inhabit many a spot—
Though with them to converse can rarely be our lot."

Oft during his sojourn in the sequestered valley do these lines occur to the young prairie merchant. And vividly; for, in very truth, he has realised the aspiration of the poet.

But, though dwelling in a desert, far different is the scene habitually before his eyes. From the front of the humble chalet that has so opportunely afforded him a shelter, seated under the spreading branches of a pecan-tree, he can look on a landscape lovely as ever opened to the eyes of man— almost as that closed against our first parents when expelled from Paradise. Above he beholds a sapphire sky, scarce ever shadowed by a cloud; a sun whose fierce, fervid beams become softened as they fall amid the foliage of evergreen oaks; among clustering groves that show all the varied tints of verdure, disporting upon green glassy glades, and glinting into arbours overshadowed by the sassafras laurel, the Osage orange, and the wild China-tree, laced together by a trellis of grape vines. A lake in the centre of this luxurious vegetation, placid as sleep itself, only stirred by the webbed feet of waterfowl, or the wings of dipping swallows, with above and below a brawling rivulet, here and there showing cascades like the tails of white horses, or the skirts of ballroom belles floating through waltz or gallopade.

In correspondence with these fair sights are the sounds heard. By day the cooing of doves, the soft tones of the golden oriole, and the lively chatter of the red cardinal; by night the booming note of the bull-bat, the sonorous call of the trumpeter swan, and that lay far excelling all—the clear song of the polyglot thrush, the famed mocking-bird of America.

No wonder the invalid, recovering from his illness, after the long dark spell that has obscured his intellect, wrapping his soul, as it were, in a shroud—no wonder he fancies the scene to be a sort of Paradise, worthy of being inhabited by Peris. One is there he deems fair as Houri or Peri, unsurpassed by any ideal of Hindoo or Persian fable—Adela Miranda. In her he beholds beauty of a type striking as rare; not common anywhere, and only seen among women in whose veins courses the blue blood of Andalusia—a beauty perhaps not in accordance with the standard of taste acknowledged in the icy northland. The *vigolite* upon her upper lip might look a little bizarre in an assemblage of Saxon dames, just as her sprightly spirit would offend the sentiment of a strait-laced Puritanism.

It has no such effect upon Frank Hamersley. The child of a land above all others free from conventionalism, with a nature attuned to the picturesque, these peculiarities, while piquing his fancy, have fixed his admiration. Long before leaving his sick couch there has been but one world for him—that where dwells Adela Miranda; but one being in it—herself.

Surely it was decreed by fate that these two should love one another! Surely for them was there a marriage in heaven! Else why brought together in such a strange place and by such a singular chain of circumstances?

For himself, Hamersley thinks of this—builds hopes upon it deeming it an omen.

Another often occurs to him, also looking like fate. He remembers that portrait on the wall at Albuquerque, and how it had predisposed him in favour of the original. The features of Spano-Mexican type—so unlike those he had been accustomed to in his own country—had vividly impressed him. Gazing upon it he had almost felt love for the likeness. Then the description of the young girl given by her brother, with the incidents that led to friendly relations between him and Colonel Miranda, all had contributed to sow the seed of a tender sentiment in the heart of the young Kentuckian. It had not died out. Neither time nor absence had obliterated it. Far off—even when occupied with the pressing claims of business—that portrait-face had often appeared upon the retina of his memory, and often also in the visions of dreamland. Now that he has looked upon it in reality—sees it in all its blazing beauty, surrounded by scenes picturesque as its own expression, amid incidents romantic as his fancy could conjure up—now that he knows it as the face of her who has saved his life, is it any wonder the slight, tender sentiment first kindled by the painted picture should become stronger at the sight of the living original?

It has done this—become a passion that pervade his soul, filling his whole heart. All the more from its being the first he has ever felt—the first love of his life. And for this also all the more does he tremble as he thinks of the possibility of its being unreciprocated.

He has been calculating the chances in his favour every hour since consciousness returned to him. And from some words heard in that very hour has he derived greater pleasure, and draws more hope than from aught that has occurred since. Constantly does he recall that soliloquy, speech spoken under the impression that it did not reach his ears.

There has been nothing afterwards—neither word nor deed—to give him proof he is beloved. The lady has been a tender nurse—a hostess apparently solicitous for the happiness of her guest—nothing more. Were the words she had so thoughtlessly spoken unfelt, and without any particular meaning? Or was the speech but an allusion, born from the still lingering distemper of his brain?

He yearns to know the truth. Every hour that he remains ignorant of it, he is in torture equalling that of Tantalus. Yet he fears to ask, lest in the answer he may have a painful revelation.

He almost envies Walt Wilder his commonplace love, its easy conquest, and somewhat grotesque declaration. He wishes he could propose with like freedom, and receive a similar response. His comrade's success should embolden him; but does not. There is no parallelism between the parties.

Thus he delays seeking the knowledge he most desires to possess, through fear it may afflict him. Not from any lack of opportunity. Since almost all the time is he left alone with her he so worships. Nothing stands in his way—no zealous watchfulness of a brother. Don Valerian neglects every step of fraternal duty—if to take such ever occurred to him. His time is fully occupied in roving around the valley, or making more distant excursions, in the companionship of the *ci-devant* Ranger, who narrates to him a strange chapter in the life-lore of the prairies.

When Walt chances to be indoors, he has companion of his own, which hinder him from too frequently intruding upon his comrade. Enough for him the company of Conchita.

Hamersley has equally as little to dread the intrusion of Don Prospero. Absorbed in his favourite study of Nature, the ex-army surgeon passes most of his hours in communion with her. More than half the day is he out of doors, chasing lizards into their crevices among the rocks, impaling insects on the spikes of the wild maguey plant, or plucking such flowers as seem new to the classified list of the botanist. In these tranquil pursuits he is perhaps happier than all around—even those whose hearts throb with that supreme passion, full of sweetness, but too often bringing bitterness.

So ever near the shrine of his adoration, having it all to himself, Hamersley worships on, but in silence.

Chapter Forty Two.
A Dangerous Design.

At length the day, the hour, is at hand when the young Kentuckian purposes taking departure. He does not anticipate this with pleasure. On the contrary, the prospect gives him pain. In that sequestered spot he could linger long—for ever, if Adela Miranda were to be with him. He is leaving it with reluctance, and would stay longer now, but that he is stirred by a sense of duty. He has to seek justice for the assassination of his teamsters, and, if possible, punish their assassins. To obtain this he intends going on to the Del Norte—if need be, to Albuquerque itself. The information given by the ex-commandant, with all the suspicious circumstances attending, have determined him how to act. He intends calling Uraga to account; but not by the honourable action of a duel, but in a court of justice, if such can be found in New Mexico.

"If it turns out as we have been conjecturing," he says, in conversation with Miranda, "I shall seek the scoundrel in his own stronghold. If he be not there, I shall follow him elsewhere—ay, all over Mexico."

"Hyar's one'll be wi' ye in that chase," cries the ex-Ranger, coming up at the moment. "Yis, Frank, go wi' ye to the heart o' Mexiko, plum centre; to the halls o' the Montezoomas, if ye like, enywhar to be in at the death o' a skunk like that."

"Surely, Colonel Miranda," continues Hamersley, gratified, though not carried away by his old comrade's enthusiastic offer of assistance, "surely there is law in your land sufficient to give redress for such an outrage as that."

"My dear Don Francisco," replies the Mexican, tranquilly twirling a cigarrito between his fingers, "there is law for those who have the power and money to obtain it. In New Mexico, as you must yourself know, might makes right; and never more than at this present time. Don Manuel Armijo is once more the governor of my unfortunate fatherland. When I tell you that he rose to his present position by just such a crime as that we've been speaking of, you may then understand the sort of law administered under his rule. Manuel Armijo was a shepherd, employed on one occasion to drive a flock of thirty thousand sheep—the property of his employer, the Señor Chavez—to the market Chihuahua. While crossing the Jornado del Muerte, he and one or two confederates, whom he had put up to his plan, disguised themselves as Apache Indians, attacked their fellow sheep-drivers, murdered them, and made themselves masters of the flock. Then pulling the plumes from their heads, and washing the paint off their faces, they drove their muttons to a different market, sold them, and returned to Chavez to tell a tale of Indian spoliation, and how they themselves had just escaped with their scalps. This is the true history of General Don Manuel Armijo, Governor of New Mexico; at least that of his first beginnings. With such and many similar deeds since, is it likely he would look with any other than a lenient eye on the doings of Gil Urago, his imitator? No, señor, not even if you could prove the present commandant of Albuquerque, in full, open court, to have been the individual who robbed yourself and murdered your men."

"I shall try, for all that," rejoins Hamersley, his heart wrung with sorrow at the remembrance of his slaughtered comrades, and bursting with the bitter thought of justice thus likely to be obstructed. "Don't suppose Colonel Miranda, that I intend resting my cause on the clemency of Don Manuel Armijo, or any chance of right to be expected at his hands. There's a wide stretch of desert between the United States and Mexico, but not wide enough to hinder the American eagle from flapping its wings across, and giving protection to all who have a right to claim it, even to a poor prairie trader. A thousand thanks, Colonel Miranda. I owe you that for twice saving my life, and now for setting me on the track of him who has twice endangered it. No use your trying to dissuade me. I shall go in search of this *forban* direct to the valley of the Del Norte. Don't fear that I shall fail in obtaining justice, whatever Don Manuel Armijo may do to defeat it."

"Well, if you are determined I shall not hold out against you. Only I fear your errand may be fruitless, if not worse. The two mules are at your service, and you can leave them at a place I shall indicate. When Manuel returns I shall send him to bring them back."

"Possibly I may bring them myself. I do not intend making stay in New Mexico; only long enough to communicate with the American Consul at Santa Fé, and take some preliminary steps for the end in view. Then I shall return to the—States to lay the whole affair before our Government."

"And you think of coming this way?"

"Walt, here, has been making explorations down the stream that runs through this valley; he has no doubt about its being one of the heads of the

Red River of Louisiana, if not the Texan Brazos. By keeping down it we can reach the frontier settlements of Texas, then on to the States."

"I'm glad you intend returning this way. It will give us the pleasure of soon again seeing you."

"Colonel Miranda," rejoins Hamersley, in a tone that tells of something on his mind, a proposition he would make to his host, and feels delicacy in declaring it, "in coming back by the Llano Estacado I have another object in view besides the idea of a direct route."

"What other object, *amago mio?*"

"The hope of inducing you to accompany me to the States—you and yours."

"Señor Don Francisco, 'tis exceedingly kind of you. But the period of our banishment may not be long. I've had late news from our friends, telling me things are taking a turn and the political wheel must soon make another revolution, the present party going below. Then I get back to my country, returning triumphant. Meanwhile we are happy enough here, and I think safe."

"In the last I disagree with you. I'm sorry to say, but have reasons. Now that I know the real character of this ruffian Uraga—his deeds actually done, and others we suspect—he's just the man who'll leave no stone unturned to discover your hiding place. He has more than one motive for doing so, but one that will move him to follow you here into the desert—aye, to the uttermost end of the earth!"

The motive in the speaker's mind is Uraga's desire to possess Adela.

After a pause, this though: passing him, he adds,—

"No, Don Valerian, you are not safe here."

Then, continuing,—

"How know you that your servant Manuel has not been recognised while executing some of those errands on which you've sent him; or that the man himself may not turn traitor? I confess, from what I've seen of the fellow, he has not favourably impressed me."

The words make an impression upon Miranda anything but pleasant. It is not the first time for him to have the thought suggested by them. More than once has he entertained suspicions about the peon's fidelity. It is possible the man might prove traitor; if not then, at some future time—aye, and probable, too, considering the reward offered for the exile's head.

Miranda, knowing and now thinking of it, admits the justice of his friend's fear. More; he sees cause for raising alarm. So does Don Prospero, who, at the moment coming up, takes part in the conference.

It ends in the refugees resolving to stay in the valley till Hamersley and Walt can return to them; then to forsake that asylum, no longer deemed safe, and retire to one certainly so—the land over which waves a flag powerful to protect its citizens and give the same to their friends—the Star-spangled Banner.

Chapter Forty Three.
The Last Appeal.

"I have news for you, *nina*."

It is Colonel Miranda speaking to his sister, shortly after the conversation reported.

"What news, Valerian?"

"Well, there are two sorts of them."

"Both good, I hope."

"Not altogether; one will be pleasant to you, the other, perhaps, a little painful."

"In that case they should neutralise one another; anyhow, let me hear them."

"I shall tell the pleasant ones first. We shall soon have an opportunity of leaving this lonely place."

"Do you call that good news? I rather think it the reverse. What will the bad be?"

"But, dear Adela, our life here, away from all society, has been a harsh experience—to you a terrible one."

"In that, *hermano mio*, you're mistaken. You know I don't care a straw for what the world calls society—never did. I prefer being free from its stupid restraints and silly conventionalities. Give me Nature for my companion— ay, in her wildest scenes and most surly moods."

"Surely you've had both to a surfeit."

"Nothing of the kind; I'm not tired of Nature yet. I have never been happier than in this wilderness home. How different from my convent school—my prison, I should rather call it! Oh, it is charming! and if I were to have my way, it should never come to an end. But why do you talk of leaving this place? Do you suppose the troubles are over, and we can return safely? I don't wish to go there, brother. After what has happened, I hate New Mexico, and would prefer staying in the Llano Estacado."

"I have no thought of going back to New Mexico."

"Where, then, brother?"

"In the very opposite direction—to the United States. Don Francisco advises me to do so; and I have yielded to his counsel."

Adela seems less disposed to offer opposition. She no longer protests against the change of residence.

"Dear sister," he continues, "we cannot do better. There seems little hope of our unfortunate country getting rid of her tyrants—at least, for some time to come. When the day again arrives for our patriots to pronounce, I shall know it in time to be with them. Now, we should only think of our safety. Although I don't wish to alarm you, I've never felt it quite safe here. Who knows, but that Uraga may yet discover our hiding-place? He has his scouts searching in all directions. Every time Manuel makes a visit to the settlements, I have fear of his being followed back. Therefore, I think it will be wiser for us to carry out our original design, and go on to the American States."

"Do you intend accompanying Don Francisco?"

She listens eagerly for an answer.

"Yes; but not now. It will be some time before he can return to us."

"He is going home first, and will then come back?"

"Not home—not to his home."

"Where, then?"

"That is the news I thought might be painful. He has resolved upon going on to our country for reasons already known to you. We suspect Uraga of having been at the head of the red robbers who have plundered him and killed his people. He is determined to find out and punish the perpetrators of that foul deed. It will be difficult; nay, more, there will be danger in his attempting it—I've told him so."

"Dear brother, try to dissuade him!"

If Hamersley could but hear the earnest tone in which the appeal is spoken it would give him gratification.

"I have tried, but to no purpose. It is not the loss of his property—he is generous, and does not regard it. His motive is a nobler, a holier one. His comrades have been murdered; he says he will seek the assassins and obtain redress, even at the risk of sacrificing his own life."

"A hero! Who could not help loving him?"

Adela does not say this aloud, nor to her brother. It is a thought, silent within the secret recesses of her own heart.

"If you wish," continues the colonel, "I will see him, and again try to turn him from this reckless course; though I know there is little hope. Stay! a thought strikes me, sister. Suppose you speak to him. A woman's words are more likely to be listened to; and I know that yours will have great weight with him. He looks upon you as the saviour of his life, and may yield to your request."

"If you think so, Valerian—"

"I do. I see him coming this way. Remain where you are. I shall send him in to you."

With a heart heaving and surging, Hamersley stands in the presence of her, the sole cause of its tumultuous excitement. For he has been summoned thither in a manner that somewhat surprises him. "Don Francisco, my sister wishes a word with you," is the speech of Colonel Miranda, an invitation promptly responded to.

What is to be the import of his interview, unexpected, unsought, apparently commanded?

He asks himself this question as he proceeds towards the place where she stands waiting to receive him. Coming up to her, he says,—

"Senorita, your brother has told me you wish to speak with me?"

"I do," she replies, without quail in her look or quiver in her voice.

In returning her glance Hamersley feels as if his case is hopeless. That very day he had thought of proposing to her. It almost passes from his mind. So cool, she cannot care for him. He remains silent, leaving her to proceed.

"Señor, it is about your going to the Rio del Norte. My brother tells me such is your intention. We wish you not to go, Don Francisco. There is danger in your doing it."

"It is my duty."

"In what respect? Explain yourself!"

"My brave comrades have been slain—assassinated. I have reason to believe that in the town of Albuquerque I may discover their assassins—at all events their chief, and perhaps bring him to justice. I intend trying, if it costs me my life."

"Do you reflect what your life is worth?"

"To me not much."

"It may be to others. You have at home a mother, brothers, and sisters. Perhaps one dearer?"

"No—not at home."

"Elsewhere, then?"

He is silent under this searching inquisition.

"Do you think that danger to your life would be unhappiness to her's—your death her life's misery?"

"My dishonour should be more, as it would to myself. It is not vengeance I seek against those who have murdered my men, only to bring them to justice. I must do that, or else proclaim myself a poltroon—I feel myself one—a self-accusation that would give me a life-long remorse. No, Señorita Adela. It is kind of you to take an interest in my safety. I already owe you my life; but I cannot permit you to save it again, at the sacrifice of honour, of duty, of humanity."

Hamersley fancies himself being coldly judged and counselled with indifference. Could he know the warm, wild admiration struggling in the breast of her who counsels him, he would make rejoinder in different fashion.

Soon after he talks in an altered tone, and with changed understanding. So also does she, hitherto so difficult of comprehension.

"Go!" she cries. "Go and get redress of your wrongs, justice for your fallen comrades; and if you can, the punishment of their assassins. But remember! if it brings death to you, there is one who will not care to live after."

"Who?" he asks, springing forward, with heart on fire and eyes aflame. "Who?"

He scarce needs to put the question. It is already answered by the emphasis on her last words.

But it is again replied to, this time in a more tranquil tone; the long, dark lashes of the speaker veiling her eyes as she pronounces her own name, —

"*Adela Miranda!*"

From poverty to riches, from a dungeon to bright daylight, from the agonising struggle of drowning to that confident feeling when the feet stand firm upon terra firma—all these are sensations of a pleasantly-exciting kind. They are dull in comparison with that delirious joy, the lot of the despairing lover on finding that his despair has been all a fancy, and that his passion is reciprocated.

Such a joy thrills through Hamersley's breast as he hears the name pronounced. It is like a cabalistic speech, throwing open to him the portals of Paradise.

Chapter Forty Four.
A Mysterious Message.

As is known, Hamersley's suspicions about the treachery of the peon are not without cause. On the contrary, they might seem second-sight. For, almost at the moment he is communicating them to Colonel Miranda, the native is telling his tale to Uraga.

Nor does the latter lose much time in acting upon the information gained—only that short interlude given to exultation as he stepped up to the portrait of Adela Miranda, and stood triumphantly regarding the likeness of her he now looks upon as sure to be his. He has no hope to get possession of her by fair means; foul are alone in his thoughts.

After delivering his half-frenzied apostrophe to the painted image, he returns to the table, beside which Roblez has already taken a seat.

They re-fill their glasses, and drink the toasts specified, with a ceremony in strange contrast to the hellish glee sparkling in the eyes of the Lancer-Colonel. His countenance beams with triumph, such as might be shown by Satan over the ruin of innocence. For he now feels sure of his victims—alike that of his love as well as those of his revenge.

Not long does he remain over his cups in the company of his subordinate. He has an important matter upon his mind which calls for reflection—in silence and by himself.

Though often admitting his adjutant to a share in his criminal schemes, the participation is only in their profits and the act of execution. Despotic even in his villainies, he keeps the planning to himself, for he has secrets even Roblez must not know. And now an idea has dawned upon his mind, a purpose he does not care to communicate to the subaltern till such time as may be necessary or seem fit to him. Not that he dreads treachery on the part of his fellow freebooter. They are mutually compromised, and long have been; too much to tell tales about one another. Besides, Roblez, though a man of undoubted courage, of the coarse, animal kind, has, neverthless, a certain moral dread of his commanding officer, and fears to offend him. He knows Gil Uraga to be one whose hostility, once provoked, will stop short at nothing, leave no means untried to take retribution—this of a terrible kind.

Hence a control which the colonel holds over him beyond that drawn from his superior military rank. Hence, also, his receiving but a small share in the proceeds of their various robberies, and his being satisfied with this, or, at all events, seeming so.

On his side, Uraga has several motives for not letting his subordinate into the knowledge of all his complicated schemes; among them one springing from a moral peculiarity. He is of a strangely-constituted nature, secretive to the last degree—a quality or habit in which he prides himself. It is his delight to practice it whenever the opportunity offers; just as the thief and detective officer take pleasure in their respective callings beyond the mere prize to be derived from their exercise.

The intelligence just received from the traitorous mule-driver, unexpected as pleasing, has opened to him the prospect of a grand success. It may enable him to strike a *coup* covering all—alike giving gratification to his love, as his hate.

But the blow must needs be dealt deftly. There are circumstances to be considered and precautions taken, not only to prevent its failing, but secure against a publicity that might cause scandal to himself, to say naught of consequent danger.

And it must be struck soon—at once. It is too ticklish a matter to admit of delay, either in the design or execution.

Already has the matter flitted before his mind in its general outlines; almost soon as receiving the report of the peon.

It is only the details that remain for consideration; and these he intends considering alone, without any aid from his adjutant.

As time is an object, he speedily terminates his carousal with the subaltern; who, dismissed, returns to the military *cuartel*.

Soon as he is gone the colonel again seats himself, and lighting a fresh cigar, continues smoking. For several minutes he remains silent, his eyes turned upwards, and his features set in a smile. One might fancy him but watching the smoke of his cigar as it rises in spiral wreaths to the ceiling. He is occupied with no such innocent amusement. On the contrary, his grim smile betokens meditation deep and devilish. He is mentally working out a problem, a nefarious scheme, which will ere long bear evil fruit.

As the cigar grows shorter he seems to draw nearer to his conclusions. And when at length there is only the stump between his teeth, he spits it out; and, taking a hand-bell from the table, rings until a domestic appears in the doorway in answer to the summons.

"Call in the guard-corporal!" is the order received by the servant, who withdraws without saying a word.

Soon the soldier shows himself, saluting as he enters the door.

"*Cabo*! Bring your prisoner before me."

The corporal retires, and shortly after returns, having the Indian in charge. He is commanded to leave the latter, and himself remain waiting without. Directed also to close the door; which he does on getting outside.

Thus closeted with the peon—still wondering why he has been made a prisoner—Uraga submits him to a process of examination, which elicits from the scared creature everything he seeds to know. Among the rest, he makes himself acquainted with the situation of the valley, where the exiles have found temporary asylum; the direction, distance, and means of access to it—in short, its complete topography.

With all the Indian is familiar, can correctly describe it, and does so. In that imposing presence he dare not attempt deception, even if inclined. But he is not. Between questioner and questioned the aim and end are similar, if not the same. Besides, the peon's blood has again been warmed up, and his tongue set loose, by a fresh infusion of aguardiente—so that his confessions are full as free. He tells about the life led by the Mexican refugees, as also their American guests—all he knows, and this is nearly everything. For trusted, unsuspected, he has had every opportunity to learn. The only thing concealed by him is his own love affair with Conchita and its disastrous ending, through the intrusion of the Texan Ranger.

This, if told, would give his listener slight concern, alongside the grave impressions made upon him by another affair; some particulars of which the peon communicates. These points refer to tender relations existing between the young prairie trader and Adela Miranda, almost proving their existence. Confirmed or not, on hearing of them Gil Uraga receives a shock which sends the blood rushing in quick current through his veins; while upon his countenance comes an expression of such bitter malignity, that the traitor, in fear for his own safety, repents having told him.

But Uraga has no spite against him—no motive for having it. On the contrary, he intends rewarding him, after he gets out of him certain other services for which he is to be retained.

When his cross-questioning is at length brought to a close, he is once more committed to the charge of the guard-corporal, with orders to be returned to the prison. At the same time a hint is given him that his incarceration is only precautionary, with a promise it will not be for long.

Immediately after his removal, Uraga seats himself before an escritoire, which stands on one side of the room. Laying open the lid, he spreads a sheet of paper upon it, and commences to write what appears an epistle.

Whatever it is, the composition occupies some considerable time. Occasionally he stops using the pen, as though pondering what to put down.

When it is at length completed, apparently to his satisfaction, he folds the sheet, thrusts a stick of wax into the flame of a candle, and seals the document, but without using any seal-stamp. A small silver coin taken from his pocket makes the necessary impression. There does not appear to be any name appended to the epistle, if one it is; and the superscription shows only two words, without any address. The words are "El Barbato."

Again ringing the bell, the same servant answers it.

"Go to the stables," commands his master, "or the corral, or wherever he may be, and tell Pedrillo I want him. Be quick about it!"

The man bows and disappears.

"It will take them—how many days to reach the Tenawas' town, and how many back to the Pecos?" soliloquises Uraga, pacing the floor, as he makes his calculations. "Three, four, five. No matter. If before them we can wait till they come. Pedrillo!"

Pedrillo has put in an appearance. He is an Indian of the tame sort, not greatly differing from the man Manuel, with a countenance quite as forbidding. But we have seen Pedrillo before; since he was one of the two muleteers who conducted the *atajo* transporting the spoil from the caravan of the prairie traders.

"Pedrillo," directs the Colonel, "catch a couple of the best roadsters in the corral—one for yourself, the other for José. Have them saddled, and get yourselves ready for a journey of two weeks, or so. Make all haste with your preparations. When ready, come here, and report yourself."

The muleteer disappears, and Uraga continues to pace the floor, apparently yet busied with a mental measurement of time and distance. At intervals he stops before the portrait on the wall, and for a second or two gazes at it. This seems to increase his impatience for the man's reappearance.

He has not a great while to wait. The scrip and staff of a New Mexican traveller of Pedrillo's kind is of no great bulk or complexity. It takes but a short time to prepare it. A few *tortillas* and *frijoles*, a head or two of *chile Colorado*, half a dozen onions, and a bunch of *tasojo*—jerked beef. Having collected these comestibles, and filled his *xuaje*, or water gourd, Pedrillo reports himself ready for the road, or trail, or whatever sort of path, and on whatever errand, it may please his master to despatch him.

"You will go straight to the Tenawa town—Horned Lizard's—on the south branch of the Goo-al-pah. You can find your way to the place, Pedrillo. You've been there before?"

The Indian nods an affirmative.

"Take this." Here Uraga hands him the sealed paper. "See you show it to no one you may chance to meet passing out from the settlements. Give it to Barbato, or hand it to the Horned Lizard himself. He'll know who it's for. You are to ride night and day, as fast as the animals can carry you. When you've delivered it you needn't wait, but come back—not here, but to the Alamo. You know the place—where we met the Tenawas some weeks ago. You will find me there. *Vaya!*"

On receiving these instructions Pedrillo vanishes from, the room; a strange sinister glance in his oblique Indian eyes telling that he knows himself to be once more—what he has often been—an emissary of evil.

Uraga takes another turn across the floor, then, seating himself by the table, seeks rest for his passion-tossed soul by drinking deep of the *mescal* of Tequila.

Chapter Forty Five.
The Staked Plain.

The elevated table-land known as Llano Estacado is in length over three hundred miles, with an average width of sixty or seventy. It extends longitudinally between the former Spanish provinces of New Mexico and Texas; their respective capitals, Santa Fé and San Antonia de Bejar, being on the opposite side of it. In the days of vice-royal rule, a military road ran across it, connecting the two provincial centres, and mule trains of traders passed to and fro between. As this road was only a trail, often obliterated by the drifting sands of the desert, tall stakes were set up at intervals to indicate the route. Hence the name "Llano Estacado"—literally, Staked Plain.

In those days Spain was a strong, enterprising nation, and her Mexican colonists could travel over most parts of their vast territory without fear of being assaulted by the savages. At a later period, when Spanish power began to decline, all this became changed. Cities fell to ruin, settlements were deserted, mission establishments abandoned, and in the provinces of Northern Mexico white travellers had to be cautious in keeping to the most frequented roads, in some districts not daring even to venture beyond the walls of their haciendas or towns. Many of these were fortified against Indian attack, and are so to this day.

Under these circumstances the old Spanish trail across the Staked Plain fell into disuse; its landmarks became lost, and of late years only expeditions of the United States army have traversed it for purposes of exploration.

In physical aspect it bears resemblance to the table lands of Abyssinia and Southern Arabia, and at its northern end many outlying spurs and detached *mesas* remind the traveller of the Abyssinian hills—known as *ambas*. A portion of this singular territory belongs to the great gypsum formation of the south-western prairies, perhaps the largest in the world; while a highly-coloured sandstone of various vivid hues, often ferruginous, forms a conspicuous feature in its cliffs. Along its eastern edge these present to the lower champaign of Texas a precipitous escarpment several hundred feet sheer, in long stretches, tending with an unbroken façade, in other places showing ragged, where cleft by canons, through which rush torrents, the heads of numerous Texan streams. Its surface is, for the most part, a dead horizontal level, sterile as the Sahara itself, in places smooth and hard as a macadamised road. Towards its southern end there is a group of *medanos* (sandhills), covering a tract of several hundred square miles, the sand ever drifting about, as with *dunes* on the seashore. High up among their summits is a lakelet of pure drinking water, though not a drop can be found upon the plateau itself for scores of miles around. Sedge and lilies grow by this tarn so singularly situated.

Here and there the plain is indented by deep fissures (*barrancas*), apparently the work of water. Often the traveller comes upon them without sign or warning of their proximity, till, standing on the edge of a precipitous escarpment, he sees yawning below a chasm sunk several hundred feet into the earth. In its bed may be loose boulders piled in chaotic confusion, as if cast there by the hands of Titans; also trunks of trees in a fossilised state such as those observed by Darwin on the eastern declivity of the Chilian Andres.

Nearly all the streams that head in the Staked Plain cut deep channels in their way to the outer world. These are often impassable, either transversely or along their course. Sometimes, however, their beds are worn out into little valleys, or "coves," in which a luxuriant vegetation finds shelter and congenial soil. There flourish the pecan, the hackberry, the black walnut, the wild china, with evergreen oaks, plums, and clustering grapevines; while in the sterile plain above are only seen those forms of the botanical world that truly indicate the desert—various species of cactaceae, agaves, and yuccas—the palmilla and lechuguilla, dwarf-cedars, and mezquites, artemisia, and the strong-smelling larrea, or "creosote plant."

Animals are rare upon the Llano Estacado, although the prong-horn antelope—true denizen of the desert—is there found, as also its enemy, the Mexican jackal, or coyote. To the rattlesnake and horned lizard (*agama*) it is a congenial home; and the singular snake-bird (*paisano*) may frequently be seen running over the arid waste, or skulking through the tortuous stems of the nopals. In the canons of the stream the grizzly bear makes his haunt, and in times not long gone by it was ascended and traversed by the unwieldy buffalo. The wild horse (*musteno*) still occasionally courses across it.

Of all the living things it is least frequented by man. Even the Indian rarely strays into its solitudes; and the white man, when necessitated to enter them, does so with fear and trembling, for he knows there is danger.

This is chiefly due to the absence of water; but there is also the chance of going astray—getting lost in the absence of landmarks. To be astray in a wilderness of any kind is a perilous predicament for the traveller—in one without water it is death.

After their affair with the Tenawas, the Texan Rangers directed their course towards the Llano Estacado. On starting, it was their intention to strike north, and get upon the main stream of the Canadian, then follow it up to the place where the prairie traders met their murderous doom. From the country of the Tenawa Comanches this would be the correct route, and was the same taken by these freebooters returning with the spoils of the caravan. But from the mouth of the Pecan Creek is one more direct, leading across a spur of the plateau itself, instead of turning its north-eastern extremity.

It was not known to the Rangers, though Cully remembered having heard something about it. But the Mexican renegade declared himself familiar with, and counselled taking it. There had been hesitation before acceding to his counsel. Of course, they could have no confidence in such a man, but rather suspicion of all he said or did. In guiding them across the Staked Plain he might have some sinister purpose—perhaps lead them into a trap.

After all, how could he? The tribe of savages with which he had been consorting was now so terribly chastised, so effectually crushed, it was not probable—scarce possible—they would be encountered again. Certainly not for a season. For weeks there would be weeping and wailing in the tents of the Tenawas. If the renegade had any hope of being rescued from his present captivity, it could not be by them. He might have some thought of escape, taking the Rangers by the route he proposed to them. On this score they had no apprehension—not the slightest. Suspicious, they would keep close watch upon him; shoot him down like a dog at the first sign of his attempting to deceive them. And, as Cully remembered having heard of this trail over the Staked Plain, it was most probable the Mexican had no other object than to bring them to the end of their journey in the shortest time and straightest course. All knew it would be a near cut, and this decided them in its favour.

After parting from Pecan Creek, with their faces set westward, they had a journey before them anything but easy or pleasant. On the contrary, one of the most difficult and irksome. For it lay across a sterile tract—the great gypsum bed of North-western Texas, on which abut the bluffs of the Llano Estacado. Mile after mile, league after league; no "land in sight," to use a prairie-man's phrase—nothing but level plain, smooth as a sleeping sea; but, unlike the last, without water—not a sheet to cheer their eyes, not a drop to quench the thirst, almost choking them. Only its resemblance, seen in the white mist always moving over these arid plains—the deluding, tantalising mirage. Lakes lay before them, their shores garlanded by green trees, their bosoms enamelled with islets smiling in all the verdure of spring—always before them, ever receding; the trees, as the water, never to be reached!

Water they do arrive at more than once—streams rushing in full flow across the barren waste. At sight they ride towards them rapidly. Their horses need not to be spurred. The animals suffer as themselves, and rush on with outstretched necks, eager to assuage their thirst. They dip their muzzles, plunge in their heads till half-buried, only to draw out again and toss them aloft with snorts of disappointment shaking the water like spray from their nostrils. It is salt!

For days they have been thus journeying. They are wearied, worn down by fatigue, hungry; but more than all, tortured by the terrible thirst—their horses as themselves. The animals have become reduced in flesh and strength; they look like skeletons staggering on, scarce able to carry their riders.

Where is the Mexican conducting them? He has brought them into a desert. Is the journey to end in their death? It looks like enough.

Some counsel killing him, and returning on their tracks. Not all; only a minority. The majority cry "Onward!" with a thought beyond present suffering. They must find the bones of Walt Wilder and bury them! Brave men, true men, these Texan Rangers! Rough in outward appearance, often rude in behaviour, they have hearts gentle as children. Of all friends the most faithful, whether it be affection or pure *camaraderie*. In this case a comrade has been killed—cruelly murdered, and in a strange manner. Its very strangeness has maddened them the more, while sharpening their desire to have a last look at his remains, and give them Christian burial. Only the fainthearted talk of retreating; the others do not think of it, and these are more than the majority.

On, therefore, they ride across treeless, grassless tracks; along the banks of streams, of whose bitter, saline waters they cannot drink, but tantalising themselves and their animals. On, on!

Their perseverance is at length rewarded. Before their eyes looms up a line of elevated land, apparently the profile of a mountain.

But no; it cannot be that.

Trending horizontally, without curvature, against the sky, they know it is not a mountain, but a mesa—a table-land.

It is the Llano Estacado.

Drawing nearer, they get under the shadow of its beetling bluffs.

They see that these are rugged, with promontories projecting far out over the plain, forming what Spanish Americans, in their expressive phraseology, call *ceja*.

Into an embayment between two of the out-stretching spurs Barbato conducts them.

Joyously they ride into it, like ships long storm-tossed entering a haven of safety; for at the inner end of the concavity there is a cleft in the precipitous wall, reaching from base to summit, out of which issues a stream whose waters are sweet!

It is a branch of the Brazos River, along whose banks they have been some time travelling, lower down finding its waters bitter as gall. That was in its course through the selenite. Now they have reached the sandstone it is clear as crystal, and to them sweeter than champagne.

"Up it lies our way," says the renegade guide, pointing to the portals of the canon through which the stream debouched from the table to the lower plain.

But for that night the Rangers care hot to travel further. There is no call for haste. They are *en route* to bury the bones of a dead man, not to rescue one still living.

.

Chapter Forty Six.
A Brilliant Band.

Just as the Texan Rangers are approaching the Staked Plain on its eastern edge, another body of horsemen, about their equal in number, ascends to the same plateau, coming from the very opposite direction—the west.

Only in point of numbers, and that both are on horseback, is there any similitude between the two troops. Individually they are unlike as human beings could be; for most of those composing the Texan party are great, strapping fellows, fair-haired, and of bright complexions; whereas they coming in the counter direction are all, or nearly all, small men, with black hair and sallow visage—many of them dark as Indians. Between the horses of the two troops there is a proportionate disparity in size; the Texans bestriding animals of nearly sixteen hands in height, while they approaching from the west are mounted on Mexican mustangs, few over fourteen. One alone at their head, evidently their leader, rides a large American horse. In point of discipline the second troop shows superiority. It is a military organisation *pur sang*, and marches in regular formation, while the men composing it are armed and uniformed alike. Their uniform is that of Mexican lancers, very similar to the French, their arms the same. And just such are they; the lancers of Colonel Uraga, himself at their head.

Having crossed the Rio Pecos bottom, and climbed up the bluffs to the higher bench of the Llano Estacado, they strike out over the sterile plain.

As it is early morning, and the air is chilly, they wear their ample cavalry cloaks of bright yellow cloth. These falling back over the flanks of their horses, with their square lancer caps, plumed, and overtopped by the points of the pennoned lances, give them an imposing martial appearance. Though it is but a detachment of not over fifty men—a single troop—riding by twos, the files stretch afar in shining array, its sheen all the more brilliant from contrast with the sombre sterility of the desert.

A warlike sight, and worthy of admiration, if one knew it to be an expedition directed against the red pirates of the plains, *en route* to chastise them for their many crimes—a long list of cruel atrocities committed upon the defenceless citizens of Chihuahua and New Mexico. But knowing it is not this—cognisant of its true purpose—the impression made is altogether different. Instead of admiration it is disgust; and, in place of sending up a prayer for its success, the spectator would feel apprehension, or earnestly desire its failure.

Its purpose is anything but praiseworthy. On the contrary, sinister, as may be learnt by listening to the conversation of the two who ride at the head of the detachment, some paces in advance of the first file. They are its chief and his confidential second, the ruffian Roblez.

Uraga is speaking.

"Won't our worthy friend Miranda be surprised when he sees us riding up to the door of his *jacal*, with these fifty fellows behind us? And the old doctor, Don Prospero? I can fancy his quizzical look through those great goggle spectacles he used to wear. I suppose they are still on his nose; but they'll fly off as soon as he sees the pennons of our lances."

"Ha! ha! ha! That will be a comical sight, colonel. But do you think Miranda will make any resistance?"

"Not likely. I only wish he would."

"Why do you wish that?"

"*Ayadante!* you ask a stupid question. You ought to have a clearer comprehension in the brisk, bright atmosphere of this upland plain. It should make your brain more active."

"Well, *Coronel mio*, you're the first man I ever saw on the way to make a prisoner who desired to meet resistance. *Carrambia!* I can't understand that."

"I don't desire to make any prisoner—at least, not Don Valerian Miranda. For the old doctor, I shan't much care one way or the other. Living or dead, he can't do any great harm. Miranda I'd rather take dead."

"Ah! now I think I comprehend you."

"If he show the slightest resistance—raise but a hand—I shall have him that way."

"Why can't you anyhow? Surely you can deal with him as you think proper—a refugee, a rebel?"

"There you again show your want of sense. You've got a thick skull, *teniente*; and would be a bad counsellor in any case requiring skilful management. This is one of the kind, and needs the most delicate manipulation."

"How so?"

"For several reasons. Remember, Roblez, we're not now acting with the Horned Lizard and his painted freebooters. Our fellows here have eyes in their heads, and tongues behind their teeth. They might wag the latter to our disadvantage if we allowed the former to see anything not exactly on the square. And if we were to shoot or cut down Miranda, he not resisting, that would be a scandal I might have difficulty in suppressing. It would spread surely, go over the country, get to the ears of the Central Government, and return to New Mexico with a weight that might overwhelm me. Besides, *amigo mio*, it would spoil my plan in several respects—notably, that with the nina and others too numerous to mention. Of course, we'll kill him if we can, with fair pretext for doing so. But unless he show fight, we must take him alive, his guests along with him. I hope he will."

"I think it likely you'll have your hopes. The two Americanos are not men to submit tamely. Remember how they fought at the attack on their waggon-train, and how they got off afterwards. They're a rough couple, and likely to give us anything but a smooth reception."

"The rougher the better. That would be just as wanted, and we'll settle everything at once. If otherwise, I have my plan fixed and complete."

"What is it, colonel?"

"Not now. I'll tell you in the proper time. First to make experiment of what's immediately before us. If it succeed, we shall return this way with only women as our prisoners. If it fail, we'll have men—four of them. A word in your ear to content you for the while. Not one of the four will ever enter the prison of Albuquerque."

"You intend sending them to some other?"

"I do."

"Where?"

"A gaol from which there can be no escape—need I name it?"

"You need not. There's but one will answer your description—the grave."

With this solemn conjecture the *sotto voce* conversation comes to a close, the ruffians riding at the head of their troop, far extending after, its files resembling the vertebrae of some grand glittering serpent on its way to seize a victim, the two in front fair types of its protruding poisonous fangs.

Chapter Forty Seven.
A Coming Cloud.

Between lovers, those who truly love, the parting is ever painful Frank Hamersley, taking leave of Adela Miranda, feels this as does Walt Wilder separating from Conchita.

There may be a difference in degree, in the intensity of their respective passions; perhaps also something in its character. Still the sentiment is the same. Both suffer at the thought of separation, feel it keenly. All the more as they reflect on what is before them—a prospect anything but cheerful. Clouds in the sky; many chances they may never see their loved ones again. No wonder they turn towards the Del Norte with gloom in their glances and dark forebodings in their breasts. Men of less loyal hearts, less prone to the promptings of humanity, would trifle and stay; spend longer time in a dalliance so surely agreeable, so truly delightful. Not so the young Kentuckian and his older companion, the Texan. Though the love of woman is enthroned in their hearts, each has kept a corner sacred to a sentiment almost as strong, and perhaps purer. The blood of their slaughtered comrades cries from the ground, from the sand through which they saw it filtering away. They cannot find peace without responding to its appeal; and for this even the fruition of their love is to be delayed. To seek retribution they must journey on to the settlements of the Del Norte; not sure of success on arrival there, but more likely to meet failure—perhaps imprisonment. In this there would be nothing new or strange. They would not be the first Americans to suffer incarceration without cause in a New Mexican *calabozo*, and lie there for long years without trial.

Once more Miranda represents the danger they are about to undergo. It does not daunt them.

"No matter," is the reckless response. "Whatever be the consequences, go we will. We must."

Thus determined to start off, after exchanging tender adieus with those left behind—two of them in tears.

According to promise, Miranda has placed his mules at their disposal, and on these they are mounted. He has, moreover, furnished them with spare dresses from his wardrobe—costumes of his native country, which will enable them to travel through it without attracting attention.

Starting at sunrise, it is still early morning when they reach the upper plain through the ravine between the two twin mountains. So far Colonel Miranda accompanies them, as also Don Prospero. There parting, the refugees return to the ranche, while the travellers strike out over the treeless waste, which spreads before their faces to the very verge of vision.

They have no landmark to guide them, neither rock nor tree; but the sky is without a cloud, and there is a sun in it gleaming like a globe of fire. To the experienced prairie man this is sufficient for telling every point of the compass, and they but want one. Their course is due west till they strike the Pecos; then along its bank to the crossing, thence west again through the Sierras, and on to Santa Fé.

Keeping the sun slightly on the left shoulder, they journey till near noon, when a dark object, seen a little to the right, attracts them. Not to surprise, for they well know what it is—a grove. They can tell, too, that the trees composing it are oaks, of the species known as black-jack. Notwithstanding their stunted growth, the black-jacks are umbrageous, and give good shade. Though the sun has not yet reached meridian, its rays are of meridian heat, and strike down with fiery fervour on the surface of the parched plain.

This determines them to seek the shelter of the grove, and there make their noontide halt. It is a little but of their way; but, far as they can see ahead, no other spot offers a chance of protection against the burning beams.

The grove is a mere copse, covering scarce half an acre, and the topmost branches rise but a few feet above their heads. Still is there shade, both for them and their animals; and cover, should they require to conceal themselves—the last a fortunate circumstance, as is soon proved. Equally fortunate their not having need to kindle a fire. In their haversacks they carry provisions already cooked.

Dismounting, they lead their males in among the trees, and there make them secure by looping the bridles to a branch. Then, laying themselves along the earth, they eat their midday meal, pull out their pipes, and follow it with a smoke.

With little thought, they are burning the last bit of tobacco which remained to the refugees. At parting, their generous host, to comfort them on their journey, presented them with the ultimate ounce of his stock; with true Spanish politeness saying nothing of this.

As they lie watching the blue film curling up among the branches of the black-jacks, as little do they reflect how fortunate for them it is not the smoke of a fire, nor visible at any great distance. Were it so, there would not be much likelihood of their ever reaching the Del Norte or leaving the Llano Estacado alive.

Not dreaming of danger in that desolate place—at least none caused by human kind—they remain tranquilly pulling at their pipes, now conversing of the past, anon speculating about their plans for the future.

Three or four hours elapse; the sun having crossed the meridian, begins to stoop lower. Its rays fall less fervently, and they think of continuing their journey. They have "unhitched" the mules, led them out to the edge of the copse, and are standing by the stirrup, ready to remount, when an object catches the quick eye of the ex-Ranger, causing him to utter a sharp ejaculation.

Something seen west, the way they want to go.

Pointing it out to Hamersley, the two stand observing. No great scrutiny needed to tell them 'tis a cloud of dust, although in breadth not bigger than a blanket. But while they are regarding it it gradually spreads out, at the same time showing higher above the surface of the plain.

It may be a swirl of the wind acting on the dry sand of the desert—the first commencement of a regular whirlwind—a thing common on the table lands of New Mexico. But it has not the round pillar-like form of the *molino*, nor do they believe it to be one. Both are too well acquainted with this phenomenon to be deceived by its counterfeit.

If they had any doubts, as they stand gazing these are resolved. The cloud presents a dense dark head, with a nucleus of something more solid than dust. And while guessing at the true character of this opaque central part, a circumstance occurs disclosing it. A puff of wind striking the dust causes it to swirl sideways, showing underneath a body of mounted men. Men, too, in military array, marching in double file, armed, uniformed, with lances borne erect, their blades glinting in the sun.

"Sogers!" exclaims the ex-Ranger.

Chapter Forty Eight.
Dread Conjectures.

It is Wilder who so emphatically proclaims the character of the cavalcade. He has no need, Hamersley having already made it out himself.

"Yes; they are soldiers," he rejoins, mechanically, adding, "Mexican, as a matter of course. None of our troops ever stray this fair west. 'Tis out of United States territory. The Texans claim it. But those are not Texans: they are uniformed, and carry lances. Your old friends, the Rangers, don't affect that sort of thing."

"No," responds Wilder, with a contemptuous toss of the head, "I shedn't think they did. We niver tuk to them long sticks; 'bout as much use as bean-poles. In coorse they're Mexikins, *lanzeeros*."

"What can they be doing out here? There are no Indians on the Staked Plain. If there were, such a small party as that, taking it to be Mexican, would not be likely to venture after them."

"Maybe it's only a advance guard, and thar's a bigger body behint. We shell soon see, as they're ridin' deerect this way. By the 'Tarnal, 'twon't do to let 'em sight us; leastwise, not till we've seen more o' them, an' know what sort they air. White men tho' they call themselves, I'd a'most as soon meet Injuns. They'd be sure to take us for Texans; and 'bout me there'd be no mistake in that. But they'd treet you the same, an' thar treetment ain't like to be civil. Pull yur mule well back among the bushes. Let's blind the brutes, or they may take it into their heads to squeal."

The hybrids are led back into the grove, tied, and *zapadoed*—the last operation performed by passing a blanket, mask fashion, over their eyes. This done, the two men return to the edge of the copse, keeping themselves screened behind the outstanding trees.

In their absence the moving cohort has drawn nearer, and still advances. But slowly, and, as when first sighted, enveloped in a cloud of dust. Only now and then, as the wind wafts this aside, can be distinguished the forms of the individuals composing it. Then but for an instant, the dust again drifting around them.

Still the *nimbus* draws nigher, and is gradually approaching the spot where the travellers had concealed themselves.

At first only surprised at seeing soldiers on the Staked Plain, they soon become seriously alarmed. The troop is advancing towards the black-jack grove, apparently intending it for a place of bivouac; if so, there will be no chance for them to escape observation. The soldiers will scatter about, and penetrate every part of the copse. Equally idle to attempt flight on their slow-footed animals, pursued by over two score of cavalry horses.

They can see no alternative but surrender, submit to be made prisoners, and receive such treatment as their captors may think fit to extend to them.

While thus despairingly reflecting, they take note of something that restores their disturbed equanimity. It is the direction in which the Mexicans are marching. The cloud moving in slow, stately progress does not approach any nearer to the copse. Evidently the horsemen do not design halting there, but will ride past, leaving it on their left.

They are, in truth, passing along the same path from which the travellers have late deflected; only in the counter direction.

Now, for the first time, a suspicion occurs to Hamersley, shared by the Texan, giving both far greater uneasiness than if the soldiers were heading direct towards them.

It is further intensified as a fresh spurt of the desert wind sweeps the dust away, displaying in clear light the line of marching horsemen. No question as to their character now. There they are, with their square-peaked corded caps, and plumes of horsehair; their pennoned spears sloped over their shoulders; their yellow cloaks folded and strapped over the cantles of their saddles; sabres lying along thighs, clinking against spurs and stirrups—all the picturesque panoply of lancers.

It is not this that strikes dismay into the minds of those who are spectators, for it is now struck into their heart of hearts. On one figure of the cavalcade the eyes of both become fixed; he who rides at its head.

Their attention had been first attracted to his horse, Wilder gasping out, soon as he set eyes on the animal, "Look yonner, Frank!"

"At what?"

"The fellur ridin' foremost. D'ye see the anymal he's on? It's the same we war obleeged to abandon on takin' to the rocks."

"By heavens! my horse!"

"Yurs, to a sartinty."

"And his rider! The man I fought with at Chihuahua, the ruffian Uraga!"

On recognising his antagonist in the duel, the Kentuckian gives out a groan. The Texan, too. For on both the truth flashes in all its fulness—all its terrible reality.

It is not the possession of Hamersley's horse, identifying its rider with the destroyers of the caravan. That is nothing new, and scarce surprises them. What pains—agonises them—is the direction in which the soldiers are proceeding.

They can have no doubt as to the purpose of the military march, or the point to which it is tending.

"Yes," says Walt, "they're strikin' straight fur the valley, goin' 'ithout guess-work, too. Thar's a guide along, an' thar's been a treetur."

"Who do you think?"

"That Injun, Manoel. Ye remember he went on a errand 'bout a week ago, to fetch them some things that war needed. Instead, he's made diskivery o' the hidin' place o' his master, and sold that master's head. That's what he's did, sure."

"It is," mutters Hamersley, in a tone that tells of affliction too deep for speech. Before his mind is a fearful forecast. Don Valerian a prisoner to Uraga and his ruffians—Don Prospero, too; both to be dragged back to Albuquerque and cast into a military prison. Perhaps worse still—tried by court-martial soon as captured, and shot as soon as tried. Nor is this the direst of his previsions. There is one darker—Adela in the company of a ribald crew, surrounded by the brutal soldiery, powerless, unprotected— she his own dear one, now his betrothed! Overcome by his emotions he remains for some time silent, scarce heeding the remarks of his comrade. One, however, restores his attention.

"I tolt ye so," says Walt. "See! yonner's the skunk himself astride o' a mule at the tail o' the gang."

Hamersley directs his eyes to the rear of the outstretched rank. There, sure enough, is a man on muleback, dressed differently from the troopers.

The coarse woollen tilma, and straw hat, he remembers as having been worn by one of Mirander's male domestics. He does not identify the man. But Walt's recollection of his rival is clearer, and he has no doubt that he on the mule is Manuel. Nor, for that matter, has Hamersley. The peon's presence is something to assist in the explanation. It clears up everything.

Hamersley breathes hard as the dark shadows sweep through his soul. For a long time absorbed in thought, he utters scarce an ejaculation. Only after the lancer troop has passed, its rearmost files just clearing the alignment of the copse, he gasps out, in a voice husky as that of one in the act of being strangled, —

"They're going straight for the place. O God!"

"Yes," rejoins the ex-Ranger, in a tone like despondent, "Thar boun' thar for sartint. The darned creetur's been tempted by the blood-money set on Kumel Miranda's head, an' air too like to git it. They'll grup him, sure; an's like as not gie him the garota. Poor gentleman! He air the noblest Mexikin I iver sot eyes on, an' desarves a better fate. As for the ole doc, he may get off arter sarvin' a spell in prison, an' the saynorita—"

A groan from Hamersley interrupts the remark. His comrade, perceiving how much he is pained, modifies what he meant to say.

"Thar's no need to be so much afeard o' what may happen to her. She ain't goin' to be rubbed out, anyhow; an' if she hasn't no brother to purtect her, I reckon she's got a frien' in you, Frank. An' hyar's another o' the same, as they say in the Psalms o' Davit."

Walt's words have a hopeful sound. Hamersley is cheered by them, but replies not. He only presses the hand of his comrade in silent and grateful grasp.

"Yis," continues the ex-Ranger with increased emphasis, "I'd lay down my life to save that young lady from harum, as I know you'd lay down yourn. An' thet air to say nothin' o' my own gurl. This chile ain't niver been much guv to runnin' arter white wheemen, an' war gen'rally content to put up wi' a squaw. But sech as them! As for yourn, I don't wonder yur heart beats like a chased rabbit's; myen air doin' the same for Concheeter. Wal, niver fear! Ef thar's a hair o' eyther o' thar heads teched, you'll hear the crack o' Walt Wilder's rifle, and see its bullet go into the breast o' him as harms 'em. I don't care who or what he air, or whar he be. Nor I don't care a durn—not the valley of a dried buffler-chip—what may come arter—

hangin', garrotin', or shootin'. At all risks, them two sweet creeturs air bound to be protected from harum; an ef it comes, they shall be reevenged. I swar that, by the Eturnal!"

"I join you in the oath," pronounces Hamersley, with emphatic fervour, once more exchanging a hand-squeeze with his companion. "Yes, Walt; the brave Miranda may be sacrificed—I fear it must be so. But for his sister, there is still a hope that we may save her; and surely heaven will help us. If not, I shall be ready to die. Ah! death would be easier to bear than the loss of Adela!"

"An' for this chile the same, rayther than he shed lose Concheeter."

Chapter Forty Nine.
A Cautious Commander.

No need saying that the cavalcade seen passing the copse is the lancer troop of Colonel Uraga.

Some thirty hours before, they ascended to the Staked Plain, and are now nearly across it. Guided by the traitor, they had no need to grope their way, and have made quick time. In a few hours more they will pounce upon the prey for which they have swooped so far.

The two men concealed in the grove expect them to ride on without stopping, till out of sight. Instead, they see them draw up at a few miles distance, though all remain mounted. Two separate from the rest keep on a couple of hundred yards ahead, then also halt.

These are Uraga himself, with his adjutant Roblez.

'Tis only a temporary pause to exchange counsel about the plan of proceeding—as a falcon expands itself in the air before its last flight towards the quarry it has selected.

Before separating from his followers, Uraga has summoned to his side the youngest commissioned officer of the troop, saying, —

"Alferes! go back to that Indian! Send the brute on to the front here."

Manuel is the individual thus coarsely indicated.

Told that he is wanted, the peon spurs his mule forward, and places himself by the side of the commanding officer, who has meanwhile dismounted.

In the countenance of the Indian there is an expression of conscious guilt, such as may appear in that of one not hardened by habitual crime. There is even something like compunction for what he is about to do, with remorse for what he has already done. Now that he is drawing near the scene, where those betrayed by him must suffer, his reflections are anything but pleasant. Rather are they tinged with regret. Don Valerian Miranda has been an indulgent master to him, and the Dona Adela a kind mistress. On both he is bringing destruction.

And what is to be his reward? From the time of his betraying them, the moment he parted with the secret of their hiding-place, he has lost control of it.

He is no longer treated with the slightest respect. On the contrary, he to whom he communicated it behaves to him as conqueror to conquered, master to slave, forcing him forward with sword pointed at his breast, or pistol aimed at his head.

If a guide, he is no longer looked upon as a voluntary one. Nor would he be this, but for a thought that inspires, while keeping him true to his treasonous intent. When he thinks of Conchita—of that scene in the cotton-wood grove—of the Texan kissing her—holding her in his fond embrace—when the Indian recalls all this, torturing his soul afresh, then no more remorse, not a spark of regret, not a ray of repentance!

No; perish the dueno—the duena too! Let die the good doctor, if need be—all whom his vengeance has devoted!

"Sirrah! are those the two peaks you spoke of?"

It is Uraga who puts this interrogatory, pointing to a pair of twin summits seen rising above the horizon to eastward.

"*Si Señor Coronel*; they are the same."

"And you say the path leads down between them?"

"Goes down through a gulch, after keeping round the cliff."

"And there's no other by which the valley may be entered?"

"Your excellency, I did not say that. There is another entrance, but not from the upper plain here. A stream runs through, and cuts it way out beyond. Following its channel through the *cañon*, the place can be reached from below; but not after it's been raining. Then the flood fills its bed, and there's no path along the edge. As it hasn't rained lately, the banks will be above water."

"And anyone could pass out below?"

"They could, Señor Coronel."

"We require to observe caution, Roblez," says Uraga, addressing himself to the adjutant; "else we may have made our long journey for nothing. 'Twill never do to enter the cage and find the birds flown. How far is it to the point where the river runs below?"

The question is put to the peon.

"*Cinco leguas, Señor*; not less. It's a long way to get round, after going down the cliff."

"Five leagues there, and five back up the canon of the stream—quite a day's journey. If we send a detachment round 'twill take all of that. Shall we do it?"

"I don't think there's the slightest need for wasting so much time," counsels the adjutant.

"But the Indian says any one going down the defile between those hills can be seen from the house. Supposing they should see us, and retreat by the opening below?"

"No need to let them see us. We can stay above till night, then descend in the darkness. As they're not likely to be expecting visitors, there should be no great difficulty in approaching this grand mansion unannounced. Let us make our call after the hour of midnight, when, doubtless, the fair Adela will be dreaming of—"

"Enough!" exclaims Uraga, a cloud suddenly coming over his countenance, as if the words of his subordinate recalled some unpleasant souvenir. "We shall do as you say, *ayadante*. Give orders for the men to dismount. We shall halt here till sunset. Meanwhile, see that this copper-skin is closely kept. To make safe, you may as well clap the manacles on him."

In obedience, Roblez takes the Indian back to the halted troop, directs him to be shackled; then gives the order for dismounting.

But not for a night camp, only for a temporary bivouac; and this without fires, or even unsaddling of the horses. The troopers are to stay by the stirrup, ready at any moment to remount.

There stay they; no longer in formation, but, as commanded, silent and motionless; only such stir as is made by snatching a morsel from their haversacks or smoking their corn-husk cigarritos.

Thus till near sundown, when, remounting, they move on.

Chapter Fifty.
Stalking the Stalker!

The spot upon which the lancer troop had halted was less than a league from the grove that gave shelter to the two Americans. In the translucent atmosphere of the tableland it looked scarce a mile. The individual forms of troopers could be distinguished, and the two who had taken themselves apart. The taller of these was easily identified as the commanding officer of the troop.

"If they'd only keep thar till arter sundown," mutters Wilder, "especially him on yur hoss, I ked settle the hul bizness. This hyar gun the doc presented to me air 'bout as good a shootin'-iron as I'd care to shet my claws on, an 'most equal to my own ole rifle. I've gin it all sorts o' trials, tharfor I know it's good for plum center at a hundred an' fifty paces. Ef yonner two squattin' out from the rest 'ill jest stay thur till the shades o' night gie me a chance o' stealin' clost enuf, thar's one o' 'em will never see daylight again."

"Ah!" exclaimed Hamersley, with a sigh of despair, and yet half hopeful, "if they would but remain there till night, we might still head them into the valley, time enough to get our friends away."

"Don't you have any sech hopes, Frank; thar's no chance o' that I kin see what the party air arter. They've made up thar mind not to 'tempt goin' inter the gully till they hev a trifle o' shadder aroun' them. They think that ef they're seen afore they git up to the house their victims might 'scape 'em. Tharfor they purpiss approachin' the shanty unobserved, and makin' a surround o' it. That's thar game. Cunnin' o' them, too, for Mexikins."

"Yes, that is what they intend doing—no doubt of it. Oh, heavens! only to think we are so near, and yet cannot give Miranda a word of warning!"

"Can't be helped. We must put our trust in Him as hes an eye on all o' us—same over these desert purairas an' mountains as whar people are livin' in large cities. Sartin we must trust to Him an' let things slide a bit, jest as He may direct 'em. To go out of our kiver now 'ud be the same as steppin' inter the heart o' a forest fire. Them sogers air mounted on swift horses, an' 'ud ketch up wi these slow critturs o' mules in the shakin' o' goat's tail. Thurfor, let's lie by till night. Tain't fur off now. Then, ef we see any chance to steal down inter the valley, we'll take edvantage o' it."

Hamersley can make no objection to the plan proposed. He sees no alternative but accede to it. So they remain watching the halted troop, regarding every movement with keen scrutiny.

For several hours are they thus occupied, until the sun begins to throw elongated shadows over the plain. Within half an hour of its setting the Mexicans again mount their horses and move onwards.

"Jest as I supposed they'd do," said Walt. "Thar's still all o' ten miles atween them and the place. They've mezyured the time it'll take 'em to git thur—an hour or so arter sundown. Thar ain't the shadder o' a chance for us to steal ahead o' 'em. We must stay in this kiver till they're clar out o' sight."

And they do stay in it until the receding horsemen, who present the appearance of giants under the magnifying twilight mist, gradually grow less, and at length fade from view under the thickening darkness.

Not another moment do Hamersley and the hunter remain within the grove, but springing to their saddles, push on after the troop.

Night soon descending, with scarce ten minutes of twilight, covers the plain with a complete obscurity, as if a shroud of crape had been suddenly thrown over it.

There is no moon, not even stars, in the sky; and the twin *buttes*, that form the portals of the pass, are no longer discerned.

But the ex-Ranger needs neither moon, nor stars, nor mountain peaks to guide him for such a short distance. Taking his bearings before starting from the black-jack copse, he rides on in a course straight as the direction of a bullet from his own rifle, until the two mounds loom up, their silhouettes seen against the leaden sky.

"We mustn't go any furrer, Frank," he says, suddenly pulling up his mule; "leastwise, not a-straddle o' these hyar conspikerous critters. Whether the sogers hev goed down inter the valley or no, they're sartin to hev left some o' the party ahind, by way o' keepin' century. Let's picket the animals out hyar, an' creep forrad afut. That'll gie us a chance o' seeing in, 'ithout bein' seen."

The mules being disposed of as Walt had suggested, the two continue their advance.

First walking erect, then in bent attitude, then crouching still lower, then as quadrupeds on all-fours, and at length, crawling like reptiles, they make their approach to the pass that leads down into the valley.

They do not enter it; they dare not. Before getting within the gape of its gloomy portals they hear voices issuing therefrom. They can see tiny sparks of fire glowing at the lips of ignited cigars. From this they can tell that there are sentries there—a line of them across the ravine, guarding it from side to side.

"It ain't no use tryin', Frank," whispers Wilder; "ne'er a chance o' our settin' through. They're stannin' thick all over the ground. I kin see by thar seegars. Don't ye hear them palaverin? A black snake kedn't crawl through among 'em 'ithout bein' observed."

"What are we to do?" asks Hamersley, in a despairing tone.

"We kin do nothin' now, 'ceptin' go back an' git our mules. We must move them out o' the way afore sun-up. 'Taint no matter o' use our squattin' hyar. No doubt o' what's been done. The main body's goed below; them we see's only a party left to guard the gap. Guess it's all over wi' the poor critters in the cabin, or will be afore we kin do anythin' to help 'em. Ef they ain't kilt, they're captered by this time."

Hamersley can scarce restrain himself from uttering an audible groan. Only the evident danger keeps him silent.

"I say agin, Frank, 'tair no use our stayin' hyar. Anythin' we kin do must be did elsewhar. Let's go back for our mules, fetch 'em away, an' see ef we kin clomb up one o' these hyar hills. Thar's a good skirtin' o' kiver on thar tops. Ef the anymals can't be tuk up, we kin leave them in some gulch, an' go on to the summut ourselves. Thar we may command a view o' all that passes. The sogers'll be sartin to kum past in the mornin', bringin' thar prisoners. Then we'll see who's along wi' 'em, and kin foller thar trail."

"Walt, I'm willing to do as you direct. I feel as if I'd lost all hope, and could give way to downright despair."

"Deespair be durned! Thar's allers a hope while thar's a bit o' breth in the body. Keep up yur heart, man! Think o' how we war 'mong them wagguns. That oughter strengthen yur gizzern. Niver say die till yur dead, and the crowner are holdin' his 'quest over yur karkidge. Thet's the doctryne o' Walt Wilder."

As if to give illustrative proof of it, he catches hold of his comrade's sleeve; with a pluck turns him around, and leads him back to the place where they had parted from the mules. These are released from their pickets, then led silently, and in a circuitous direction, towards the base of one of the buttes.

Its sides appear too steep for even a mule to scale them; but a boulder-strewed ravine offers a suitable place for secreting the animals.

There they are left, their lariats affording sufficient length to make them fast to the rocks, while a *tapado* of the saddle-blankets secures them against binneying.

Having thus disposed of the animals, the two men scramble on up the ravine, reach the summit of the hill, and sit down among the cedar-scrub that crowns it, determined to remain there and await the "development of events."

Chapter Fifty One.
Approaching the Prey.

Were we gifted with clairvoyance, it might at times spare us much misery, thought at other times it would make it. Perhaps 'tis better we are as we are.

Were Frank Hamersley and Walt Wilder, keeping watch on the summit of the mound, possessed of second sight, they would not think of remaining there throughout all the night—not for an hour—nay, not so much as a minute, for they would be aware that within less than ten miles of them is a party of men with friendly hearts and strong arms, both at their disposal for the very purpose they now need such. Enough of them to strike Uraga's lancers and scatter them like chaff.

And could the man commanding these but peep over the precipitous escarpment of the Llano Estacado and see those stalwart Texans bivouacked below, he would descend into the valley with less deliberation, and make greater haste to retire out of it. He and his know nothing of the formidable foes so near, any more than Hamersley and Wilder suspect the proximity of such powerful friends. Both are alike unconscious that the Texans are encamped within ten miles. Yet they are; for the gorge at whose mouth they have halted is the outlet of the valley stream, where it debouches upon the Texan plain.

Without thought of being interfered with, the former proceed upon their ruthless expedition; while the latter have no alternative but await its issue. They do so with spirits impatiently chafing, and hearts sorely agonised.

Both are alike apprehensive for what next day's sun will show them—perchance a dread spectacle.

Neither shuts eye in sleep. With nerves excited and bosoms agitated they lie awake, counting the hours, the minutes; now and then questioning the stars as to the time.

They converse but little, and only in whispers. The night is profoundly still. The slightest sound, a word uttered above their breath, might betray them.

They can distinctly hear the talk of the lancers left below. Hamersley, who understands their tongue, can make out their conversation. It is for the most part ribald and blasphemous, boasts of their *bonnes fortunes* with the damsels of the Del Norte, commingled with curses at this ill-starred expedition that for a time separates them from their sweethearts.

Among them appears a gleam greater than the ignited tips of their cigarittos. 'Tis the light of a candle which they have stuck up over a serape spread along the earth. Several are seen clustering around it; while their conversation tells that they are relieving the dull hours with a little diversion. They are engaged in gambling, and ever and anon the cries, "*Soto en la puerta!*" "*Cavallo mozo!*" ascending in increased monotone, proclaim it to be the never-ending national game of montè.

Meanwhile Uraga, with the larger body of the lancers, has got down into the glen, and is making way towards the point aimed at. He proceeds slowly and with caution. This for two distinct reasons—the sloping path is difficult even by day, at night requiring all the skill of experienced riders to descend it. Still with the traitor at their head, who knows every step, they gradually crawl down the cliff, single file, again forming "by twos" as they reach the more practicable causeway below.

Along this they continue to advance in silence and like caution. Neither the lancer colonel nor his lieutenant has forgotten the terrible havoc made among the Tenawas by the two men who survived that fearful affray, and whom they may expect once more to meet. They know that both have guns—the traitor has told them so—and that, as before, they will make use of them. Therefore Uraga intends approaching stealthily, and taking them by surprise. Otherwise he may himself be the first to fall—a fate he does not wish to contemplate. But there can be no danger, he fancies as he rides forward. It is now the mid-hour of night, a little later, and the party to be surprised will be in their beds. If all goes well he may seize them asleep.

So far everything seems favourable. No sound comes from the direction of the lonely dwelling, not even the bark of a watch dog. The only noises that interrupt the stillness of the night are the lugubrious cry of the coyoté and the wailing note of the whip-poor-will; these, at intervals blending with the sweeter strain of the tzenzontle—the Mexican nightingale—intermittently silenced as the marching troop passes near the spot where it is perched.

Once more, before coming in sight of the solitary jacal, Uraga commands a halt. This time to reconnoitre, not to rest or stay. The troopers sit in their saddles, with reins ready to be drawn; like a flock of vultures about to unfold their wings for the last swoop upon their victims—to clutch, tear, kill, do with them as they may wish!

Chapter Fifty Two.
A Bloodless Capture.

A house from which agreeable guests have just taken departure is rarely cheerful. The reverse, if these have been very agreeable—especially on the first evening after.

The rude sheiling which gives shelter to the refugees is no exception. Everyone under its roof is afflicted with low spirits, some of them sad—two particularly so.

Thus has it been since the early hour of daybreak, when the guests regretted spoke the parting speech.

In the ears of Adela Miranda, all day long, has been ringing that painful word, "Adios!" while thoughts about him who uttered it have been agitating her bosom.

Not that she has any fear of his fealty, or that he will prove traitor to his troth now plighted. On the contrary, she can confide in him for that, and does—fully, trustingly.

Her fears are from a far different cause; the danger he is about to dare.

Conchita, in like manner, though in less degree, has her apprehensions. The great Colossus who has captured her heart, and been promised her hand, may never return to claim it. But, unacquainted with the risk he is going to run, the little mestiza has less to alarm her, and only contemplates her lover's absence, with that sense of uncertainty common to all who live in a land where every day has its dangers.

Colonel Miranda is discomforted too. Never before since his arrival in the valley have his apprehensions been so keen. Hamersley's words, directing suspicion to the peon, Manuel, have excited them. All the more from his having entertained something of this before. And now still more, that his messenger is three days overdue from the errand on which he has sent him.

At noon he and Don Prospero again ascend to the summit of the pass, and scan the table plain above—to observe nothing upon it, either westwardly or in any other direction. And all the afternoon has one or the other been standing near the door of the jacal, with a lorgnette levelled up the ravine through which the valley is entered from above.

Only as the shades of night close over them do they desist from this vigil, proving fruitless.

Added to the idea of danger, they have another reason for desiring the speedy return of the messenger. Certain little luxuries he is expected to bring—among the rest a skin or two of wine and a few boxes of cigars. For neither the colonel himself nor the ex-army surgeon are anchorites, however much they have of late been compelled to the habit. Above all, they need tobacco, their stock being out; the last ounce given to their late guests on leaving.

These are minor matters, but yet add to the cheerlessness of the time after the strangers have gone. Not less at night, when more than ever one feels a craving for the nicotian weed, to consume it in some way—pipe, cigar, or cigaritto.

As the circle of three assemble in their little sitting-room, after a frugal supper, tobacco is the Colonel's chief care, and becomes the first topic of conversation.

"Carramba!" he explains, as if some new idea had entered his head, "I couldn't have believed in a man suffering so much from such a trifling cause."

"What are you referring to?" interrogates the doctor.

"The thing you're thinking of at this moment, *amigo mio.* I'll make a wager it's the same."

"As you know, colonel, I never bet."

"Nor I upon a certainty, as in this case it would be. I know what your mind's bent upon—tobacco."

"I confess it, colonel. I want a smoke, bad as ever I did in my life."

"Sol."

"But why don't you both have it, then?"

It is Adela who thus innocently interrogates.

"For the best of all reasons," rejoins her brother. "We haven't the wherewith."

"What! no cigarittos? I saw some yesterday on one of the shelves."

"But not to day. At this moment there isn't a pinch of tobacco within twenty miles of where we sit, unless our late guests have made a very short day's march. I gave them the last I had to comfort them on the journey."

"Yes, senorita," adds the doctor, "and something quite as bad, if not worse. Our bottles are empty. The wine is out as well as the weed."

"In that," interrupts the Colonel, "I'm happy to say you're mistaken. It's not so bad as you think, doctor. True, the pigskin has collapsed; for the throat of the huge Texan was as difficult to saturate as the most parched spot on the Staked Plain. Finding it so, I took occasion to abstract a good large gourd, and set it surreptitiously aside. I did that to meet emergencies. As one seems to have arisen, I think the hidden treasure may now be produced."

Saying this, the colonel steps out of the room, soon returning with a large calabash bottle.

Conchita is summoned, and directed to bring drinking cups, which she does.

Miranda, pouring out the wine says,—

"This will cheer us; and, in truth, we all need cheering. I fancy there's enough to last us till Manuel makes his reappearance with a fresh supply. Strange his not having returned. He's had time to do all his bargainings and been back three days ago. I hoped to see him home before our friends took departure, so that I could better have provided them for their journey. They'll stand a fair chance of being famished."

"No fear of that," puts in Don Prospero.

"Why do you say so, doctor?"

"Because of the rifle I gave to Señor Gualtero. With it he will be able to keep both provisioned. 'Tis marvellous how he can manage it. He has killed bits of birds without spoiling their skins or even ruffling a feather. I'm indebted to him for some of my best specimens. So long as he carries a gun, with ammunition to load it, you need have no fear he or his companion will perish from hunger, even on the Llano Estacado."

"About that," rejoins Miranda, "I think we need have no uneasiness. Beyond lies the thing to be apprehended—not on the desert, but amid cultivated fields, in the streets of towns, in the midst of so-called civilisation. There will be their real danger."

For some time the three are silent, their reflections assuming a sombre hue, called forth by the colonel's words.

But the doctor, habitually light-hearted, soon recovers, and makes an effort to imbue the others with cheerfulness like his own.

"Senorita," he says, addressing himself to Adela, "your guitar, hanging there against the wall, seems straining its strings as if they longed for the touch of your fair fingers. You've been singing every night for the last month, delighting us all I hope you won't be silent now that your audience is reduced, but will think it all the more reason for bestowing your favours on the few that remain."

To the gallant speech of pure Castilian idiom, the young lady answers with a smile expressing assent, at the same time taking hold of her guitar. As she reseats herself, and commences tuning the instrument, a string snaps.

It seems an evil omen; and so all three regard it, though without knowing why. It is because, like the strings of the instrument, their hearts are out of tune, or rather attuned to a presentiment which oppresses them.

The broken string is soon remedied by a knot; this easily done. Not so easy to restore the tranquillity of thought disturbed by its breaking.

No more does the melancholy song which succeeds. Even to that far land has travelled the strain of the "Exile of Erin." Its appropriateness to their own circumstances suggesting itself to the Mexican maiden, she sings—

> Sad is my fate, said the heart-broken stranger,
> The wild deer and wolf to the covert can flee,
> But I have no refuge from famine and danger,
> A home and a country remain not to me.

"Dear Adela!" interrupts Miranda. "That song is too sad. We're already afflicted with its spirit. Change it for one more cheerful. Give us a lay of the Alhambra—a battle-song of the Cid or the Campeador—something patriotic and stirring."

Obedient to her brother's request, the young girl changes tune and song, now pouring forth one of those inimitable lays for which the language of Cervantes is celebrated.

Despite all, the heaviness of heart remains, pressing upon those who listen as on her who sings. Adela's voice appears to have lost its accustomed sweetness, while the strings of her guitar seem equally out of tune.

All at once, while in the middle of her song, the two bloodhounds, that have been lying on the floor at her feet, start from their recumbent position, simultaneously giving utterance to a growl, and together rush out through the open door.

The singing is instantly brought to an end; while Don Valerian and the doctor rise hastily from their chairs.

The bark of watch-dog outside some quiet farmhouse, amidst the homes of civilisation, can give no idea of the startling effect which the same sound calls forth on the far Indian frontier—nothing like the alarm felt by the dwellers in that lone ranche. To add to it, they hear a hoof striking on the stones outside—that of either horse or mule. It cannot be Lolita's; the mustang mare is securely stalled, and the hoof-stroke comes not from the stable. There are no other animals. Their late guests have taken away the two saddle mules, while the *mulas de carga* are with the messenger, Manuel.

"It's he come back!" exclaims the doctor. "We ought to be rejoiced instead of scared. Come, Don Valerian! we shall have our smoke yet before going to bed."

"It's not Manuel," answers Miranda. "The dogs would have known him before this. Hear how they keep on baying! Ha! what's that? Chico's voice! Somebody has caught hold of him!"

A cry from the peon outside, succeeded by expostulations, as if he was struggling to escape—his voice commingled with shrill screams from Conchita—are sounds almost simultaneous.

Don Valerian strides back into the room and lays hold of his sword, the doctor clutching at the first weapon that presents itself.

But weapons are of no avail where there are not enough hands to wield them.

Into the cabin lead two entrance doors—one front, the other back—and into both is seen pouring a stream of armed men, soldiers in uniform.

Before Miranda can disengage his sword from its scabbard, a perfect *chevaux-de-frise* of lance-points are within six inches of his breast, while the doctor is similarly menaced.

Both perceive that resistance will be idle. It can only end in their instant impalement.

"Surrender, rebels!" cries a voice rising above the din.

"Drop your weapons, and at once, if you wish your lives spared! Soldiers, disarm them!"

Miranda recognises the voice. Perhaps, had he done so sooner, he would have held on to his sword, and taken the chances of a more protracted and desperate resistance.

It is too late. As the weapon is wrested from his grasp, he sees standing before him the man of all others he has most reason to fear—Gil Uraga!

Chapter Fifty Three.
A Sleepless Night.

All night long Hamersley and the hunter remain upon the summit of the mound. It is a night of dread anxiety, seeming to them an age.

They think not of taking sleep—they could not. There is that in their minds that would keep them wakeful if they had not slept for a week. Time passing does not lessen their suspense. On the contrary, it grows keener, becoming an agony almost unendurable.

To escape from it, Hamersley half forms the resolution to descend the hill and endeavour to steal past the sentinels. If discovered, to attack them boldly, and attempt cutting a way through; then on into the valley, and take such chances as may turn up for the rescue of the refugees.

Putting it to his companion, the latter at once offers opposing counsel. It would be more than rashness—sheer madness. At least a dozen soldiers have been left on picket at the summit of the pass. Standing or sitting, they are scattered all over the ground. It would be impossible for anyone going down the gorge to get past them unperceived; and for two men to attack twelve, however courageous the former and cowardly the latter, the odds would be too great.

"I wouldn't mind it for all that," says Walt, concluding his response to the rash proposal, "ef thar war nothin' more to be did beyont. But thar is. Even war we to cut clar through, kill every skunk o' 'em, our work 'ud be only begun. Thar's two score to meet us below. What ked we do wi' 'em? No, Frank; we mout tackle these twelve wi' some sort o' chance, but two agin forty! It's too ugly a odds. No doubt we ked drop a good grist o' 'em afore goin' under, but in the eend they'd git the better o' us—kill us to a sartinty."

"It's killing me to stay here. Only to think what the ruffians may be doing at this moment! Adela—"

"Don't gie yur mind to thinkin' o' things now. Keep your thoughts for what we may do arterward. Yur Adela ain't goin' to be ate up that quick, nor yet my Concheeter. They'll be tuk away 'long wi' t'others as prisoners.

We kin foller, and trust to some chance o' bein' able to git 'em out o' the clutches o' the scoundrels."

Swayed by his comrade's counsel, somewhat tranquillised by it, Hamersley resigns himself to stay as they are. Calmer reflection convinces him there is no help for it. The alternative, for an instant entertained, would be to rush recklessly on death, going into its very jaws.

They lie along the ground listening, now and then standing up and peering through the branches at the sentries below. For a long while they hear nothing save the calls of the card-players, thickly interlarded with *carajoz, chingaras,* and other blasphemous expressions. But just after the hour of midnight other sounds reach their ears, which absorb all their attention, taking it away from the gamesters.

Up out of the valley, borne upon the buoyant atmosphere, comes the baying of bloodhounds. In echo it reverberates along the façade of the cliff, for a time keeping continuous. Soon after a human voice, quickly followed by a second; these not echoes or repetitions of the same; for one is the coarse guttural cry of a man, the other a scream in the shrill treble of of a woman. The first is the shout of surprise uttered by Chico, the second the shriek of alarm sent forth by Conchita.

With hearts audibly beating, the listeners bend their ears to catch what may come next, both conjecturing the import of the sounds that have already reached them, and this with instinctive correctness. Walt is the first to give speech to his interpretation of it.

"They're at the shanty now," he says, in a whisper. "The two houn's guv tongue on hearin' 'em approach. That fust shout war from the Injun Cheeko; and the t'other air hern—my gurl's. Durnation! if they hurt but a he'r o' her head—Wagh! what's the use o' my threetenin'?"

As if seeing his impotence, the hunter suddenly ceases speech, again setting himself to listen. Hamersley, without heeding him, is already in this attitude.

And now out of the valley arise other sounds, not all of them loud. The stream, here and there falling in cataracts, does something to deaden them. Only now and then there is the neigh of a horse, and intermittently the bark of one of the bloodhounds, as if these animals had yielded, but yet remain hostile to the intruders. They hear human voices, too, but no shout following that of Chico, and no scream save the one sent up by Conchita.

There is loud talk, a confusion of speakers, but no report of firearms. This last is tranquillising. A shot at that moment heard by Hamersley would give him more uneasiness than if the gun were aimed at himself.

"Thank God!" he gasps out, after a long spell of listening, "Miranda has made no resistance. He's seen it would be no use, and has quietly surrendered. I suppose it's all over now, and they are captives."

"Wal, better thet than they shed be corpses," is the consolatory reflection of the hunter. "So long as thar's breath left in thar bodies we kin hev hope, as I sayed arready. Let's keep up our hearts by thinkin' o' the fix we war in atween the wagguns, an' arterwards thet scrape in the cave. We kim clar out o' both in a way we mout call mirakelous, an' we may yit git them clar in someat the same fashion. 'Slong's I've got my claws roun' the stock o' a good gun, wi' plenty o' powder and lead, I ain't a-goin' to deespar. We've both got that, tharfor niver say die!"

The hunter's quaint speech is encouraging; but for all, it does not hinder him and his comrade from soon after returning to a condition of despondency, if not actual despair.

A feeling which holds possession of them till the rising of the sun, and on till it reaches meridian.

When the day breaks, with eyes anxiously scrutinising, they look down into the valley. A mist hangs over the stream, caused by the spray of its cataracts.

Lifting at length, there is displayed a scene not very different from what they have been expecting.

Around the ranche they see horses picketed and soldiers moving among them or standing in groups apart; in short, a picture of military life in "country quarters."

Their point of view is too far off to identify individual forms or note the exact action carried on. This last, left to conjecture, is filled up by fancies of the most painful kind.

For long hours are they constrained to endure them—up to that of noon. Then, the notes of a bugle, rising clear above the hissing of the cascades, foretell a change in the spectacle. It is the call, "Boots and saddles!" The soldiers are seen caparisoning their horses and standing by the stirrup.

Another blast gives the order to "Mount!" Soon after, the "Forward!" Then the troop files off from the front of the jacal, disappearing under the trees like a gigantic glittering serpent. The white drapery of a woman's dress is seen fluttering at its head, as if the reptile had seized upon some tender prey—a dove from the cote—and was bearing it off to its slimy lair.

For another half-hour the two men on the mound wait with nervous impatience. It requires this time to make the ascent from the centre of the valley to the upper plain. After entering among the trees, the soldiers and their captives are out of sight; but the clattering of their horses' hoofs can be heard as they strike upon the rock-strewn path. Once or twice a trumpet sound proclaims their movements upon the march.

At length the head of the troop appears, the leading files following one after the other along the narrow ledge. As they approach the summit of the pass the track widens, admitting a formation "by twos." At the trumpet call they change to this, a single horseman riding at their head.

He is now near enough for his features to be distinguished, and Hamersley's heart strikes fiercely against his ribs as he recognises them. If he had any doubt before, it is set at rest now. He sees Gil Uraga, certain of his being the man who caused the destruction of his caravan. His own horse, ridden by the robber, is proof conclusive of the crime.

He takes note that the lancer colonel is dressed in splendid style, very different from the dust-stained cavalier who the day before passed over the desert plain. Now he appears in a gorgeous laced uniform, with lancer cap and plume, gold cords and aiguillettes dangling adown his breast; for he has this morning made his toilet with care, in consideration of the company in which he intends travelling.

Neither Hamersley nor the hunter hold their eyes long upon him; they are both looking for another individual—each his own. These soon make their appearance, their white dresses distinguishable amid the darker uniforms. During the march their position has been changed. They are now near the centre of the troop, the young lady upon her own mare Lolita, while the Indian damsel is mounted on a mule. They are free, both hand and limb, but a file in front, with another behind, have charge of them. Farther rearward is another group, more resembling captives. This is composed of three men upon mules, fast bound to saddle and stirrup, two of them having their arms pinioned behind their backs. Their animals are led each by a trooper who rides before. The two about whose security such precaution has been taken are Don Valerian and the doctor, the third, with his arms free, is Chico. His fellow-servant Manuel, also on mule-back, is following not far behind, but in his attitude or demeanour there is nothing to tell of the captive. If at times he looks gloomy, it is when he reflects upon his black treason and infamous ingratitude. Perhaps he has repented, or deems the prospect not so cheerful as expected. After all, what will be his reward? He has ruined his master and many others beside, but this will not win him the love of Conchita.

The spectators feel somewhat relieved as Colonel Miranda comes in sight. Still more as the march brings him nearer, and it can be seen that he sits his horse with no sign of having received any injury; and neither has Don Prospero. The elaborate fastenings are of themselves evidences that no hurt has happened to them. It has been a capture without resistance, as their friends hoped it would, their fears having been of a conflict to end in the death of the exiles.

One by one, and two by two, the troops come filing on, till the leader is opposite the spot where the two spectators stand crouching among the trees. These are dwarf cedars, and give the best cover for concealment. Thoroughly screened by their thickly-set boughs and dense dark foliage, Hamersley and the hunter command a clear view of everything below. The distance to the summit of the pass is about two hundred yards in a slanting direction.

As the lancer colonel approaches the spot where the picket is posted, he halts and gives an order. It is for the guard to fall in along with the rest of the troop.

At this moment a similar thought is in the minds of the two men whose eyes are upon him from above. Wilder is the first to give expression to it. He does so in an undertone,—

"Ef we ked trust the carry o' our rifles, Frank."

"I was thinking of it," is the rejoinder, equally earnest. "We can't I'm afraid it's too far."

"I weesh I only had my old gun; she'd a sent a bullet furrer than that. A blue pill inter his stomach 'ud simplerfy matters consid'rable. 'Tall events it 'ud git your gurl out o' danger, and mayhap all on 'em. I b'lieve the hul clanjamfery o' them spangled jay birds 'ud run at hearin' a shot. Then we ked gie 'em a second, and load an' fire half a dozen times afore they could mount up hyar—if they'd dar to try it. Ah! it's too fur. The distance in these hyar high puraipras is desprit deceivin'. Durned pity we kedn't do it. I fear we can't."

"If we should miss, then—"

"Things 'ud only be wuss. I reck'n we'd better let'm slide now, and foller arter. Thar boun' straight for the Del Norte; but whether or no, we kin eesy pick up thar trail."

Hamersley still hesitates, his fingers alternately tightening on his gun, and then relaxing. His thoughts are flowing in a quick current—too quick for cool deliberation. He knows he can trust his own aim, as well as that of his comrade. But the distance is doubtful, and the shots might fall short. Then it would be certain death to them; for the situation is such that there could be no chance to escape, with fifty horsemen to pursue, themselves mounted upon mules, and therewith be reached without difficulty. They might defend themselves on the mound, but not for long. Two against fifty, they would soon be overpowered. After all, it will be better to let the troop pass on. So counsels the ex-Ranger, pointing out that the prisoners will be carried on to New Mexico—to Albuquerque, of course. He and his comrade are Americans, and not proscribed there. They can follow without fear. Some better opportunity may arise for rescuing the captives. Their prison may offer this; and from what they have heard of such places it is probable enough. A golden key is good for opening the door of any gaol in Mexico.

Only one thought hinders Hamersley from at once giving way to this reasoning—the thought of his betrothed being in such company—under such an escort, worse than unprotected!

Once more he scans the distance that separates him from the soldiers, his gun tightly grasped.

Could their colonel but suspect his proximity at that moment, and what is passing through his mind, he would sit with little confidence in his saddle, bearing himself less pompously.

Caution, backed by the ex-Ranger's counsel, asserts its sway, and the Kentuckian relaxes his grasp on the gun, dropping its butt to the ground.

The last files, having cleared the gap, are formed into a more compact order; when, the bugle again sounding "Forward," the march is resumed, the troop striking off over the plain in the direction whence it came.

Chapter Fifty Four.
A Man and a Mule.

Carefully as ever, Hamersley and the Texan keep to their place of concealment. They dare not do otherwise. The slope by which they ascended is treeless, the cedars only growing upon the summit. The gorge, too, by which they went up, and at the bottom of which their mules were left, debouches westwardly on the plain—the direction in which the lancers have ridden off. Any of these chancing to look back would be sure to catch sight of them if they show themselves outside the sheltering scrub. They have their apprehensions about their animals. It is a wonder these have not been seen by the soldiers. Although standing amid large boulders, a portion of the bodies of both are visible from the place mentioned. Fortunately for their owners, their colour closely resembled the rocks, and for which the troopers may have mistaken them. More probably, in their impatience to proceed upon the return route, none of them turn their eyes in that direction.

An equally fortunate circumstance is the fact of the mules being muffled. Otherwise they might make themselves heard. Not a sound, either snort or hinney, escape them; not so much as the stamping of a hoof. They stand patient and silent, as if they themselves had fear of the men who are foes to their masters.

For a full hour after the lancers have left these stay crouching behind the cedars. Even an hour does not take the troop out of sight. Cumbered with their captives, they march at slow, measured pace—a walk. Moreover, the pellucid atmosphere of the Staked Plain makes objects visible at double the ordinary distance. They are yet but five miles from the buttes, and, looking back, could see a man at their base, more surely one mounted.

The two who are on the summit allow quite twenty minutes more to elapse before they think of leaving it. Then, deeming it safe, they prepare to descend.

Still they are in no haste. Their intention is to follow the cavalcade, but by no means to overtake it. Nor do they care to keep it in sight, but the contrary, since that might beget danger to themselves. They anticipate no difficulty in taking up the trail of a troop like that Walt confidently declares he could do so were he blindfolded as their mules, adding, in characteristic phraseology, "I ked track the skunks by thar smell."

Saying this he proposes a "bit o' brakwist," a proposition his comrade assents to with eagerness. They have not eaten since dinner of the day before, their provisions having been left below, and the sharp morning air has given additional edge to their appetites. This at length draws them down to their mules.

Taking off the *tapados* to relieve the poor animals, who have somewhat suffered from being so scurvily treated, they snatch a hasty repast from their haversacks, then light their pipes for a smoke preparatory to setting forth. It is not yet time, for the soldiers are still in sight. They will wait till the last lance pennon sinks below the horizon.

Whilst smoking, with eyes bent upon the receding troop, a sound salutes their ears, causing both to start. Fortunately they draw back behind one of the boulders, and there remain listening. What they heard was certainly a hoofstroke, whether of horse or mule—not of either of their own; these are by their sides, while the sound that has startled them appears to proceed from the other side of the mound, as if from the summit of the pass leading up out of the valley.

They hear it again. Surely it is in the gorge that goes down, or at the head of it.

Their conjecture is that one of the lancers has lagged behind, and is now *en route* to overtake the troop.

If it be thus what course are they to pursue? He may look back and see themselves or their animals, then gallop on and report to his comrades.

'Twould be a sinister episode, and they must take steps to prevent it.

They do so by hastily restoring the *tapados* and leading the mules into a *cul-de-sac*, where they will be safe from observation.

Again they hear the sound, still resembling a hoofstroke, but not of an animal making way over the ground in walk, trot, or gallop, but as one that refused to advance, and was jibbing.

Between them and it there seems great space, a projecting spur of the butte from which they have just descended. By climbing the ridge for a score of yards or so they can see into the gorge that goes down to the valley.

As the trampling still appears steadfast to the same point, their alarm gives place to curiosity, then impatience. Yielding to this, they scramble up the ridge that screens the kicking animal from their view.

Craning their heads over its crest, they see that which, instead of causing further fear, rather gives them joy.

Just under their eyes, in the gap of the gorge, a man is struggling with a mule. It is a contest of very common occurrence. The animal is saddled, and the man is making attempts to get his leg over the saddle. The hybrid is restive, and will not permit him to put foot in the stirrup. Ever as he approaches it shies back, rearing and pitching to the full length and stretch of the bridle-rein.

Soon as seeing him, they upon the ridge recognise the man thus vexatiously engaged. He is the peon Manuel.

"The durned scoundrel," hissed Walt, through clenched teeth. "What's kep him ahint, I wonder?"

Hamersley responds not—he, too, conjecturing.

"By Jehorum!" continues the hunter, "it looks like he'd stayed back apurpose. Thar ked been nothin' to hinder him to go on 'long wi' the rest. The questyun air what he's stayed for. Some trick o' trezun, same as he's did afore."

"Something of the kind, I think," rejoins Hamersley, still considering.

"Wal, he's wantin' to get on bad enuf now, if the mule 'ud only let him. Say, Frank, shell I put a payriud to their conflict by sendin' a bit o' lead that way, I kin rub the varmint out by jest pressin' my finger on this trigger."

"Do you mean the man or the mule?"

"The man, in coorse. For what shed I shoot the harmless critter that's been carryin' him? Say the word, an' I'll send him to kingdom come in the twinklin' o' a goat's tail. I've got sight on him. Shall I draw the trigger?"

"For your life, don't look yonder! They're not yet out of sight. They might see the smoke, perhaps hear the crack. Comrade, you're taking leave of your senses!"

"Contemplatin' that ugly anymal below air enough to make me. It a'most druv me out o' my mind to think o' his black ungratefulness. Now, seein' hisself through the sight of a rifle 'ithin good shootin' distance, shurely ye don't intend we shud let him go!"

"Certainly not. That would be ruin to ourselves. We must either kill or capture him. But it must be done without noise, or at least without firing a shot. They're not far enough off yet."

"How d'ye devise, then?"

"Let's back to our mules, mount, and get round the ledge. We must head him before he gets out of the gap. Come on!"

Both scramble back down the slope quicker than they ascended it, knowing there is good reason for haste—the best for their lives—every thing may depend on capturing the peon. Should he see them, and get away, it will be worse both for them and their dear ones.

In two minutes the mules are again unmuffled and mounted. In two more they are entering the gap from outside, their masters on their backs.

These, spurring the animals to speed, enter the gorge, their eyes everywhere. They reach the spot where the peon was so late seen, striving to get into his saddle. They see the turf torn up by the hybrid's hoofs, but no man, no mule.

Chapter Fifty Five.
A Lagger Lagged.

The surprise of the two men is but momentary; for there can be no mystery about the peon's disappearance. He has simply gone down the ravine, and back into the valley. Is he on return to the house, which they know is now untenanted, and, if so, with what intent? Has he become so attached to the place as to intend prolonging his sojourn there? or has something arisen to make him discontented with the company he has been keeping, and so determined to get quit of it by hanging behind?

Something of this sort was on their minds as they last saw him over the crest of the ridge. While in conflict with his mule, he was ever and anon turning his eyes towards the point where the soldiers must have been last seen by him; for from the gap in which he was these were no longer visible. Both Hamersley and Wilder had noticed an uneasy air about him at the time, attributing it to his vexation at being delayed by the obstinacy of the animal and the fear of being left behind. Now that he had mounted and taken the back-track, the cause must be different.

"Thar's somethin' queery in what the coyoats doin'," is Walt's half-soliloquised observation; adding, "Though what he's arter tain't so eezy to tell. He must be tired o' their kumpany, and want to get shet o' it. He'll be supposin' they ain't likely to kum back arter him; an' I reck'n they won't, seein' they've got all out o' him they need care for. Still, what ked he do stayin' hyar by himself?"

Walt is still ignorant of the peon's partiality for his own sweetheart. He has had a suspicion of something, but not the deep, dire passion that burns in the Indian's heart. Aware of this, he would not dwell on the probability of the man having any intention, any more than himself, remain behind now that Conchita is gone.

"Arter all," he continues, still speaking in half soliloquy, "I don't think stayin's his game. There's somethin' else at the bottom on't."

"Can Uraga have sent him back on any errand?"

"No, that ain't it eyther. More like he's good on a errand o' his own. I reckon I ken guess it now. The traitur intends turnin' thief as well—doin' a leetle bit o' stealin' along wi' his treason. Ye remember, Frank, thar war a goodish grit o' valleyables in the shanty—the saynorita's jeweltry an' the like. Jest possyble, in the skrimmage, whiles they war making capter o' thar prisoners, this ugly varmint tuk devantage o' the confusion to secret a whun o' thar gimcracks, an's now goed back arter 'em."

"It seems probable enough. Still, he might have some other errand, and may not go on as far as the house. In which case, we may look for his return this way at any moment. It will never do for us to start upon their trail, leaving him coming in our rear. He would see us, and in the night might slip past and give them warning they were followed."

"All that air true. We must grup him now."

"Should we go down after him, or stay here till he comes up?"

"Neythur o' the two ways'll do. He moutn't kum along no time. If he's got plunder he won't try to overtake the sogers, but wait till they're well out o' his way. He knows the road to the Del Norte, and kin travel it by hisself."

"Then we should go down after him."

"Only one o' us. If we both purceed to the shanty there's be a chance o' passin' him on the way. He mout be in the timmer, an', seein' us, put back out hyar, an' so head us. There'd no need o' both for the capterin' sech a critter as that. I'll fetch him on his marrowbones by jest raisin' this rifle. Tharfor, s'pose you stay hyar an' guard this gap, while I go arter an' grup him. I'm a'most sartin he'll be at the shanty. Anyhow, he's in the trap, and can't get out till he's hed my claws roun' the scruff o' his neck an' my thumb on his thropple."

"Don't kill him if you can help it. True he deserves to die; but we may want a word with him first. He may give information that will afterwards prove useful to us."

"Don't be afeared, Frank. I shan't hurt a har o' his head, unless he reesists, then I must kripple him a bit. But he ain't like to show fight, such a coyoat as he!"

"All right, Walt. I'll wait for you."

"You won't hev long. Ye'd better take kiver back o' them big stones to make sure o' not bein' seen by him, shed he by any chance slip past me. An' keep yur ears open. Soon as I've treed him I'll gie a whistle or two. When ye hear that ye can kim down."

After delivering this chapter of suggestions and injunctions, the ex-Ranger heads his mule down the pass, and is soon lost to his comrade's sight as he turns off along the ledge of the cliff.

Hamersley, himself inclined to caution, follows the direction last given, and rides back behind one of the boulders. Keeping in the saddle, he sits in silent meditation. Sad thoughts alone occupy his mind. His prospects are gloomy indeed; his forecast of the future dark and doubtful. He has but little hope of being able to benefit Don Valerian Miranda, and cannot be sure of rescueing his sister—his own betrothed—in time to avert that terrible catastrophe which he knows to be impending over her. He does not give it a name—he scarce dares let it take shape in his thoughts.

Nearly half-an-hour is spent in this painful reverie. He is aroused from it by a sound which ascends out of the valley. With a start of joy he recognises the signal his comrade promised to send him. The whistle is heard in three distinct "wheeps," rising clear above the hoarser sibillations of the cascades. From the direction he can tell it comes from the neighbourhood of the house; but, without waiting to reflect whither, he spurs his mule out, and rides down the pass as rapidly as possible.

On reaching the level below he urges the animal to a gallop, and soon arrives at the ranche.

There, as expected, he finds his companion, with the peon a captive.

The two, with their mules, form a tableau in front of the untenanted dwelling.

The ex-Ranger is standing in harangue attitude, slightly bent forward, his body propped by his rifle, the butt of which rests upon the ground. At his feet is the Indian, lying prostrate, his ankles lashed together with a piece of cowhide rope, his wrists similarly secured.

"I ked catched him a leetle sooner," says Walt to his comrade, coming up, "but I war kewrious to find out what he war arter, an' waited to watch him. That's the explication o' it."

He points to a large bag lying near, with its contents half poured out—a varied collection of articles of bijouterie and virtu, resembling a cornucopia; spilling its fruits. Hamersley recognises them as part of the *penates* of his late host.

"Stolen goods," continues Walt, "that's what they air. An' stole from a master he's basely betrayed, may be to death. A mistress, besides, that's been too kind to him. Darnation! that's a tortiss-shell comb as belonged to my Concheeter, an' a pair o' slippers I ken swar wur here. What shed we do to him?"

"What I intended," responds Hamersley, assuming a curious air; "first make him confess—tell all he knows. When we've got his story out of him we can settle that next."

The confession is not very difficult to extract. With Wilder's bowie-knife gleaming before his eyes, its blade within six inches of his breast, the wretch reveals all that has passed since the moment of his first meditating treason. He even makes declaration of the motive, knowing the nobility of the men who threatened him, and thinking by this means to obtain pardon.

To strengthen his chances he goes still farther, turning traitor against him to whom he had sold himself—Uraga. He has overheard a conversation between the Mexican colonel and his adjutant, Lieutenant Roblez. It was to the effect that they do not intend taking their prisoners all the way back to Albuquerque. How they mean to dispose of them the peon does not know.

He had but half heard the dialogue relating to Don Valerian and the doctor.

The female prisoners! Can he tell anything of what is intended with them? Though not in these terms, the question is asked with this earnestness.

The peon is unable to answer it. He does not think they are prisoners—certainly not Conchita. She is only being taken back along with her mistress. About the senorita, his mistress, he heard some words pass between Uraga and Roblez, but without comprehending their signification.

In his own heart Hamersley can supply it—does so with dark, dire misgivings.

Chapter Fifty Six.
"The Norte."

Westward, across the Liana Estacado, Uraga and his lancers continue on their return march. The troop, going by twos, is again drawn out in an elongated line, the arms and accoutrements of the soldiers glancing in the sun, while the breeze floats back the pennons of their lances. The men prisoners are a few files from the rear, a file on each flank guarding them. The women are at the head, alongside the guide and sub-lieutenant, who has charge of the troop.

For reasons of his own the lancer colonel does not intrude his company on the captives. He intends doing so in his own time. It has not yet come. Nor does he take any part in directing the march of the men. That duty has been entrusted to the *alferez*; he and Roblez riding several hundred paces in advance of the troop.

He has thus isolated himself for the purpose of holding conversation with his adjutant, unembarrassed by any apprehension of being overheard.

"Well, *ayadante*," he begins, as soon as they are safe beyond earshot, "what's your opinion of things now?"

"I think we've done the thing neatly, though not exactly the way you wanted it."

"Anything but that. Still, I don't despair of getting everything straight in due time. The man Manuel has learnt from his fellow-servant that our American friends have gone on to the settlements of the Del Norte. Strange if we can't find them there; and stranger still if, when found, I don't bring them to book at last. *Caraja*! Neither of the two will ever leave New Mexico alive."

"What about these two—our Mexican friends?"

"For them a fate the very reverse. Neither shall ever reach it alive."

"You intend taking them there dead, do you?"

"Neither living nor dead. I don't intend taking them there at all."

"You think of leaving them by the way?"

"More than think; I've determined upon it."

"But surely you don't mean to kill them in cold blood?"

"I won't harm a hair of their heads—neither I, nor you, nor any of my soldiers. For all that, they shall die."

"Colonel, your speech is somewhat enigmatical. I don't comprehend it."

"In due time you will. Have patience for four days more—it may be less. Then you will have the key to the enigma. Then Don Valerian Miranda and the old rascal Don Prospero shall cease to trouble the dreams of Gil Uraga."

"And you are really determined on Miranda's death?"

"A silly question for a man who knows me as you. Of course I am."

"Well, for my part, I don't care much one way or the other, only I can't see what benefit it will be to you. He's not such a bad sort of a fellow, and has got the name of being a courageous soldier."

"You're growing wonderfully sentimental, *ayadante*. The tender glances of the senorita seem to have softened you."

"Not likely," rejoins the adjutant with a grim smile. "The eyes that could make impression upon the heart of Gaspar Roblez don't exist in the head of woman. If I have any weaknesses in the feminine way, it's for the goddess Fortuna. So long as I can get a pack of playing cards, with some rich *gringo* to face me in the game, I'll leave petticoats alone."

In turn the colonel smiles. He knows the idiosyncracy of his confederate in crime. Rather a strange one for a man who has committed many robberies, and more than once imbued his hands in blood. Cards, dice and drink are his passions, his habitual pleasure. Of love he seems incapable, and does not surrender himself to its lure, though there has been a chapter of it in his life's history, of which Uraga is aware, having an unfortunate termination, sealing his heart against the sex to contempt, almost hatred. Partially to this might be traced the fact of his having fallen into evil courses, and, like his colonel, become a robber. But, unlike the latter, he is not all bad. As in the case of Conrad, linked to a thousand crimes, one virtue is left to him—courage. Something like a second remains in his admiration of the same quality in others. This it is that leads him to put in a word for Colonel Miranda, whose bravery is known far and wide throughout the Mexican army. Continuing to plead for him, he says—

"I don't see why you should trouble yourself to turn States' executioner. When we get to Santa Fé our prisoners can be tried by court-martial. No doubt they'll be condemned and shot."

"Very great doubt of it, *ayadante*. That might have done when we first turned their party out. But of late, things are somewhat changed. In the hills of the Moctezumas matters are again getting complicated, and just now our worthy chief, El Cojo, will scarce dare to sign a sentence of death, especially where the party to be *passado por les armes* is a man of note like Don Valerian Miranda."

"He must die?"

"*Teniente*! Turn your head round and look me straight in the face."

"I am doing so, colonel. Why do you wish me?"

"You see that scar on my cheek?"

"Certainly I do."

"Don Valerian Miranda did not give the wound that's left it, but he was partly the cause of my receiving it. But for him the duel would have ended differently. It's now twelve months gone since I got that gash, at the same time losing three of my teeth. Ever since the spot has felt aflame as if hell's fire were burning a hole through my cheek. It can only be extinguished by the blood of those who kindled it. Miranda is one of them. You've asked the question, 'Must he die?' Looking at this ugly scar, and into the eye above it, I fancy you will not think it necessary to repeat the question."

"But how is it to be done without scandal? As you yourself have said, it won't do for us to murder the man outright. We may be held to account—possibly ourselves called before a court-martial. Had he made resistance, and given us a pretext—"

"My dear *ayadante*, don't trouble yourself about pretexts. I have a plan which will serve equally as well—my particular purpose, much better. As I've promised, you shall know it in good time—participate in its execution. But, come, we've been discoursing serious matters till I'm sick of them. Let's talk of something lighter and pleasanter—say, woman. What think you of my charmer?"

"The Dona Adela?"

"Of course. Could any other charm me? Even you, with your heart of flint, should feel sparks struck out of it at the sight of her."

"Certainly she's the most beautiful captive I've ever assisted at the taking of."

"Captive!" mutters Uraga, in soliloquy. "I wish she were, in a sense different."

Then, with a frown upon his face, continuing,—

"What matters it! When he is out of the way, I shall have it all my own way. Woo her as Tarquin did Lucretia, and she will yield not as the Roman matron, but as a Mexican woman—give her consent when she can no longer withhold it. What is it, *cabo*?"

The interrogatory is addressed to a corporal who has ridden alongside, and halts, saluting him.

"Colonel, the *alferez* sends me to report that the Indian is no longer with us."

"What! the man Manuel?"

"The same, colonel."

"Halt!" commands Uraga, shouting aloud to the troop, which instantly comes to a stand. "What's this I hear, *alferez*?" he asks, riding back, and speaking to the sub-lieutenant.

"Colonel, we miss the fellow who guided us. He must have dropped behind as we came out of the gorge. He was with us on leaving the house, and along the valley road."

"It don't much signify," says Uraga, in an undertone to Roblez; "we've got all out of him we need care for. Still, it may be better to bring him along. No doubt he slipped off to settle some affair of his own—some pilferings, I presume; and will be found at the ranche. *Cabo*! take a file of men, go back to the valley, and bring the loiterer along with you. As I intend marching slowly, you'll easily overtake us at our night camp."

The corporal, singling out the file as directed, rides back towards the buttes, still in sight, while the troop continues its uninterrupted march. Uraga and Roblez again go in advance, the former making further disclosure of his plans to his *particeps criminis*.

Their confidential dialogue has lasted about an hour, when another of the lancers riding up again interrupts it. He is a grizzled old veteran, who has once been a *cibolero*, and seen life upon the plains.

"What is it, Hernandez?" demands the colonel.

"*Señor coronel*," says the man, pointing to a little speck in the sky, that has just shown itself above the north-eastern horizon, "do you see yonder cloud?"

"Cloud! I see no cloud, unless you mean that spot on the horizon, scarce so large as the crown of my hat Is it that you mean?"

"It is, colonel. And small as it seems, there may come trouble from it. It don't look much now, but in ten minutes time it will be big enough to spread all over the sky, and over us too."

"You think so? Why, what is it, Hernandez? El Norte?"

"I'm sure of it. *Carramba!* I've seen it too often. Trust me, colonel, we're going to have a storm."

"In that case we'd better bring to a halt and get under shelter. I see nothing here that would screen a cat, save yonder clump of dwarf oaks. In a way it'll keep the blast off us, and, as we may as well stay under it for the night, it will furnish fuel for our fires. Ride back to the troop. Tell the *alferez* to bring on the men to yonder grove, and quickly. Let the tents be pitched there. *Vaya!*"

The *ci-devant* cibolero does as directed, going at a gallop; while the colonel and his adjutant trot on to the clump of blackjacks, standing some three hundred paces out of the line of march. It was the same copse that gave shade and concealment to Frank Hamersley and Walt Wilder on the day preceding.

On arriving at its edge, which they do before their followers, Uraga and Roblez see the tracks of the two mules. Not without surprise, and they exchange some words regarding them. But the fast-darkening sky drives the subject out of their thoughts, and they occupy themselves in choosing a spot for pitching the tents.

Of these there are too—one which Urago owns, the other, found in the ranche, an old marquee Miranda had carried with him in his flight. This has been brought along for the accommodation of his sister, whom Uraga has reason to treat tenderly.

Both tents are soon set up in the shelter of the black-jacks; the marquee, as ordered by Uraga, occupied by the female captives.

The lancers, having hastily dismounted, picket their horses and make other preparations for the storm, predicted by the ex-cibolero as something terrific.

Before long they see his prediction verified to the spirit and the letter.

The sky, hitherto shining like a sapphire and blue as a turquoise, becomes changed to the sombre hue of lead; then darker, as if night had suddenly descended over the sterile plain. The atmosphere, but a moment before unpleasantly hot, is now cold as winter; the thermometer is less than twenty minutes falling over forty degrees—almost to freezing point!

It is not night which causes the darkness, nor winter the cold. Both come from an atmospheric phenomenon peculiar to the table-lands of Texas, and far more feared by the traveller. It is that called by Mexicans and styled by the ex-cibolero *El Norte*; by Texans known as "The Norther."

Alike dreaded by both.

Chapter Fifty Seven.
A Cumbersome Captive.

Having made prisoner of the peon, and drawn out of him all he is able to tell, his captors have a difficulty in deciding what to do with him. It will hamper them to take him along. Still they cannot leave him behind; and the young Kentuckian is not cruel enough to kill him, though convinced of his deserving death.

If left to himself, Walt might settle the question quickly. Indignant at the Indian's treason, he has now a new reason to dislike him—as a rival.

With the ex-Ranger this last weighs little. He is sure of having the affections of Conchita. He has her heart, with the promise of her hand, and in his own confiding simplicity has no fear of failure in that sense—not a pang of jealousy. The idea of having for a rival the abject creature at his feet, whom he could crush out of existence with the heel of his horseskin boot, is too ridiculous for him to entertain. He can laugh it to scorn.

Not for that would he now put an end to the man's life, but solely from a sense of outraged justice, with the rough-and-ready retribution to which, as a Texan Ranger, he has been accustomed.

His comrade, less prone to acts of high-handed punishment, restrains him; and the two stand considering what they are to do with their prisoner, now proving so inconvenient.

While still undecided a sound reaches their ears causing them to start and turn pale. It is the trampling of horses; there can be no mistaking it for aught else. And many of them; not two or three, or half a dozen, but a whole troop.

Uraga and his lancers have re-entered the valley! They are riding up to the ranche! What but this can it be? No other party of horsemen could be expected in that place.

And no other thought have the two men hearing the hoof strokes. They are sure it is the soldiers returning.

Instinctively they retreat into the house, without taking their prisoner along with them. Tied, he cannot stir from the spot. If he could it would make little difference now. Their determination is to defend themselves, if need be, to the death; and the hut, with its stout timber walls, is the best place they can think of. It has two doors, opening front and back, both of heavy slabs—split trunks of the palmilla. They have been constructed strongly and to shut close, for the nights are sometimes chilly, and grizzly bears stray around the ranche.

Hastily shutting to the doors and barring them they take stand, each at a window, of which there are also two, both being in front. They are mere apertures in the log wall, and of limited dimensions, but on this account all the better for their purpose, being large enough to serve as loopholes through which they can deliver their fire.

The position is not unfavourable for defence. The cabin stands close to a cliff, with but passage way behind. In front the ground is open, a sort of natural lawn leading down to the lake; only here and there a tree diversifies its smooth surface. Across this anyone approaching must come, whether they have entered the valley from above or below. On each flank the façade of the precipice projects outward, so that the abutting points can be seen from either of the windows; and, as they are both within rifle range, an assailant attempting to turn the cabin so as to enter from the back would be exposed to the enfilading fire of those inside. For security against a surround, the spot could not have been better chosen, and with anything like a fair proportion between besiegers and besieged the former would fail. Under the circumstances, however, there is not likely to be this, and for the two men to attempt defending themselves would seem the certain sealing of their doom.

What chance for them to hold the hut against a force of fifty armed men—soldiers—for if the whole of the troop is returning there is this number? It may be not all have re-entered the valley—only a party sent back to bring on the pilferer, who has been missed upon the march. In that case there will be some chance of withstanding their attack. At all hazards it is to be withstood.

What else can the two men do? Surrender, and become the prisoner of Uraga? Never! They know the relentless ruffian too well, and with too good reason. After their experience of him they need expect no mercy. The man who could leave them buried alive to die a lingering death in the gloomy recesses of a cavern, would be cruel enough not only to kill but torture them. They have to "go under," anyhow, as the prairie hunter expresses it, adding, "Ef we must die let's do so, killin' them as kills us. I'm good for half a score o' them leetle minikin Mexikins, an' I reck'n you, Frank, kin wipe out as many. We'll make it a bloody bizness for them afore the last breath leeves our bodies. Air you all churged an' riddy?"

"I am," is the response of the Kentuckian, in stern, solemn tones, showing that he, as the Texan, has made up his mind to "die killing."

Says the latter, "They'll come out through the trees yonder, where the path runs in. Let's take the fust as shows, an' drop him dead. Gie me the chance, Frank. I'm dyin' to try the doctor's gun."

"By all means do so."

"You fetch the second out o' his saddle, if a second show. That'll gie the others a scare, an' keep 'em back a bit, so's we'll hev good time to get loaded agin."

All this—both speech and action—has not occupied over two minutes of time. The rush inside the cabin, the closing of the doors, and taking stand at the windows, have been done in that haste with which men retreat from a tiger or flee before a prairie fire.

And now, having taken all the precautions possible, the two men wait behind the walls, gun in hand, prepared for the approach of the assailants—themselves so sheltered by the obscurity inside as not to be seen from without.

As yet no enemy has made appearance. No living thing is seen outside, save the lump of copper-coloured humanity prostrate on the sward, beside the bag and swag he has been hindered from taking away. Still the shod hoofs are heard striking against stones, the click sounding clearer and nearer. They inside the *jacal* listen with bated breath, but hearts beating audibly. Hearts filled with anxiety. How could it be else? In another minute they may expect to engage in a life-and-death conflict—for themselves too likely a death one.

Something more than anxiety stirs within them. Something of apprehension, perhaps actual fear. If so, not strange; fear, under the circumstances, excusable, even in the hearts of heroes. Stranger were it otherwise.

Whatever their emotions at the moment, they experience a sudden change, succeeded by a series. The first is surprise. While listening to the hoof strokes of the horses, all at once it appears to them that these are not coming down the valley, but up it from below. Is it a sonorous deception, caused by the sough of the cascade or reverberation from the rocks?

More intently they bend their ears, more carefully note the quarter whence proceeds the sound. Soon to answer the above question, each to himself, in the negative. Unquestionably it comes from below.

They have recovered from this, their first surprise, before a second seizes upon them. Mingling with the horses' tramp they hear voices of men. So much they might expect; but not such voices. For amidst the speeches exchanged arise roars of laughter, not such as could come from the slender gullets of puny Mexicans, nor men of the Spanish race. Nor does it resemble the savage cachinnation of the Comanche Indians. Its rough aspirate, and rude, but hearty, tone could only proceed from Celtic or Anglo-Saxon throats.

While still wondering at the sound ringing in their ears, a sight comes before their eyes which but lessens their surprise by changing it into gladness. Out of the trees at the lower end of the lake a horseman is seen riding—after him a second. Both so unlike Uraga or any of his lancers, so different from what they would deem enemies, that the rifles of Hamersley and the hunter, instead of being aimed to deliver their fire, are dropped, butts to the ground.

Before clearing the skirt of timber, the two horsemen make halt—only for an instant, as if to reconnoitre. They appear surprised at seeing the hut, and not less at sight of a man lying along the ground in front of it. For they are near enough to perceive that he is tied hand and foot, and to note the spilled paraphernalia beside him.

As they are men not easily to be daunted, the tableau, though it somewhat mystifies, does not affright or drive them back. Instead, they advance without the slightest show of fear. And behind the two first showing themselves follow two others, and two more, till fifty have filed out of the timber, and ride across the clear ground, heading direct for the house.

Clad in rough coats of sombre hue, jeans, blanket, and buckskin, not a few of them ragged, with hats of all shapes and styles; carrying rifles in their hands, with revolving pistols and bowie-knives in their belts, there could be no mistaking them for the gaudily-bedizened troop whose horses at sunrise of that same day trampled over the same turf. To the spectators no two cohorts could present a *coup d'oeil* more dissimilar. Though about equal in numbers, the two bodies of men were unlike in everything else—arms, dresses, accoutrements; even their horses having but slight resemblance. The horsemen late upon the spot would seem dwarfs beside those now occupying it, who in comparison might be accounted giants.

Whatever the impression made upon the young prairie merchant by the sight of the newly-arrived troop, its effect upon the ex-Ranger might be compared to a shock of electricity, or the result that succeeds the inspiration of laughing-gas.

Long before the first files have reached the centre of the cleared space he has sprung to the door, pulled the bar back, slammed open the slabs, almost smashing them apart, and rushed out; when outside sending forth a shout that causes every rock to re-echo it to the remotest corner of the valley. It is a grand cry of gladness like a clap of thunder, with its lightning flash bursting forth from the cloud in which in has been pent up.

After it some words spoken more coherently give the key to its jubilant tone.

"Texas Rangers! Ye've jest come in time. Thank the Lord!"

Chapter Fifty Eight.
Old Acquaintances.

Not necessary to say that the horsemen riding up to the ranche are Captain Haynes and his company of Rangers. They have come up the canon guided by Barbato.

Even more than they is the renegade surprised at seeing a house in that solitary spot. It was not there on his last passing through the valley in company with his red-skinned confederates, the Tenawas, which he did some twelve months before. Equally astonished is he to see Walt Wilder spring out from the door, though he hails the sight with a far different feeling. At the first glance he recognises the gigantic individual who so heroically defended the waggon-train, and the other behind—for Hamersley has also come forth—as the second man who retreated along with him. Surely they are the two who were entombed!

The unexpected appearance produces on the Mexican an effect almost comical, though not to him. On the contrary, he stands appalled, under the influence of a dark superstitious terror, his only movement being to repeatedly make the sign of the Cross, all the while muttering Ave Marias.

Under other circumstances his ludicrous behaviour would have elicited laughter from the Rangers—peals of it. But their eyes are not on him, all being turned to the two men who have issued out of the cabin and are coming on towards the spot where they have pulled up.

Several of them have already recognised their old comrade, and in hurried speech communicate the fact to the others.

"Walt Wilder!" are the words that leap from a dozen pairs of lips, while they, pronouncing the name with glances aghast, look as if a spectre had suddenly appeared to them.

An apparition, however, that is welcome; altogether different to the impression it has produced upon their guide.

Meanwhile, Wilder advances to meet them; as he comes on, keeping up a fire of exclamatory phrases, addressed to Hamersley, who is close behind.

"Air this chile awake, or only dreaming? Look thar, Frank! That's Ned Haynes, my old captin'. An' thar's Nat Cully, an' Jim Buckland. Durn it, thar's the hul strenth o' the kumpany."

Walt is now close to their horses' heads, and the rangers, assured it is himself and not his ghost, are still stricken with surprise. Some of them turn towards the Mexican for explanation. They suppose him to have lied in his story about their old comrade having been closed up in a cave, though with what motive they cannot guess. The man's appearance does not make things any clearer. He still stands affrighted, trembling, and repeating his Paternosters. But now in changed tone, for his fear is no longer of the supernatural. Reason reasserting itself, he has given up the idea of disembodied spirits, convinced that the two figures coming forward are real flesh and blood; the same whose blood he assisted in spilling, and whose flesh he lately believed to be decaying in the obscurity of a cave. He stands appalled as ever; no more with unearthly awe, but the fear of an earthly retribution—a terrible one, which he is conscious of having provoked by the cruel crime in which he participated.

Whatever his fears and reflections they are not for the time intruded upon. The rangers, after giving a glance to him, turn to the two men who are now at their horses' heads; and, springing from their saddles, cluster around them with questions upon their tongues and eager expectations in their eyes.

The captain and Cully are the two first who interrogate.

"Can we be sure it's you, Walt?" is the interrogatory put by his old officer. "Is it yourself?"

"Darn me ef I know, cap. Jess now I ain't sure o' anythin', arter what's passed. Specially meetin' you wi' the rest o' the boys. Say, cap, what's fetched ye out hyar?"

"You."

"Me!"

"Yes; we came to bury you."

"Yis, hoss," adds Cully, confirming the captain's statement. "We're on the way to gie burial to your bones, not expecting to find so much flesh on 'em. For that purpiss we've come express all the way from Peecawn Crik. An' as I know'd you had a kindly feelin' for yur ole shootin'-iron, I've brought that along to lay it in the grave aside o' ye."

While speaking, Cully slips out of his saddle and gives his old comrade a true prairie embrace, at the same time handing him his gun.

Neither the words nor the weapon makes things any clearer to Walt, but rather add to their complication. With increased astonishment he cries out,—

"Geehorum! Am I myself, or somebody else? Is't a dream, or not? That's my ole shootin' stick, sartin. I left it over my hoss, arter cuttin' the poor critter's throat. Maybe you've got him too? I shedn't now be surprised at anythin'. Come, Nat; don't stan' shilly-shallyin', but tell me all about it. Whar did ye git the gun?"

"On Peecawn Crik. Thar we kim acrost a party o' Tenawa Kimanch, unner a chief they call Horned Lizart, o' the whom ye've heern. He han't no name now, seein' he's rubbed out, wi' the majority of his band. We did that. The skrimmage tuk place on the crik, whar we foun' them camped. It didn't last long; an' arter 'twere eended, lookin' about among thar bodies, we foun' thar beauty o' a chief wi' this gun upon his parson, tight clutched in the death-grup. Soon's seeing it I know'd 'twar yourn; an' in coorse surspected ye'd had some mischance. Still, the gun kedn't gie us any informashun o' how you'd parted wi' it. By good luck, 'mong the Injuns we'd captered a Mexikin rennygade—thet thing ye see out thar. He war joined in Horned Lizart's lot, an' he'd been wi' 'em some time. So we put a loose larzette roun' his thrapple, an' on the promise o' its bein' tightened, he tolt us the hul story; how they hed attackted an' skuttled a carryvan, an' all 'bout entoomin' you an' a kimrade—this young fellur, I take it—who war wi' ye. Our bizness out hyar war to look up yur bones an' gie 'em a more Christyun kind o' beril. We were goin' for that cave, the rennygade guidin' us. He said he ked take us a near cut up the gully through which we've just come—arter ascendin' one o' the heads o' the Loosyvana Rod. Near cut! Doggone it, he's been righter than I reck'n he thort o'. Stead o' your bones thar's yur body, wi' as much beef on't as ever. Now I've told our story, we want yourn, the which appears to be a darned deal more o' a unexplainable mistry than ourn. So open yur head, ole hoss, and let's have it."

Brief and graphic as is Cully's narrative, it takes Walt still less time to put his former associates in possession of what has happened to himself and Hamersley, whom he introduces to them as the companion of his perilous adventures—the second of the two believed to have been buried alive!

Chapter Fifty Nine.
Mutual Explanations.

The arrival of the Rangers at that particular time is certainly a contingency of the strangest kind. Ten minutes later, and they would have found the jacal deserted; for Hamersley and Wilder had made up their minds to set off, taking the traitor along with them. The Texans would have discovered signs to tell of the place having been recently occupied by a large body of men, and from the tracks of shod horses these skilled trailers would have known the riders were not Indians. Still, they would have made delay around the ranche and encamped in the valley for that night. This had been their intention, their horses being jaded and themselves wearied making their way up the canon. Though but ten miles in a direct line, it was well nigh twenty by the winding of the stream—a good, even difficult, day's journey.

On going out above they would have seen the trail of Uraga's party, and known it to be made by Mexican soldiers. But, though these were their sworn foemen, they might not have been tempted to follow them. The start of several hours, their own animals in poor condition, the likelihood of a larger force of the enemy being near—all this would have weighed with them, and they would have continued on to the cave whither the renegade was guiding them—a direction altogether different. A very singular coincidence, then, their coming up at that exact instant. It seemed the hand of Providence opportunely extended; and in this light Hamersley looked upon it, as also the ex-Ranger.

Briefly as may be they make known to the new-comers all that had transpired, or as much as for the time needs to be told. Then appeal to them for assistance.

By the Texans their cause is instantly espoused—unanimously, without one dissenting voice. On the contrary, all are uttered with an energy and warmth that give Hamersley a world of hope. Here are friends, whose enemies are his own. And they are in strength sufficient to pursue Uraga's troop and destroy it. They may overtake it that very night; if not, on the morrow. And if not then, they will pursue it to the borders of New Mexico—to the banks of the Del Norte itself.

His heart is no more depressed. The chance of rescuing his friends from death and saving his betrothed from dishonour is no longer hopeless. There is now a probability—almost a certainty—of its success. Backed by Wilder, he proposes instant pursuit.

To the Texans the proposal is like an invitation to a ball or frontier fandango. Excitement is the breath of their life, and a fight with Mexicans their joy; a pursuit of these their supremest delight. Such as this, moreover, having for its object not only the defeat of a hated foe, but the recovery of captives, beautiful women, as their old comrade Walt enthusiastically describes them, is the very thing to rouse the Rangers to energetic action, rekindling in their hearts the spirit of frontier chivalry—the same which led them to become Rangers.

Notwithstanding their wild enthusiasm they do not proceed rashly. Haynes, their captain, is an old "Indian fighter," one of the most experienced chiefs of that Texan border warfare, so long continued.

Checking their impatience to pursue at once, he counsels prudence and deliberate action. Cully also recommends this course.

"But why should we lose a moment?" inquires the hot-blooded Kentuckian, chafing at the delay; "they cannot yet be more than ten miles off. We may overtake them before sunset."

"That's just what we mustn't do," rejoins the Ranger chief. "Suppose they get sight of us before we're near? On the naked plain, you say it is, they'd be sure to do that. What then? Their horses, I take it, are fresh, compared with ours. They might gallop off and leave us gazing after them like so many April fools. They'd have time, too, to take their prisoners along with them."

This last speech makes an impression upon all. Even Hamersley no longer offers opposition.

"Let the sun go down," continues the Texan captain; "that's just what we want. Since they're bound due west I reckon we can easily keep on their trail, clear night or dark one. Here's Nat Cully can do that; and if our friend Walt hasn't lost his old skill he can be trusted for the same."

The Ranger and ex-Ranger, both standing by, remain modestly silent.

"Our plan will be," pursues Haynes, "to approach their camp under cover of night, surround, and so make certain of them. They'll have a camp; and these Mexican soldiers are such greenhorns, they're sure to keep big fires burning, if it is only to give them light for their card-playing. The blaze'll guide us to their squatting-ground, wherever they may make it."

The captain's scheme seems so rational that no one opposes it. Walt Wilder in words signifies assent to it, and Hamersley, with, some reluctance, is at length constrained to do the same.

It is resolved to remain two hours longer in the valley, and then start for the upper plain. That will give time to recruit their horses on the nutritious *gramma* grass, as themselves on the game they have killed before entering the canon. This hangs plentifully over the horns of their saddles, in the shape of wild turkeys, haunches of venison, and pieces of bear meat.

The fire on the cabin hearth and those kindled by the soldiers outside are still smouldering. They are quickly replenished, and the abandoned cooking utensils once more called into use. But pointed saplings, and the iron ramrods of their rifles—the Ranger's ordinary spit—are in greater demand, and broiling is the style of *cuisine* most resorted to.

The turkeys are plucked and singed, the venison and bear meat cut into collops, and soon two score pieces are sputtering in the flames of half-a-dozen bivouac fires, while the horses, unbridled, are led out upon their lariats, and given to the grass.

Chapter Sixty.
Cross-Questioning.

While the Rangers are preparing for their Homeric repast, a group gathered in front of the jacal is occupied with an affair altogether different.

The individuals most conspicuous in it are the Texan captain, the guide Cully, Walt Wilder, and the young Kentuckian, though several besides take part in the conference.

Two others are concerned in it, though not forming figures in the group. They are some paces apart, lying on the grass, both bound. These are the traitor Manuel and the renegade Barbato.

Both Indian and Mexican appear terribly cowed and crestfallen, for both feel themselves in what Cully or Walt Wilder would call a "bad fix." They are, in truth, in a dangerous predicament; for, now that Walt and the Kentuckian have turned up alive, what with the story they have to tell, added to that already known to the Rangers—comparing notes between the two parties—new light is let in, floods of it, falling upon spots hitherto dark, and clearing up points confused and obscure. The two culprits are again cross-examined, and, with pistols held to their heads, forced to still further confession.

The peon repeats what he has already told, without adding much, not having much to add. With the renegade it is different. He has kept much back concerning the part played by Uraga and his lieutenant in the affair of the destroyed waggon train.

But with Hamersley, who speaks his own native tongue, now cross-questioning him, and Walt Wilder to extract his testimony by the persuasive influence of a knife-blade glistening in his eyes, he goes further, and admits the unnatural confederation that existed between the white and red robbers—the Mexican colonel and Comanche chief. In short, to save his life, he makes a much cleaner breast of it than before, this time only keeping back his own special guiltiness in being their willing go-between.

While he is repeating his confession, all the other Rangers gather around the group to listen to him. They stand silent, with bated breath and brows contracted.

When at length they become possessed of the tale in all its diabolical atrocity, all its completeness, their anger, already excited, become almost ungovernable; and it is as much as their captain can do to restrain them from at once starting in pursuit. Some fling their spits in the fire with the meat upon them still untouched; others drop the pieces roasted and partly eaten; most demanding to be led on.

The counsels of the more prudent prevail; and again tranquillised, they recover the morsels of meat and continue their repast.

Not long, till they have reason to regret the delay and deem the prudence misplaced. Though this arises not from any mistake on the part of their counsellors, but from a circumstance entirely accidental.

While they are still in the midst of their meal, the sky, all day long of cerulean clearness, becomes suddenly clouded. Not as this term is understood in the ordinary sense, but absolutely black, as if the sun were instantly eclipsed, or had dropped altogether out of the firmament. Scarce ten minutes after its commencement the obscurity has reached completeness— that of a total solar eclipse or as in a starless night.

Though troubled at the change, none of the Rangers are dismayed by it, or even surprised. The old prairie men are the least astonished, since they know what it means. At the first portentous sign Cully is heard crying out,—

"A hurricane!—A norther!"

Wat Wilder has observed it at the same time, and confirms the prognostic. This is before any of the others have noticed aught peculiar in the aspect of the sky, and when there is just the selvedge of a cloud seen above the cliff.

All Texans understand the significance of the word "norther"—a storm or tornado, usually preceded by a hot, stifling atmosphere, with drifting dust, accompanied by sheet or forked lightning and claps of terrific thunder, followed by wind and rain, sometimes hail or sleet, as if the sluices of heaven were drawn open, ending in a continued blast of more regular direction, but chill as though coming direct from the Arctic regions.

In less than ten minutes after its first sign, the tempest is around them. Down into the valley pours the dust, swept from the surface of the upper plain, along with it the leaves and stalks of the wild wormwood, with other weeds of the desert. Simultaneously the wind, at first in low sighs, like the sound of a distant sea; then roaring against the rocks, and swooping down among the trees, whose branches go crashing before its blast. Then succeed lightning, thunder, and rain—the last falling, not in drops, but in sheets, as if spilled from a spout.

For shelter the Rangers rush inside the ranche, leaving their horses to take care of themselves. The latter stand cowering under the trees, neighing with affright—the mules among them giving vent to their plaintive hinney. There are dogs, too, that howl and bark, with other sounds that come from farther off—from the wild denizens of the wilderness; cries of the cougar in contralto, wolf-barkings in mezzo-soprano, screaming of eagles in shrill treble, snorting of bears in basso, and hooting of scared owls in lugubrious tone, to be likened only to the wailing of agonised spirits in Purgatory.

Crowded within the hut, so thickly as to have scarce standing room, the Rangers wait for the calming of the tempest. They submit with greater resignation, knowing it will not long continue. It is far from being their first experience of a "norther."

The only thought that troubles them is the delay—being hindered from setting forth on the pursuit. True, the party to be pursued will be stayed by the same obstruction. The soldiers will have to halt during the continuance of the storm, so that the distance between will remain the same.

But then their tracks will be obliterated—every vestige of them. The wind, the rain, and dust will do this. How is their trail to be taken up? "That will be easy enough," says one, whose self-esteem is greater than his prairie experience. He adds: "As they're going due west, we can't make any mistake by steering the same way."

"How little he knows about it!" is the muttered remark exchanged between Wilder and Cully. For they know that the deflection of a single point upon the prairies—above all, upon the Staked Plain—will leave the traveller, like a ship at sea without chart or compass, to steer by guesswork, or go drifting at sheer chance.

To most, the consoling thought is that the Mexicans will halt near, and stay till the storm is over. They have some baggage—a tent or two, with other camp equipage. This is learnt from the Indian; and Hamersley, as also Wilder, have themselves made note of it.

To the returning soldiers there can be no great reason for haste, and they will not likely resume their march till the sky is quite clear. Therefore they will gain nothing in distance.

Satisfied by such assurance given by the sager ones of the party, the Rangers remain inside the hut, on the roof of which the rain dashes down, without experiencing any keen pangs of impatience. Some of them even jest—their jokes having allusion to the close quarters in which they are packed, and other like trifles incidental to the situation.

Walt Wilder for a while gives way to this humour. Whatever may be the danger of Don Valerian and the others, he does not believe his sweetheart much exposed. The little brown-skinned damsel is not in the proscribed list; and the ex-Ranger, strong in the confidence of having her heart, with the promise of her hand, has less reason to be apprehensive about the consequences. Besides, he is now in the midst of his former associates, and the exchange of new histories and old reminiscences is sufficient to fill up the time, and keep him from yielding to impatient longing.

Of all Hamersley alone is unhappy. Despite the assurances spoken, the hopes felt, there is yet apprehension for the future. The position, however, is endurable, and only passes this point as a thought comes into his mind—a memory that flashes across his brain, as if a bullet had struck him between the temples.

It causes him to spring suddenly to his feet, for he has been seated, at the same time wringing from him a cry of peculiar signification.

"What is it, Mr Hamersley?" asks the Ranger Captain, who is close by his side.

"My God!" exclaims the Kentuckian. "I'd forgotten. We must be off at once, or we shall be too late—too late!"

Saying this, he makes a dash for the door, hurtling his way through the crowd close standing between.

The Rangers regard him with glances of astonishment, and doubts about his sanity. Some of them actually think he has gone mad!

One alone understands him—Walt Wilder; though he, too, seems demented. With like incoherent speech and frantic gesture, he follows Hamersley to the door.

Both rush outside; as they do so calling back, "Come on! come on!"

Chapter Sixty One.
Into the Storm.

Lightning flashes, thunder rolls, wind bellows, and rain pours down in sheets, as if from sluices; for the storm is still raging as furiously as ever. Into it have rushed the two, regardless of all.

The Texans are astounded—for a time some of them still believing both men mad. But soon it is seen they are acting with method, making straight for the horses, while shouting and gesticulating for the Rangers to come after.

These do not need either the shouts or signs to be repeated. Walt's old comrades know he must have reason, and, disregarding the tempest, they strike out after. Their example is electric, and in ten seconds the jacal is empty.

In ten more they are among their horses, drawing in the trail-ropes and bridling them.

Before they can get into their saddles they are made aware of what it is all about.

Hamersley and Walt, already mounted and waiting, make known to the Ranger captain the cause of their hurried action, apparently so eccentric. A few words suffice.

"The way out," says the Kentuckian, "is up yonder ravine, along the bed of the stream that runs through. When it rains as it's doing now, then the water suddenly rises and fills up the channel, leaving no room, no road. If we don't get out quick we may be kept here for days."

"Yis, boys!" adds Wilder, "we've got to climb the stairs right smart, rain or shine, storm or no storm. Hyar's one off for the upper storey, fast as his critter kin carry him."

While speaking, he jobs his heels against the ribs of his horse—for he is now mounted on one, as also Hamersley—supernumeraries of the Texan troop. Then, dashing off, with the Kentuckian by his side, they are soon under the trees and out of sight. Not of the Rangers, who, themselves now in the saddle, spur after in straggling line, riding at top speed.

Once again the place is deserted, for, despite their precipitate leave-taking, the Texans have carried the prisoners along with them. No living thing remains by the abandoned dwelling. The only sign of human occupation is the smoke that ascends through its kitchen chimney, and from the camp fires outside, these gradually getting extinguished by the downpour.

Still the lightning flashes, the thunder rolls, the wind bellows, and the rain pours down as from dishes. But not to deter the Texans, who, drenched to their shirts, continue to ride rapidly on up the valley road. There is in reality no road, only a trail made by wild animals, occasionally trodden by the domesticated ones belonging to Colonel Miranda; later still by Uraga's lancers.

Soaked by the rain, it has become a bed of mud, into which the horses of the Rangers sink to their saddle girths, greatly impeding their progress. Whip and spur as they may, they make but slow time. The animals baulk, plunge, stumble, some going headforemost into the mire, others striking their shoulders against the thick-standing trees, doing damage to themselves and their riders. For with the norther still clouding the sky, it is almost dark as night.

Other dangers assail them from falling trees. Some go down bodily before the blast, while from others great branches are broken off by the wind, and strike crashing across the path. One comes near crushing half a dozen horsemen under its broad, spreading avalanche of boughs.

Notwithstanding all, they struggle on fearlessly, and fast as they can, Hamersley and Wilder at their head, Haynes, Cully, and the best mounted of the troop close following. Walt and the Kentuckian well know the way. Otherwise, in the buffeting of that terrible storm, they might fail to find it.

They succeed in keeping it, on to the head of the valley, where the stream comes in between the cliffs. A tiny runlet as they last looked upon it—a mere brook, pellucid and sparkling as the sand on its bed. Now it is a torrent, deep, red and roaring; only white on its surface, where the froth sweeps on, clouting the cliffs on each side. Against these it has risen quite six feet, and still creeps upward. It has filled the channel from side to side, leaving not an inch of roadway between the river and rock.

To wade it would be impossible; to attempt swimming it destruction. The staunchest steed could not stem its surges. Even the huge river-horse of Africa would be swept off his feet and tossed to the surface like one of its froth-flakes.

Arriving on its edge, Hamersley sees this at a glance. As he checks up his horse, the exclamation that leaps from his lips more resembles the anguished cry of a man struggling in the torrent than one seated safely in a saddle on its bank.

After it, he gives utterance to two words in sad despairing tone, twice repeated,—

"Too late—too late!"

Again repeated by Walt Wilder, and twenty times again by a score of the Rangers who have ridden up, and reined their horses crowdingly behind.

There is no response save echo from the rocks, scarce audible through the hoarse sough of the swollen surging stream, that rolls relentlessly by, seeming to say, as in scorn, "Ford me! swim across me if you can!"

Chapter Sixty Two.
A Short Shrift.

Difficult—indeed, impossible—for pen to describe the scene consequent upon the arrival of the Rangers by the banks of the swollen stream, and finding it unfordable.

Imagine a man who has secured passage by a ship bound for some far-off foreign land, and delayed by some trifling affair, comes upon the pier to see the hawser cast off, the plank drawn ashore, the sails spread, himself left hopelessly behind!

His chagrin might be equal to that felt by the Texans, but slight compared with what harrows the hearts of Hamersley and Walt Wilder. To symbolise theirs, it must be a man missing his ship homeward bound, with sweetheart, wife, child awaiting him at the end of the voyage, and in a port from which vessels take departure but "few and far between."

These two, better than any of the Texans, understand the obstruction that has arisen, in the same proportion as they are aggrieved by it. Too well do they comprehend its fatal import. Not hours, but whole days, may elapse before the flood subsides, the stream can be forded, the ravine ascended, and the pursuit continued.

Hours—days! A single day—an hour—may seal the fate of those dear to them. The hearts of both are sad, their bosoms racked with anguish, as they sit in their saddles with eyes bent on the turbid stream, which cruelly forbids fording it.

In different degree and from a different cause the Texans also suffer. Some only disappointment, but others real chagrin. These last men, whose lives have been spent fighting their Mexican foemen, hating them from the bottom of their hearts. They are those who knew the unfortunate Fanning and the lamented Bowie, who gave his name to their knives; some of themselves having escaped from the red massacre of Goliad and the savage butchery of the Alamo.

Ever since they have been practising the *lex talionis*—seeking retaliation, and oft-times finding it. Perhaps too often wreaking their vengeance on victims that might be innocent. Now that guilty ones—real Mexican soldiers in uniform, such as ruthlessly speared and shot down their countrymen at Goliad and San Antonio—now that a whole troop of these have but the hour before been within reach—almost striking distance—it is afflicting, maddening, to think they may escape.

And the more reflecting on the reason, so slight and accidental—a shower of rain swelling a tiny stream. For all this, staying their pursuit as effectively as if a sea of fire separated them from the foe, so despised and detested.

The lightning still flashes, the thunder rolls, the wind bellows, and the rain pours down.

No use staying any longer by the side of the swollen stream, to be tantalised by its rapid, rushing current, and mocked by its foam-flakes dancing merrily along.

Rather return to the forsaken ranche, and avail themselves of such shelter as it may afford.

In short, there seems no alternative; and, yielding to the necessity, they rein round, and commence the backward march, every eye glancing gloomily, every brow overcast.

They are all disappointed, most of them surly as bears that had been shot in the head, and have scratched the place to a sore. They are just in the humour to kill anyone, or anything, that should chance in their way.

But there is no one, and nothing; and, in the absence of an object to spend their spite upon, some counsel wreaking it on their captives—the traitor and renegade.

Never during life were these two men nearer their end. To all appearance, in ten minutes more both will be dangling at the end of a rope suspended from a limb of a tree.

They are saved by a circumstance for them at least lucky, if unfortunate for some others.

Just as a half-score of the Rangers have clumped together under a spreading pecan-tree, intending to hang them upon one of its branches, a horse is heard to neigh. Not one of their own, but an animal some way off the track, amid the trees. The hail is at once responded to by the steeds they are bestriding; and is promptly re-answered, not by one horse, but three neighing simultaneously.

A strange thing this, that calls for explanation. What horses can be there, save their own? And none of the Rangers have ridden in the direction whence the "whighering" proceeds.

A dozen of them do so now; before they have gone far, finding three horses standing under the shadow of a large live oak, with three men mounted on their backs, who endeavour to keep concealed behind its broad buttressed trunk.

In vain. Guided by the repeated neighing and continuous tramp of their horses, the Rangers ride up, close around, and capture them.

Led out into the light, the Texans see before them three men in soldier garb—the uniform of Mexican lancers. It is the corporal squad sent back by Uraga to bring on the truant traitor.

Of their errand the Rangers know nought, and nothing care. Enough that three of their hated foemen are in their hands, their hostility intensified by the events of the hour.

No more fuel is needed to fire them up. Their vengeance demands a victim, and three have offered ready to hand.

As they ride back to the road, they leave behind them a tableau, telling of a spectacle just passed—one having a frightful finale. From a large limb of the live oak, extending horizontally, hang three men, the Mexican lancers. They are suspended by the neck, dangling, dead!

Chapter Sixty Three.
A Split Trail.

The Texans ride on to the ranche. They still chafe at being thwarted of a vengeance; by every man of them keenly felt, after learning the criminality of the Lancer Colonel. Such unheard of atrocity could not help kindling within their breasts indignation of the deepest kind.

The three soldiers strung up to the trees have been its victims.

But this episode, instead of appeasing the executioners, has only roused them, as tigers who have tasted blood hindered from banqueting on flesh.

They quite comprehend the position in which the norther has placed them. On the way Hamersley and Wilder, most discomforted of all, have made them aware of it. The swollen stream will prevent egress from the valley till it subsides.

There is no outlet save above and below, and both these are now effectually closed, shutting them up as in a strong-walled prison. On each side the precipice is unscalable. Even if men might ascend, horses could not be taken along; and on such a chase it would be hopeless for them to set out afoot.

But men could not go up the cliff.

"A cat kedn't climb it," says Walt, who during his sojourn in the valley has explored every inch of it. "We've got to stay hyar till the flood falls. I reckon no one kin be sorrier to say so than this chile. But thar's no help for 't."

"Till the flood falls? When will that be?"

No one can answer this, not even Wilder himself. And with clouded brows, sullen, dispirited, they return to the jacal.

Two days they stay there, chafing with angry impatience. In their anger they are ready for the most perilous enterprise. But, although bitterly cursing the sinister chance that hinders pursuit, deeming each hour a day, they can do nought save wait till the swollen stream subsides.

They watch it with eager solicitude, constantly going to the bank to examine it, as the captain of a ship consults his weather-glass to take steps for the safety of his vessel. All the time one or another is riding to, or returning from, the head of the valley, to bring back report of how the subsidence progresses.

And long ere the stream has returned to its regular channel, they plunge their horses into it, breasting a current that almost sweeps them off their feet. But the Texan horses are strong, as their riders are skilful; the obstacle is surmounted, and the Rangers at length escape from their prolonged and irksome imprisonment.

It is mid-day, as filing up the pass, they reach the higher level of the Llano. Not many moments do they remain there; only long enough for the rear files to get out of the gorge, when those in front move forward across the plain, guided by the two best trackers in Texas, Nat Cully and Walt Wilder.

At first there is no following of a trail, since there is none visible. Wind, rain, and drifted dust have obliterated every mark made by the returning soldiers. Not a sign is left to show the pursuers the path Uraga's troop has taken.

They know it should be westward, and strike out without waiting to look for tracks.

For the first ten or twelve miles they ride at a rapid rate, often going in a gallop. Their horses, rested and fresh, enable them to do so. They are only stayed in their pace by the necessity of keeping a straight course—not so easy upon a treeless plain, when the sun is not visible in the sky. Unluckily for them, the day is cloudy, which renders it more difficult. Still, with the twin buttes behind—so long as these are in sight they keep their course with certainty; then, as their summits sink below the level of the plain, another landmark looms up ahead, well known by Walt Wilder and Hamersley. It is the black-jack grove where, two days before, they made their midday meal.

The Rangers ride towards it, with the intention also to make a short halt there and snatch a scrap from their haversacks.

When upon its edge, before entering among the trees, they see that which decides them to stay even less time than intended—the hoof-prints of half a hundred horses!

Going inside the copse, they observe other signs that speak of an encampment. Reading these with care, they can tell that it has not long been broken up. The ashes of the bivouac fires are scarce cold, while the hoof-marks of the horses show fresh on the desert dust, for the time converted into mud. Wilder and Cully declare that but one day can have passed since the lancers parted from the spot; for there is no question as to who have been bivouacking among the black-jacks.

A day—only a day! It will take full five before the soldiers can cross the Sierras and enter the valley of the Del Norte. There may still be a chance of overtaking them. All the likelier, since, cumbered with their captives, and not knowing they are pursued, they may be proceeding at a leisurely pace.

Cheered by this hope, and freshly stimulated, the Texans do not even dismount, but, spurring forth upon the plain, again ride rapidly on, munching a mouthful as they go.

They are no longer delayed by any doubt as to course. The trail of the lancer troop is now easily discernible, made since the storm passed over. Any one of the Rangers could follow it in a fast gallop.

At this pace they all go, only at intervals drawing in to a walk, to breathe their blown steeds for a fresh spurt.

Even after night has descended they continue on, a clear moonlight enabling them to lift the trail.

As next morning's sun breaks over the Llano Estacado they descend its western slope into the valley of the Rio Pecos.

Traversing its bottom, of no great breadth, they reach the crossing of the old Spanish trail, from Santa Fé to San Antonio de Bejar.

Fording the stream, on its western bank, they discover signs which cause them to come to a halt, for some time perplexing them. Nothing more than the tracks of the troop they have been all the while pursuing, which entered the river on its left side. Now on its right they are seen the same, up the sloping causeway of the bank. But on reaching the bottom, a little aback from the water's edge, the trail splits into two distinct ramifications, one continuing westward towards the Sierras, the other turning north along the stream. The first shows the hoof-marks of nigh forty horses, the second only ten or twelve.

Unquestionably the Mexican colonel had here divided his troop, the main body proceeding due west, the detachment striking up stream.

The route taken by this last would be the old Spanish road for Santa Fé, the first party proceeding on to Albuquerque.

For a time the pursuing Texans are at fault, as foxhounds by a fence, over which Reynard has doubled back to mislead them. They have halted at the bifurcation of the trails, and sit in their saddles, considering which of the two they should take.

Not all remain mounted. Cully and Wilder have flung themselves to the ground, and, in bent attitudes, with eyes close to the surface, are scanning the hoof-marks of the Mexican horses.

The others debate which of the two troops they ought to take after, or whether they should themselves separate and pursue both. This course is opposed by a majority, and it is at length almost decided to continue on after the main body, which, naturally enough, they suppose to have Uraga at its head, with the captives in keeping.

In the midst of their deliberations a shout calls the attention of all, concentrating it on Walt Wilder. For it is he who has uttered the cry. The ex-Ranger is seen upon his knees, his great body bent forward, with his chin almost touching the ground. His eyes are upon the hoof-marks of a horse—one of those that went off with the smaller detachment along the river's bank.

That he has identified the track is evident from the speech succeeding his ejaculation.

"Yur hoss, Hamersley! Hyar's his futprint, sure. An', as he's rud by Urager, the scoundrel's goed this way to a sartinty. Eqwally sartin, he's tuk the captives along wi' him."

On hearing their old comrade declare his prognosis, the Rangers wheel their horses and ride towards him.

Before reaching the spot where he is still prospecting, they see him give a sudden spring forward, like a frog leaping over meadow sward, then pause again, scrutinising a track.

A second examination, similar to the first, tells of another discovery. In like manner explained, by his speech close following, —

"An' hyar's the track o' the mare—the yeller mustang as war rid by the saynorita. An', durn me, that's the hoof-mark o' the mule as carried my Concheter. Capting Haynes! Kumrades! No use botherin' 'bout hyar any longer. Them we want to kum up wi' are goed north 'long this trail as leads by the river bank."

Not another word is needed. The Rangers, keen of apprehension and quick to arrive at conclusions, at once perceive the justness of those come to by their old comrade. They make no opposition to his proposal to proceed after the smaller party.

Instead, all signify assent; and in ten seconds after they are strung out into a long line, going at a gallop, their horses' heads turned northward up the right bank of the Rio Pecos.

Chapter Sixty Four.
A Sylvan Scene.

Perhaps no river on all the North American continent is marked with interest more romantic than that which attaches to the Rio Grande of Mexico. On its banks has been enacted many a tragic scene—many an episode of Indian and border war—from the day when the companions of Cortez first unfurled Spain's *pabellon* till the Lone Star flag of Texas, and later still the banner of the Stars and Stripes, became mirrored on its waves.

Heading in the far-famed "parks" of the Rocky Mountains, under the name of Rio Bravo del Norté, it runs in a due southerly direction between the two main ranges of the Mexican "Sierre Madre;" then, breaking through the Eastern Cordillera, it bends abruptly, continuing on in a south-easterly course till it espouses ocean in the great Mexican Gulf.

Only its lower portion is known as the "Rio Grande;" above it is the "Bravo del Norté."

The Pecos is its principal tributary, which, after running through several degrees of latitude parallel to the main stream, at length unites with it below the great bend.

In many respects the Pecos is itself a peculiar river. For many hundred miles it courses through a wilderness rarely traversed by man, more rarely by men claiming to be civilised. Its banks are only trodden by the savage, and by him but when going to or returning from a raid. For this turbid stream is a true river of the desert, having on its left side the sterile tract of the Llano Estacado, on its right dry table plains that lead up to the Sierras, forming the "divide" between its waters and those of the Bravo del Norte.

On the side of the Staked Plain the Pecos receives but few affluents, and these of insignificant character. From the Sierras, however, several streams run into it through channels deeply cut into the plain, their beds being often hundreds of feet below its level. While the plateau above is often arid and treeless, the bottom lands of these tributaries show a rich luxuriant vegetation, here and there expanding into park-like meadows, with groves and copses interspersed.

On the edge of one of these affluents, known as the *Arroyo Alamo* (Anglice "Cottonwood Creek"), two tents are seen standing—one a square marquee, the other a "single pole," of the ordinary conical shape.

Near by a half score of soldiers are grouped around a bivouac fire, some broiling bits of meat on sapling spits, others smoking corn-husk cigarettes, all gaily chatting. One is some fifty paces apart, under a spreading tree, keeping guard over two prisoners, who, with legs lashed and hands pinioned, lie prostrate upon the ground.

As the soldiers are in the uniform of Mexican lancers, it is needless to say they belong to the troop of Colonel Uraga. Superfluous to add that the two prisoners under the tree are Don Valerian Miranda and the doctor.

Uraga himself is not visible, nor his adjutant, Roblez. They are inside the conical hut, the square one being occupied by Adela and her maid.

After crossing the Pecos, Uraga separated his troop into two parties. For some time he has sent the main body, under command of his alferez, direct to Albuquerque, himself and the adjutant turning north with the captives and a few files as escort and guard. Having kept along the bank of the Pecos till reaching the Alamo, he turned up the creek, and is now *en bivouac* in its bottom, some ten miles above the confluence of the streams.

A pretty spot has he selected for the site of his encampment. A verdant mead, dotted with groves of leafy *alamo* trees, that reflect their shadows upon crystal runlets silently coursing beneath, suddenly flashing into the open light like a band of silver lace as it bisects a glade green with *gramma* grass. A landscape not all woodland or meadow, but having also a mountain aspect, for the basaltic cliffs that on both sides bound the valley bottom rise hundreds of feet high, standing scarce two hundred yards apart, grimly frowning at each other, like giant warriors about to begin battle, while the tall stems of the *pitahaya* projecting above might be likened to poised spears.

It is a scene at once soft and sublime—an Eden of angels beset by a serried phalanx of fiends; below, sweetly smiling; above, darkly frowning and weirdly picturesque. A wilderness, with all its charms, uninhabited; no house in sight; no domestic hearth or chimney towering over it; no smoke, save that curling aloft from the fire lately kindled in the soldiers' camp. Beasts and birds are its only habitual denizens; its groves the chosen perching place of sweet songsters; its openings the range of the prong-horn antelope and black-tailed deer; while soaring above, or seated on prominent points of the precipice, may be seen the *caracara*, the buzzard, and bald-headed eagle.

Uraga has pitched his tents in an open glade of about ten acres in superficial extent, and nearly circular in shape, lying within the embrace of an umbrageous wood, the trees being mostly cotton woods of large dimensions. Through its midst the streamlet meanders above, issuing out of the timber, and below again entering it.

On one side the bluffs are visible, rising darkly above the tree-tops, and in the concavity underneath stand the tents, close to the timber edge, though a hundred paces apart from each other. The troop horses, secured by their trail-ropes, are browsing by the bank of the stream; and above, perched upon the summit of the cliff, a flock of black vultures sun themselves with out-spread wings, now and then uttering an ominous croak as they crane their necks to scan what is passing underneath.

Had Uraga been influenced by a sense of sylvan beauty, he could not have chosen a spot more suitable for his camping-place.

Scenic effect has nought to do with his halting there. On the contrary, he has turned up the Alamo, and is bivouacking on its bank, for a purpose so atrocious that no one would give credit to it unacquainted with the military life of Mexico in the days of the Dictator Don Antonio Lopez de Santa Anna. This purpose is declared in a dialogue between the lancer colonel and his lieutenant, occurring inside the conical tent shortly after its being set up.

But before shadowing the bright scene we have painted by thoughts of the dark scheme so disclosed, let us seek society of a gentler kind. We shall find it in the marquee set apart for Adela Miranda and her maid.

It scarce needs to say that a change is observable in the appearance of the lady. Her dress is travel-stained, bedraggled by dust and rain; her hair, escaped from its coif, hangs dishevelled; her cheeks show the lily where but roses have hitherto bloomed. She is sad, drooping, despondent.

The Indian damsel seems to suffer less from her captivity, having less to afflict her—no dread of that terrible calamity which, like an incubus, broods upon the mind of her mistress.

In the conversation passing between them Conchita is the comforter.

"Don't grieve so, senorita," she says, "I'm sure it will be all right yet. Something whispers me it will. It may be the good Virgin—bless her! I heard one of the soldiers say they're taking us to Santa Fé, and that Don Valerian will be tried by a court martial—I think that's what he called it. Well, what of it? You know well he hasn't done anything for which they can condemn him to death—unless they downright assassinate him. They dare not do that, tyrants as they are."

At the words "assassinate him," the young lady gives a start. It is just that which is making her so sad. Too well she knows the man into whose hands they have unfortunately fallen. She remembers his design, once nigh succeeding, only frustrated by that hurried flight from their home. Is it likely the fiend will be contented to take her brother back and trust to the decision of a legal tribunal, civil or military? She cannot believe it; but shudders as she reflects upon what is before them.

"Besides," pursues Conchita, in her consolatory strain, "your gallant Francisco and my big, brave Gualtero have gone before us. They'll be in Albuquerque when we get there, and will be sure to hear of our arrival. Trust them for doing something to save Don Valerian."

"No, no," despondingly answers Adela, "they can do nothing for my brother. That is beyond their power, even if he should ever reach there. I fear he never will—perhaps, none of us."

"*Santissima*! What do you mean, senorita? Surely these men will not murder us on the way?"

"They are capable of doing that—anything. Ah! Conchita, you do not know them. I am in as much danger as my brother, for I shall choose death rather than—"

She forbears speaking the word that would explain her terrible apprehension. Without waiting for it, Conchita rejoins—

"If they kill you, they may do the same with me. Dear *duena*, I'm ready to die with you."

The *duena*, deeply affected by this proffer of devotion, flings her white arms around the neck of her brown-skinned maid, and imprints upon her brow a kiss, speaking heartfelt gratitude.

For a time the two remain enlocked in each other's arms, murmuring words of mutual consolation. Love levels all ranks, but not more than misery—perhaps not so much. In the hour of despair there is no difference between prince and peasant, between the high-born dame and the lowly damsel accustomed to serve her caprices and wait upon her wishes.

Adela Miranda has in her veins the purest *sangre azul* of Andalusia. Her ancestors came to New Spain among the proud *conquistadores*; while those of Conchita, at least on the mother's side, were of the race conquered, outraged, and humiliated.

No thought of ancestral hostility, no pride of high lineage on one side, or shame of low birth on the other, as the two girls stand inside the tent with arms entwined, endeavouring to cheer one another.

Under the dread of a common danger, the white *doncella* and the dusky damsel forget the difference in the colour of their skins; and for the first time feel themselves sisters in the true sisterhood of humanity.

Chapter Sixty Five.
Two Scoundrels in Council.

Simultaneous with the scene in the square marquee a dialogue is taking place within the conical tent, the speakers being Uraga and Roblez.

The colonel is reclining on a bearskin, spread over the thick sward of grass, which forms a soft couch underneath. The lieutenant sits on a camp-stool beside.

Both are smoking; while from a canteen and two cups, resting upon the top of a bullock trunk, comes a perfume which tells they have also been indulging in a drink.

Uraga is thoughtful and silent; Roblez patiently waiting for him to speak. The adjutant has but late entered the tent and delivered his report about the pitching of the camp, the arrangements of which he has been superintending.

"You've stationed a look-out as I directed?" the Colonel inquires, after a long silence.

"I have."

"I hope you've placed him so that he can command a good view of the valley below?"

"He's on a spur of the cliff, and can see full five miles down stream. May I ask, colonel, whom we may expect to come that way? Not pursuers, I take it?"

Uraga does not make immediate reply. There is evidently something in his thoughts he hesitates to communicate to his subordinate. The answer he at length vouchsafes is evasive.

"Whom may we expect? You forget those fellows left behind on the Llano. The corporal and two men, whether they've found the Indian or not, will make all haste after us. Fear of falling in with some party of Apaches will stimulate their speed. I wonder why they haven't got up long ago. Something strange about that."

"No doubt the storm has detained them."

"Do you think it's been that, ayadante?"

"I can't think of anything else, colonel. Anyhow, they wouldn't be likely to come here, but go on straight to Albuquerque. The corporal is a skilled *rastrero*, and, reaching the place where the troop separated, he'd be pretty sure to follow the trail of the larger party. All the more from his knowing it the safer one, so far as savages are concerned."

"I hope he has done so. We don't want him here."

Saying this, Uraga resumes his thoughtful attitude and silently puffs away at his cigar, apparently watching the smoke as it curls up and spreads against the canvas.

Roblez, who appeared anxious about something, after a time again essays speech. He puts the interrogatory,—

"How long are we to remain here?"

"That will depend on—"

Uraga does not complete the response—at least not till after taking several whiffs at his weed.

"On what?" asks the impatient subordinate.

"Many matters—circumstances, events, coincidences."

"May I know what they are. You promised to tell me, colonel."

"I did—in time. It has not yet come. One thing I may now make known. When we leave this camping-place we shall take no prisoners along with us."

"You intend setting them free?" The question is asked, not with any idea that this is Uraga's design, but to draw out the explanation.

"Free of all cares in this world, whatever may be their troubles in the next."

"They are to die, then?"

"They are to die."

"You mean only the men—Don Valerian and the doctor?"

"What a ruffian you are, Roblez! By your question you must take me for the same—a sanguinary savage. I'm not so bloodthirsty as to think of killing women, much less one so sweet as the Senorita Miranda. Men don't desire the deaths of their own wives—at least, not till after the honeymoon. The Dona Adela is to be mine—shall, and must!"

"I am aware that is your wish, and as things stand you have a fair chance of obtaining it. You can have her without spilling her brother's blood. Excuse me, colonel, but I can see no reason why he should not be let live, at least till we take him to Santa Fé, There a prison will hold him safe, and a court-martial can be called, which, with the spirit just now abroad, will condemn him in one day, and execute him on the morning of the next. That would keep you clear from all suspicion of over-haste, which may attach to you if you take the thing into your own hands here."

"Bah! you talk like a child, teniente! The security of a prison in New Mexico, or the chances of a prisoner being condemned, far less executed, are things merely imaginary. All the more now that there's some probability of a change in the political sky. Clouds have shown themselves on the horizon at the capital—talk that our good friend Gameleg is going out again. Before the storm comes I for one intend making myself secure. As the husband of Adela Miranda, owning all that belongs to her brother, and which will be hers after his death, I shall care but little who presides in the Halls of the Moctezumas. Priest-party or patriots, 'twill be all the same to me."

"Why not become her husband and let the brother live?"

"Why? Because that cannot be."

"I don't see any reason against it. Both are in your power. You may easily make terms."

Uraga, impressed with the observation, remains for a while silent, considering. To aid reflection he smokes harder than ever.

Resuming speech, he asks,—

"How do you counsel?"

"As I've said, colonel. Make terms with Miranda. Knowing his life to be in your hands, he will listen to reason. Extract from him a promise—an oath, if need be—that he will consent to his sister becoming your wife; at the same time settling a portion of his property on the newly married pair. It's big enough to afford all of you a handsome income. That's what I would do."

"He might promise you here. What security against breaking his word when we get to Albuquerque?"

"No need waiting for Albuquerque to give him the chance. You seem to forget that there are churches between, and priests not over-scrupulous. For instance, the cure of Anton Chico, and his reverence who saves souls in the pueblita of La Mora. Either one will make man and wife of you and the Senorita Adela without asking question beyond whether you can produce coin sufficient to pay the marriage fees. Disbursing freely, you may ensure the ceremonial in spite of all protest, if any should arise. There can be none."

Uraga lights a fresh cigar, and continues smoking, reflecting. The counsel of his subaltern has made an impression on him—put the thing in a new light. After all, what harm in letting Miranda live? Enough of revenge compelling him to consent that his sister shall be the wife of one she has scornfully rejected. If he refuse—if both do so—what then?

The interrogatory is addressed to Roblez.

"Your position," answers the adjutant, "will be no worse than now. You can still carry out the design you've hinted at without doing me the honour to entrust it to me. Certainly no harm can arise from trying my plan first. In ten minutes you may ascertain the result."

"I shall try it," exclaims Uraga, springing to his feet and facing towards the entrance of the tent. "You're right, Roblez. It's a second string to the bow I had a thought about. If it snap, let it. But if it do, before long—aye, before to-morrow's sun shines into our camp—the proud beauty may find herself brotherless, her sole chance of protection being the arms of Gil Uraga."

Saying this, he pitches away the stump of his cigar, and strides forth from the tent, determined to extract from Adela Miranda a promise of betrothal, or in lieu of it decree her brother's death.

Chapter Sixty Six.
A Brother Sorely Tempted.

After stepping forth from the tent Uraga pauses to reflect. The course counselled by Roblez seems reasonable enough. If he can but force the girl's consent, it will not be difficult to get it sealed. There are priests in the frontier pueblitas who will be obedient to a power superior to the Church— even in Mexico, that Paradise of padres. Gold will outweigh any scruples about the performance of the marriage ceremony, however suspicion! the circumstances under which the intending bride and bridegroom may prevent themselves at the altar. The lancer colonel is well aware of this.

But there are other points to be considered before he can proceed farther with the affair. His escort must not know too much. There are ten of them, all thorough cut-throats, and, as such, having a fellow-feeling for their commanding officer. Not one of them but has committed crime, and more than one stained his soul with murder. Nothing strange for Mexican soldiers under the regime of Santa Anna. Not rare even among their officers.

On parting with the main body Uraga selected his escort with an eye to sinister contingencies. They are the sort to assist in any deed of blood. If ordered to shoot or hang the captives they would obey with the eagerness of bloodhounds let loose from the leash, rather relishing it as cruel sport.

For all, he does not desire to entrust them with the secret of his present scheme.

They must not overhear the conversation which he intends holding with his captives; and to prevent this a plan easily suggests itself.

"Holla!" he hails a trooper with chevroned sleeves, in authority over the others. "Step this way, *sergente*."

The sergeant advances, and saluting, awaits further speech from the colonel.

"Order boots and saddles!" directs the latter.

The order is issued; and the soldiers soon stand by their stirrups ready to mount, wondering what duty they are so unexpectedly to be sent upon.

"To horse!" commands the Colonel, vicariously through his non-commissioned officer. "Ride up the creek, and find if there is a pass leading out above. Take all the men with you; only leave Galvez to keep guard over the prisoners."

The sergeant, having received these instructions, once more salutes. Then, returning to the group of lancers, at some distance off, gives the word "Mount!" The troopers, vaulting into their saddles, ride away from the ground, Galvez alone staying behind, who, being a "familiar" with his colonel, and more than once his participator in crimes of deepest dye, can be trusted to overhear anything.

The movement has not escaped the observation of the two men lying tied under the tree. They cannot divine its meaning, but neither do they augur well of it. Still worse, when Uraga, calling to Galvez to come to him, mutters some words in his ear.

Their apprehensions are increased when the sentry returns to them, and, unfastening the cord from the doctor's ankles, raises him upon his feet, as if to remove him from the spot.

On being asked what it is for, Galvez does not condescend to give an answer, except to say in a gruff voice that he has orders to separate them.

Taking hold of the doctor's arm, he conducts him to a distance of several hundred yards, and, once more laying him along the ground, stands over him as before in the attitude of a sentry. The action is suspicious, awe-inspiring—not more to Don Prospero than Miranda himself.

The latter is not left long to meditate upon it. Almost instantly he sees the place of his friend occupied by his enemy. Gil Uraga stands beside him.

There is an interval of silence, with only an interchange of glances; Don Valerian's defiant, Uraga's triumphant. But the expression of triumph on the part of the latter appears held in check, as if to wait some development that may either heighten or curb its display.

Uraga breaks silence—the first speech vouchsafed to his former commanding officer since making him a prisoner.

"Señor Miranda," he says, "you will no doubt be wondering why I have ordered your fellow-captive to be taken apart from you. It will be explained by my saying that I have words for you I don't wish overheard by anyone—not even by your dear friend, Don Prospero."

"What words, Gil Uraga?"

"A proposal I have to make."

Miranda remains silent, awaiting it.

"Let me first make known," continues the ruffian, "though doubtless you know it already, that your life is in my power. If I put a pistol to your head and blow out your brains there will be no calling me to account. If there was any danger of that, I could avoid it by giving you the benefit of a court-martial. Your life is forfeit to the state; and our military laws, as you are aware, can be stretched just now sufficiently to meet your case."

"I am aware of it," rejoins Miranda, his patriotic spirit roused by the reflection; "I know the despotism that now rules my unfortunate country. It can do anything, without respect for either laws or constitution."

"Just so," assents Uraga; "and for this reason I approach you with my proposal."

"Speak it, then. Proceed, sir, and don't multiply words. You need not fear of their effect. I am your prisoner, and powerless."

"Since you command me to avoid circumlocution, I shall obey you to the letter. My proposal is that, in exchange for your life—which I have the power to take, as also to save—you will give me your sister."

Miranda writhes till the cords fastening his wrists almost cut through the skin. Withal, he is silent; his passion too intense to permit of speech.

"Don't mistake me, Don Valerian Miranda," pursues his tormentor, in a tone intended to be soothing. "When I ask you to give me your sister I mean it in an honourable sense. I wish her for my wife; and to save your life she will consent to become so, if you only use your influence to that end. She will not be a faithful sister if she do not. I need not tell you that I love her; you know that already. Accept the conditions I offer, and all will be well. I can even promise you the clemency of the State; for my influence in high places is somewhat different from what it was when you knew me as your subordinate. It will enable me to obtain free pardon for you."

Miranda still remains silent—long enough to rouse the impatience of him who dictates, and tempt the alternative threat already shaping itself on his tongue.

"Refuse," he continues, his brow suddenly clouding, while a light of sinister significance flashes from his eyes, "Refuse me, and you see not another sun. By that now shining you may take your last look of the earth; for this night will certainly be your last on it alive. Observe those vultures on the cliff! They are whetting their beaks, as if they expected a banquet. They shall have one, on your body, if you reject the terms I've offered. Accept them, Don Valerian Miranda; or before to-morrow's sun reaches meridian the birds will be feeding upon your flesh, and the wild beasts quarrelling over your bones. Answer me, and without prevarication. I demand plain speech, yes or no."

"No!" is the monosyllable shouted, almost shrieked, by him so menaced. "No!" he repeats; "never shall I consent to that. I am in your power, Gil Uraga. Put your pistol to my head, blow out my brains, as you say you can do with impunity. Kill me any way you wish, even torture. It could not be more painful than to see you the husband of my sister, either by my consent or her own. You cannot force mine upon such disgraceful conditions, nor yet gain her's. My noble Adela! She would rather see me die, and die along with me."

"Ha! ha!" responded Uraga, in a peal of mocking laughter, mingled with a whine of chagrin, "we shall see about that. Perhaps the senorita may not treat my offer quite so slightingly as yourself. Women are not so superbly stupid. They have a keener comprehension of their own interests. Your sister may better appreciate the honour I am intending her. If not, Heaven help her and you! She will soon be without a brother. Adios, Don Valerian! I go to pour speech into softer ears. For your own sake, hope—pray—that my proposal may be more favourably received."

Saying this, Uraga turns upon his heel and abruptly walks away, leaving behind his captive with hands tied and heart in a tumult of anguished emotion.

Chapter Sixty Seven.
A Sister Sorely Tried.

The marquee occupied by Adela Miranda and her maid is not visible from the spot where her brother lies bound. The other tent is between, with some shrubbery further concealing it.

But from the tenour of his last speech, Don Valerian knows that Uraga has gone thither, as also his object.

Chagrined by the denial he has received from the brother, roused to recklessness, he resolves on having an answer from the sister, point-blank, upon the instant.

With slight ceremony he enters her tent. Once inside, he mutters a request, more like a command, for Conchita to withdraw. He does this with as much grace as the excited state of his feelings permits, excusing himself on the plea that he wishes a word with the senorita—one he is sure she would not wish to be heard by other ears than her own.

Aroused from a despondent attitude, the young lady looks up, her large round eyes expressing surprise, anger, apprehension, awe. The mestiza glances towards her mistress for instructions. The latter hesitates to give them. Only for an instant. It can serve no purpose to gainsay the wishes of one who has full power to enforce them, and whose demeanour shows him determined on doing so.

"You can go, Conchita," says her mistress; "I will call you when you are wanted."

The girl moves off with evident reluctance, but stops not far from the tent.

"Now, Don Gil Uraga," demands the lady, on being left alone with the intruder, "what have you to say to me that should not be overheard?"

"Come, senorita! I pray you will not commence so brusquely. I approach you as a friend, though for some time I may have appeared in the character of an enemy. I hope, however, you'll give me credit for good intentions. I'm sure you will when you know how much I'm distressed by the position I'm placed in. It grieves me that my instructions compel such harsh measures towards my two prisoners: but, in truth, I can say no discretion has been left me. I act under an order from headquarters."

"Señor," she rejoins, casting upon him a look of scornful incredulity, "you have said all this before. I suppose you had something else to speak of."

"And so I have, senorita. Something of a nature so unpleasant I hesitate to tell it, fearing it may sadly shock you."

"You need not. After what has passed I am not likely to be nervous."

Despite her natural courage, and an effort to appear calm, she trembles, as also her voice. There is an expression on the face of the man that bodes sinister risings—some terrible disclosure.

The suspense is too painful to be borne; and in a tone more firm and defiant she demands the promised communication.

"Dona Adela Miranda," he rejoins, speaking in a grave, measured voice, like a doctor delivering a prognosis of death, "it has been my duty to make your brother a prisoner—a painful one, as I have said. But, alas! the part I've already performed is nothing compared with that now required of me. You say you are prepared for a shock. What I'm going to say will cause you one."

She no longer attempts to conceal alarm. It is now discernible in her large, wondering eyes.

"Say it!"

The words drop mechanically from her lips, drawn forth by the intensity of her apprehension.

"You are soon to be without a brother!"

"What mean you, señor?"

"Don Valerian dies within the hour."

"You are jesting, sir. My brother has not been sick? He is not wounded? Why should he die?"

She speaks hurriedly, and with an incredulous stare at Uraga; while at the same time her heaving, palpitating bosom shows she too truly believes what he said.

"Don Valerian is not sick," continues the unfeeling wretch, "nor yet has he received any wound. For all this, in less than an hour he must die. It is decreed."

"*Madre de Dios!* You are mocking me. His death decreed! By whom?"

"Not by me, I assure you. The military authorities of the country have been his judges, and condemned him long ago, as also Don Prospero. It only needed their capture to have the sentence carried out. This disagreeable duty has been entrusted to me. My orders at starting were to have both shot on the instant of making them captives. For your sake, senorita, I've so far disobeyed the rigorous command—an act which may cost me my commission. Yes, Dona Adela, for your sake."

The tale is preposterous, and might seem to her who hears it a lie, but for her knowledge of many similar occurrences in the history of her native land, "Cosas de Mexico." Besides, her own and her brother's experience render it but too probable.

"*Dios de mi alma!*" she cries out in the anguish of conviction, "can this be true?"

"It is true."

"Colonel Uraga, you will not carry out this cruel sentence! It is not an execution—it is an assassination! You will not stain your soul with murder?"

"I must obey orders."

"My poor brother! Have mercy! You can save him?"

"I can."

"You will? You will?"

"I will!"

The emphasis with which these two words are pronounced brings a flush of gratefulness over her face, and she makes a forward movement as if to thank him by a pressure of the hand. She might have given it but for the cast upon his features, telling his consent not yet obtained, nor his speech finished. There is more to come—two other words. They are—

"Upon conditions!"

They check her bursting gratitude. Conditions! She knows not what they may be. But she knows the character of Gil Uraga, and can predict they will be hard.

"Name them!" she demands. "If it be money, I'm ready to give it. Though my brother's property is taken from him, as we've heard, not so mine. I have wealth—houses, lands. Take all, but save Valerian's life."

"You can save it without expending a single *claco*; only by giving a grace."

"What mean you, señor?"

"To explain my meaning I'll repeat what I've said. Your brother's head is forfeit. It can be saved by a hand."

"Still I do not understand you. A hand?"

"Yes, your hand."

"How?"

"Grasped in mine—united with it in holy wedlock. That is all I ask."

She starts as if a serpent had stung her, for she now comprehends all.

"All I ask," he continues in a strain of fervid passion, "I who love you with my whole soul; who have loved you for long hopeless years—aye, senorita, ever since you were a schoolgirl; myself a rough, wild youth, the son of a ranchero, who dared only gaze at you from a distance. I am a peasant no longer, but one who has wealth; upon whom the State has bestowed power to command; made me worthy to choose a wife from among the proudest in our land—even to wed with the Dona Adela Miranda, who beholds him at her feet!"

While speaking he has knelt before her, and remains upon his knees awaiting her response.

She makes none. She stands as if petrified, deprived of the power of speech.

Her silence gives him hope.

"Dona Adela," he continues in an appealing tone, as if to strengthen the chances of an affirmative answer, "I will do everything to make you happy—everything a husband can. And remember your brother's life! I am risking my own to save it. I have just spoken to him on the subject. He does not object; on the contrary, has given consent to you being mine."

"You say so?" she inquires, with a look of incredulity. "I do not believe it—will not, without hearing it from his own lips."

While speaking, she springs past the kneeling suppliant, and, before he can get upon his legs or stretch forth a hand to detain her, she has glided out of the tent, and makes for the place where she supposes the prisoners to be kept.

Starting to his feet, Uraga rushes after. His intent is to overtake and bring her back, even if he have to carry her.

He is too late. Before he can come up with her she has reached the spot where her brother lies bound, and kneels beside him with arms embracing, her lips pressing his brow, his cheeks moistened by her tears.

Chapter Sixty Eight.
A Terrible Intention.

Not for long does the scene of agonised affection remain uninterrupted. In a few seconds it is intruded on by him who is causing its agony.

Uraga, hastening after, has reached the spot and stands contemplating it. A spectacle to melt a heart of stone, it has no softening effect on his. His brow his black with rage, his eyes shining like coals of fire.

His first impulse is to call Galvez and order him to drag brother and sister apart. His next to do this himself. He is about seizing Adela's wrist, when a thought restrains him. No melting or impulse of humanity. There is not a spark of it in his bosom. Only a hope, suddenly conceived, that with the two now together he may repeat his proposal with a better chance of its being entertained.

From the expression upon their countenances he can see that in the interval before his coming up words have passed between them—few and hastily spoken, but enough for each to have been told what he has been saying to the other. It does not daunt; on the contrary, but determines him to renew his offer, and, if necessary, reiterate his threats.

There is no one within earshot for whom he need care. Galvez has taken Don Prospero far apart. Roblez is inside the tent, though he thinks not of him; while the Indian damsel, who stands trembling by, is not worth a thought. Besides, he is now more than ever regardless of the result.

"Don Valerian Miranda!" he exclaims, recovering breath after his chase across the camp-ground. "I take it your sister has told you what has passed between us. If not, I shall tell you myself."

"My sister has communicated all—even the falsehood by which you've sought to fortify your infamous proposal."

"*Carramba!*" exclaims Uraga, upon whose cheeks there is no blush of shame for the deception practised. "Does the offer to save your life, at risk of my own—to rescue you from a felon's death—does that deserve the harsh epithet with which you are pleased to qualify it? Come, señor, you are wronging me while trifling with your own interests. I have been honest, and declared all. I love the Dona Adela, as you've known, long. What do I ask? Only that she shall become my wife, and, by so doing, save the life of her brother. As your brother-in-law it will be my duty, my interest, my pleasure, to protect you."

"That you shall never be!" firmly rejoins Miranda. "No, never!" he adds, with kindling fervour, "never, on such conditions!"

"Does the senorita pronounce with the same determination?" asks Uraga, riveting his eyes on Adela.

It is a terrible ordeal for the girl. Her brother lying bound by her side, his death about to be decreed, his end near as if the executioner were standing over him—for in this light does Uraga appear. Called upon to save his life by promising to become the wife of this man—hideous in her eyes as the hangman himself; knowing, or believing, that if she does not, in another hour she may be gazing upon a blood-stained corpse—the dead body of her own brother! No wonder she trembles from head to foot, and hesitates to endorse the negative he has so emphatically pronounced.

Don Valerian notes her indecision, and, firmly as before, repeats the words,—

"No—never!" adding, "Dear sister, think not of me. Do not fear or falter; I shall not. I would rather die a hundred deaths than see you the wife of such a ruffian. Let me die first!"

"*Chingara!*" hisses the man thus boldly defied, using the vilest exclamation known to the Spanish tongue. "Then you shall die first. And, after you're dead, she shall still be my wife, or something you may not like so well—my *Margarita!*"

The infamous meaning conveyed by this word, well understood by Miranda, causes him to start half-upright, at the same time wrenching at the rope around his wrists. The perspiration forced from him by the agony of the hour has moistened the raw-hide thong to stretching. It yields to the convulsive effort, leaving his hands released.

With a quick lurch forward he clutches at the sword dangling by Uraga's side. Its hilt is in his grasp, and in an instant he has drawn the blade from its scabbard!

Seeing himself thus suddenly disarmed, the Lancer Colonel springs back shouting loudly for help. Miranda, his ankles bound, is at first unable to follow, but with the sword-blade he quickly cut the thongs, and is on his feet—free!

In another instant he is chasing Uraga across the camp-ground, the latter running like a scared hound.

Before he can be overtaken, the trampling of hoofs resound upon the grassy turf, and the returned lancers, with Roblez and the sentry, close around the prisoner.

Don Valerian sees himself encircled by a *chevaux de frise* of lances, with cocked carbines behind. There is no chance of escape, no alternative but surrender. After that—

He does not stop to reflect. A wild thought flashes across his brain—a terrible determination. To carry it out only needs the consent of his sister. She had rushed between their horses and stands by his side, with arms outstretched to protect him.

"Adela!" he says, looking intently into her eyes, "dear sister, let us die together!"

She sees the sword resolutely held in his grasp. She cannot mistake the appeal.

"Yes; let us, Valerian!" comes the quick response, with a look of despairing resignation, followed by the muttered speech of "Mother of God, take us both to thy bosom! To thee we commit our souls!"

He raises the blade, its point towards his sister—in another moment to be buried in her bosom, and afterwards in his own!

The sacrifice is not permitted, though the soldiers have no hand in hindering it. Dismayed or careless, they sit in their saddles without thought of interfering. But between their files rushes a form in whose heart is more of humanity.

The intruder is Conchita—opportune to an instant.

Two seconds more, and the fratricidal sword would have bereft her of a mistress and a master, both alike beloved.

Both are saved by her interference; for grasping the upraised arm, she restrains it from the thrust.

Roblez, close following, assists her, while several of the lancers, now dismounted, fling themselves upon Miranda and disarm him.

The intending sororicide and suicide is restored to his fastenings; his sister taken back to her tent; a trooper detailed to stand sentry beside and frustrate any attempt at a second escapade.

Chapter Sixty Nine.
An Intercepted Dispatch.

While the thrilling incident described is occurring in Uraga's camp, the Rangers, *en route* along the banks of the Pecos, are making all the haste in their power to reach it, Hamersley and Wilder every now and then saying some word to urge them on.

In pursuit of such an enemy the Texans need no pressing. 'Tis only the irrestrainable impatience of the two whose souls are tortured by the apprehension of danger hovering over the heads of those dear to them. There is no difficulty in lifting the trail of the soldiers. Their horses are shod, and the late storm, with its torrent of rain, has saturated the earth, obliterating all old hoof-marks, so that those later made are not only distinct but conspicuous. So clear, that the craft of Cully and Wilder is not called into requisition. Every Ranger riding along the trail can take it up as fast as his horse is able to carry him.

All see that Uraga has taken no pains to blind the track of his party. Why should he? He can have no suspicion of being pursued; certainly not by such pursuers.

Along the trail, then, they ride rapidly; gratified to observe that it grows fresher as they advance for they are travelling thrice as fast as the men who made it.

All at once they come to a halt—summoned to this by a sight which never fails to bring the most hurried traveller to a stand. They see before them the dead body of a man!

It is lying on a sand-spit, which projects into the river. Upon this it has evidently been washed by the waters, now subsiding after the freshet, due to the late tornado. Beside it shows the carcase of a mule, deposited in similar manner. Both are conspicuous to the Rangers as they ride abreast of the spit; but their attention has been called to them long before by a flock of buzzards, some hovering above, others alighting upon the sandbank.

Six or seven of the Texans, heading their horses down the sloping bank, ride towards the "sign"—so sad, yet terribly attractive. It would tempt scrutiny anywhere; but in the prairie wilderness, in that dangerous desert, it may be the means of guiding to a path of safety, or warding from one that is perilous.

While those who have detached themselves proceed out upon the sandbar, the main body remains upon the high bank, awaiting their return.

The dead man proves to be an Indian, though not of the *bravos*, or savage tribes. Wearing a striped woollen *talma*, with coarse cotton shirt underneath, wide sheep-skin breeches, ex tending only a little below the knee, and rude raw-hide sandals upon his feet, he is evidently one of the Christianised aboriginals.

There are no marks of violence on his body, nor yet on the carcase of the mule. The case is clear at a glance. It is one of drowning; and the swollen stream, still foaming past, is evidence eloquent of how it happened. On the man's body there are no signs of rifling or robbery. His pockets, when turned inside out, yield such contents as might be expected on the person of an *Indio manso*.

Only one thing, which, in the eyes of the examinators, appears out of place; a sheet of paper folded in the form of a letter, and sealed as such. It is saturated with water, stained to the hue of the still turbid stream. But the superscription can be read, "Por Barbato."

So much Cully and Wilder, who assist at the examination, can make out for themselves. But on breaking open the seal, and endeavouring to decipher what is written inside, both are at fault, as also the others along with them. The letter is in a language that is a sealed book to all. It is in Spanish.

Without staying to attempt translating it, they return to the river's bank, taking the piece of paper along, for the superscription has touched a tender point, and given rise to strange suspicions.

Walt carries the wet letter, which, soon as rejoining their comrades, he places in the hands of Hamersley. The latter, translating, reads aloud:

> "Señor Barbato,—As soon as you receive this, communicate
> its contents to the chief. Tell him to meet me on the Arroyo
> de Alamo—same place as before—and that he is to bring

with him twenty or thirty of his painted devils. The lesser number will be enough, as it's not an affair of fighting. Come yourself with them. You will find me encamped with a small party—some female and two male captives. No matter about the women. It's the men you have to deal with; and this is what you are to do. Charge upon our camp the moment you get sight of it; make your redskins shout like fiends, and ride forward, brandishing their spears. You won't meet resistance, nor find any one on the ground when you've got there, only our two prisoners, who will be fast bound, and so cannot flee with us. What's to be done with them, amigo mio, is the important part—in fact, the whole play. Tell the chief they are to be speared upon the spot, thrust through as soon as you get up to them. See to this yourself, lest there be any mischance; and I'll take care you shall have your reward."

Made acquainted with the contents of this vile epistle, the rage of the Rangers, already sufficiently aroused, breaks from all bounds, and, for a while, seeks vent in fearful curses and asseverations. Though there is no name appended to the diabolical chapter of instructions, they have no doubt as to who has dictated it. Circumstances, present and antecedent, point to the man of whom they are in pursuit—Gil Uraga.

And he to whom the epistle is superscribed, "Por Barbato."

A wild cry ascends simultaneously from the whole troop as they face round towards the renegade, who is still with them, and their prisoner. The wretch turns pale, as if all the blood of his body were abruptly drawn out. Without comprehending the exact import of that cry, he can read in fifty pairs of eyes glaring angrily on him that his last hour has come.

The Rangers can have no doubt as to whom the letter has been addressed, as they can also tell why it has miscarried. For the renegade has already disclosed his name, not thinking it would thus strangely turn up to condemn him to death.

Yes—to death; for, although promised life, with only the punishment of a prison, these conditions related to another criminality, and were granted without the full knowledge of his guilt—of connivance at a crime unparalleled for atrocity. His judges feel absolved from every stipulation of pardon or mercy; and, summoning to the judgment seat the quick, stem decreer—Lynch—in less than five minutes after the trembling wretch is launched into eternity!

There is reason for this haste. They know that the letter has miscarried; but he who could dictate such a damnable epistle is a wild beast at large, who cannot be too soon destroyed.

Leaving the body of Barbato to be devoured by wolves and vultures, they spur on along the Pecos, only drawing bridle to breathe their horses as the trail turns up at the bottom of a confluent creek—the Arroyo de Alamo.

Chapter Seventy.
A Scheme of Atrocity.

Discomfited—chagrined by his discomfiture—burning with shame at the pitiful spectacle he has afforded to his followers—Uraga returns within his tent like an enraged tiger. Not as one robbed of its prey—he is still sure of this as ever; for he has other strings to his bow, and the weak one just snapped scarce signifies.

But for having employed it to no purpose he now turns upon Roblez, who counselled the course that has ended so disastrously.

The adjutant is a safe target on which to expend the arrows of his spleen, and to soothe his perturbed spirit he gives vent to it.

In time, however, he gets somewhat reconciled; the sooner by gulping down two or three glasses of Catalan brandy. Along with the liquor, smoking, as if angry at his cigar, and consuming it through sheer spite, Roblez endeavours to soothe him by consolative speech.

"What matters it, after all!" puts in the confederate. "It may be that everything has been for the best. I was wrong, no doubt, in advising as I did. Still, as you see, it's gained us some advantage."

"Advantage! To me the very reverse. Only to think of being chased about my own camp by a man who is my prisoner! And before the eyes of everybody! A pretty story for our troopers to tell when they get back to Albuquerque! I, Colonel commanding, will be the jest of the *cuartel!*"

"Nothing of the kind, colonel! There is nothing to jest about. Your prisoner chanced to possess himself of your sword—a thing no one could have anticipated. He did it adroitly, but then you were at the time unsuspecting. Disarmed, what else could you do but retreat from a man, armed, desperate, determined on taking your life. I'd like to see anyone who'd have acted otherwise. Under the circumstances only an insane man would keep his ground. The episode has been awkward, I admit. But it's all nonsense—excuse me for saying so—your being sensitive about that part of it. And for the rest, I say again, it's given us an advantage; in short, the very one you wanted, if I understand your intentions aright."

"In what way?"

"Well, you desired a pretext, didn't you?"

"To do what?"

"Court-martial your prisoners, condemn, and execute them. The attempt on your life will cover all this, so that the keenest scandal-monger may not open his lips. It will be perfectly *en regie* for you to hang or shoot Don Valerian Miranda—and, if you like, the doctor, too—after ten minutes' deliberation over a drum's head. I'm ready to organise the court according to your directions."

To this proposal Uraga replies with a significant smile, saying:

"Your idea is not a bad one; but I chance to have a better. Much as I hate Miranda and wish him out of the way, I don't desire to imbrue my hands in his blood; don't intend to, as I've already hinted to you."

Roblez turns upon his superior officer a look of incredulous *surprise, interrogating,*—

"You mean to take him back, and let him be tried in the regular way?"

"I mean nothing of the kind."

"I thought it strange, after your telling me he would never leave this place alive."

"I tell you so still."

"Colonel! you take pleasure in mystifying me. If you're not going to try your prisoners by court-martial, in what way are your words to be made good? Surely you don't intend to have them shot without form of trial?"

"I've said I won't imbrue my hands in their blood."

"True, you've said that more than once, but without making things any clearer to me. You spoke of some plan. Perhaps I may now hear it?"

"You shall. But first fill me out another *capita* of the Catalan. That affair has made me thirsty as a sponge."

The adjutant, acting as Ganymede, pours out the liquor and hands the cup to his colonel, which the latter quaffs off. Then, lighting a fresh cigar, he proceeds with the promised explanation.

"I spoke of events, incidents, and coincidences—didn't I, *ayadante*?"

"You did, Colonel."

"Well, suppose I clump them altogether, and give you the story in a simple narrative—a monologue? I know, friend Roblez, you're not a man greatly given to speech; so it will save you the necessity of opening your lips till I've got through."

Roblez, usually taciturn, nods assent.

"Before coming out here," continues the Colonel, "I'd taken some steps. When you've heard what they are I fancy you'll give me credit for strategy, or cunning, if you prefer so calling it. I told you I should take no prisoners back, and that Don Valerian and the doctor are to die. They will go to their graves without causing scandal to any of us. To avoid it I've engaged an executioner, who will do the job without any direct orders from me."

"Who?" asks the adjutant, forgetting his promise to be silent.

"Don't interrupt!"

The subordinate resumes silence.

"I think," continues Uraga, in a tone of serio-comicality, "you have heard of a copper-coloured gentleman called 'Horned Lizard.' If I mistake not, you have the honour of his acquaintance. And, unless I'm astray in my reckoning, you'll have the pleasure of seeing him here this evening, or at an early hour to-morrow morning. He will make his appearance in somewhat eccentric fashion. No doubt, he'll come into our camp at a charging gallop, with some fifty or a hundred of his painted warriors behind him. And I shouldn't wonder if they should spit some of our gay lancers on the points of their spears. That will depend on whether these *valientes* be foolish enough to make resistance. I don't think they will. More likely we shall see them gallop off at the first whoop of the Indian assailants. You and I, Roblez, will have to do the same; but, as gallant gentlemen, we must take the women along with us. To abandon them to the mercy of the savages, without making an effort to save them, were absolute poltroonery, and would never bear reporting in the settlements. Therefore, we must do our best to take the ladies along. Of course, we can't be blamed for not being able to save our male prisoners. Their fate, I fear, will be for each to get half a dozen Comanche spears thrust through his body, or it may be a dozen. It's sad to think of it, but such misfortunes cannot always be avoided. They are but the ordinary incidents of frontier life. Now, *señor ayadante*, do you comprehend my scheme?"

"Since I am at length permitted to speak, I may say I do—at least, I have an obscure comprehension of it. Fairly interpreted, I take it to mean this. You have arranged with the Horned Lizard to make a counterfeit attack upon our camp—to shoot down or spear our poor devils of soldiers, if need be?"

"Not the slightest need of his doing that, nor any likelihood of his being able to do it. They'll run like good fellows at the first yell of the Indians. Have no apprehensions about them."

"In any case, the Horned Lizard is to settle the question with our captives, and take the responsibility off our hands. If I understand aright, that is the programme."

"It is."

Chapter Seventy One.
A Bootless Journey.

Having returned to his original design—the scheme of atrocity so coolly and jestingly declared, Uraga takes steps towards its execution.

The first is, to order his own horse, or rather that of Hamersley, to be saddled, bridled, and tied behind his own tent. The same for that ridden by Roblez. Also the mustang mare which belongs to Adela Miranda—her own "Lolita"—and the mule set apart for the *mestiza*. The troop horses already caparisoned are to remain so.

Ignorant of their object, the troopers wonder at these precautions, though not so much as might be expected. They are accustomed to receive mysterious commands, and obey them without cavil or question.

Not one of the ten but would cut a throat at Gil Uraga's bidding, without asking the reason why.

The picket placed on a spin of the cliff has orders to signal if any one is seen coming up the creek. If Indians appear he is to gallop into the camp, and report in person.

The alarm thus started will easily be fostered into a stampede, and at the onslaught of the savages the lancers will rush to their horses and ride off without offering resistance. In the *sauve qui peut* none of them will give a thought to the two prisoners lying tied under the tree. These are to be left behind to the tender mercies of the Tenawa chief. It will be an act of gallantry to save the female captives by carrying them off. This Uraga reserves for himself, assisted by Roblez.

Such is his scheme of vicarious assassination; in the atrocity of conception unequalled, almost incredible. He has no anxiety as to its success. For himself he is more than ever determined; while Roblez, restrained by the fiasco following his advice, no longer offers opposition.

Uraga has no fear the Tenawa chief will fail him. He has never done so before, and will not now.

The new proposal, which the colonel supposes to have reached the hands of Horned Lizard in that letter carried by Pedrillo, will be eagerly accepted. Barbato will bring the chief with his cut-throats to the Arroyo de Alamo, sure as there is a sun in the sky.

It is but a question of time. They may come up at any hour—any minute; and having arranged all preliminaries, Uraga remains in his tent to await the cue for action. He little dreams at the moment he is thus expecting his red-skinned confederate, that the latter, along with the best braves of his band, has gone to the happy hunting grounds, while his go-between, Barbato, is in safe keeping elsewhere.

As the hours pass, and no one is reported as approaching, he becomes impatient; for the time has long elapsed since the Tenawa chief should have been upon the spot.

Chafing, he strides forth from the tent, and proceeds towards the place where the look-out has been stationed. Reaching it, he reconnoitres for himself, with a telescope he has taken along, to get a better view down the valley.

At first, levelling the glass, no one can be seen. In the reach of open ground, dotted here and there with groves, there are deer browsing, and a grizzly bear is seen crossing between the cliffs, but no shape that resembles a human being.

He is about lowering the telescope when a new form comes into its field of view—a horseman riding up the creek. No the animal is a mule. No matter the rider is a man.

Keenly scrutinising, he perceives it is an Indian, though not one of the wild sort. His garb betokens him of the tamed.

Another glance through the glass and his individuality declares itself, Uraga recognising him as one of the messengers sent to the Tenawas' town. Not the principal, Pedrillo, but he of secondary importance, José.

"Returning alone!" mutters the Mexican to himself. "What does that mean? Where can Pedrillo be? What keeps him behind, I wonder?"

He continues wondering and conjecturing till José has ridden up to the spot, when, perceiving his master, the latter dismounts and approaches him.

In the messenger's countenance there is an expression of disappointment, and something more. It tells a tale of woe, with reluctance to disclose it.

"Where is Pedrillo?" is the first question asked in anxious impatience.

"Oh, *señor coronel!*" replies José, hat in hand, and trembling in every joint. "Pedrillo! *Pobre Pedrillito!*"

"Well! Poor Pedrillito—what of him? Has anything happened to him?"

"Yes, your excellency, a terrible mischance I fear to tell it you."

"Tell it, sirrah, and at once! Out with it, whatever it is!"

"Alas, Pedrillo is gone!"

"Gone—whither?"

"Down the river."

"What river?"

"The Pecos."

"Gone down the Pecos? On what errand?" inquired the colonel, in surprise.

"On no errand, your excellency."

"Then what's taken him down the Pecos? Why went he?"

"*Señor coronel*, he has not gone of his own will. It is only his dead body that went; it was carried down by the flood."

"Drowned? Pedrillo drowned?"

"*Ay de mi*! 'Tis true, as I tell you—too true, *pobrecito*."

"How did this happen, José?"

"We were crossing at the ford, señor. The waters were up from a *norte* that's just passed over the plains. The river was deep and running rapid, like a torrent, Pedrillo's *macho* stumbled, and was swept off. It was as much as mine could do to keep its legs. I think he must have got his feet stuck in the stirrups, for I could see him struggling alongside the mule till both went under. When they came to the surface both were drowned—dead. They floated on without making a motion, except what the current gave them as their bodies were tossed about by it. As I could do nothing there, I hastened here to tell you what happened. *Pobre Pedrillito!*"

The cloud already darkening Uraga's brow grows darker as he listens to the explanation. It has nothing to do with the death of Pedrillo, or compassion for his fate—upon which he scarce spends a thought—but whether there has been a miscarriage of that message of which the drowned man was the bearer. His next interrogatory, quickly put, is to get satisfied on this head.

"You reached the Tenawa town?"

"We did, *señor coronel*."

"Pedrillo carried a message to the Horned Lizard, with a letter for Barbato. You know that, I suppose?"

"He told me so."

"Well, you saw him deliver the letter to Barbato?"

"He did not deliver it to Barbato."

"To the chief, then?"

"To neither, your Excellency. He could not."

"Could not! Why?"

"They ere not there to receive it. They are no longer in this world—neither the Horned Lizard nor Barbato. Señor Coronel, the Tenawas have met with a great misfortune. They've had a fight with a party of Tejanos. The chief is killed, Barbato is killed, and nearly half of their braves. When Pedrillo and I reached the town we found the tribe in mourning, the women all painted black, with their hair cut off; the men who had escaped the slaughter cowed, and keeping concealed within their lodges."

A wild exclamation leaps from the lips of Uraga as he listens to these disclosures, his brow becoming blacker than ever.

"But, Pedrillo," he inquires, after a pause; "what did he say to them? You know the import of his message. Did he communicate it to the survivors?"

"He did, your Excellency. They could not read your letter, but he told them what it was about. They were to meet you here, he said. But they refused to come. They were in too great distress about the death of their chief, and the chastisement they had received. They were in fear that the Tejanos would pursue them to their town; and were making preparations to flee from it when Pedrillo and myself came away. *Pobre Pedrillito!*"

Uraga no longer stays listening to the mock humanity of his whining messenger. No more does he think of the drowned Pedrillo. His thoughts are now given to a new design. Murder by proxy has failed. For all that, it must still be done. To take counsel with his adjutant about the best mode of proceeding, he hastens back to the camp; plunges into his tent; and there becomes closeted—the lieutenant along with him.

Chapter Seventy Two.
A Mock Court-Martial.

For the disaster that was overtaken the Tenawa chief and his warriors, Gil Uraga does not care a jot. True, by the death of Horned Lizard he has lost an ally who, on some future scheme of murder, might have been used to advantage; while Barbato, whose life he believes also taken, can no more do him service as agent in his intercourse with the red pirates of the prairie.

It matters not much now. As military commander of a district he has attained power, enabling him to dispense with any left-handed assistance; and of late more than once has wished himself rid of such suspicious auxiliaries. Therefore, but for the frustration of his present plans, he would rather rejoice than grieve over the tidings brought by the returned emissary.

His suit scorned, his scheme of assassination thwarted, he is as much as ever determined on the death of the two prisoners.

In the first moments of his anger, after hearing José's tale, he felt half inclined to rush upon Miranda, sword in hand, and settle the matter at once. But, while returning to the camp-ground, calmer reflections arose, restraining him from the dastardly act, and deciding him to carry out the other alternative, already conceived, but kept back as a *dernier ressort*.

"Sit down, *camarado*!" he says, addressing the adjutant on entering. "We must hold a court-martial, and that is too serious a ceremonial to be gone through without the customary forms. The members of the court should be seated."

The grim smile which accompanies his words shows that he means them in jest only as regards the manner of proceeding. For the earnestness of his intention there is that in his eyes—a fierce, lurid light, which Roblez can read.

In rejoinder the adjutant asks,—

"You are still resolved upon the death of the prisoners?"

"Still resolved! Carramba! An idle question, after what has occurred! They die within the hour. We shall try, condemn, and then have them shot."

"I thought you had arranged it in a different way?"

"So I had. But circumstances alter cases. There's many a slip 'twixt cup and lip, and I've just heard of one. The Horned Lizard has failed me."

"How so, colonel?"

"You see that Indian outside. He's one of my muleteers I'd sent as a messenger to the Tenawa town. He returns to tell me there's no Horned Lizard in existence, and only a remnant of his tribe. Himself, with the best of his braves, has gone to the happy hunting grounds; not voluntarily, but sent thither by a party of Tejanos who fell foul of them on a foray."

"That's a strange tale," rejoins Roblez, adding, "And Barbato?"

"Dead, too—gone with his red-skinned associates."

"Certainly a singular occurrence—quite a coincidence."

"A coincidence that leaves me in an awkward predicament, without my expected executioners. Well, we must supply their places by substituting our own cut-throats."

"You'll find them willing, colonel. The little interlude of Miranda getting loose, and making to run you through, has been all in your favour. It affords sufficient pretext for court-martialling and condemning both prisoners to be shot I've heard the men say so, and they expect it."

"They shall not be disappointed, nor have long to wait. The court has finished its sitting, and given its verdict. Without dissenting voice, the prisoners are condemned to death. So much for the sentence. Now to carry it into execution."

"How is the thing to be done?"

"Call in the sergeant. With him I shall arrange that. And when you're out, go among the men and say a word to prepare them for the measure. You may tell them we've been trying the prisoners, and the result arrived at."

The adjutant steps out of the tent; and while Uraga is swallowing another cup of Catalan to fortify him for his fearful purpose, the sergeant enters.

"*Sergente*! there's some business to be done of a delicate nature, and you must take direction of it."

The Serjeant salutes, and stands awaiting the explanation. The colonel continues:—

"We intend taking our prisoners no farther—the men, I mean. With the women we have nothing to do—as prisoners. After what you saw, we deem it necessary that Don Valerian Miranda should die; and also the other, who is equally incriminated as a traitor to the State—a rebel, an old conspirator, well known. Lieutenant Roblez and I have held a court, and decreed their death. So order the men to load their carbines, and make ready to carry out the sentence."

The sergeant simply nods assent, and, again saluting, is about to retire, when Uraga stays him with a second speech.

"Let all take part in the firing except Galvez. Post him as sentry over the square tent. Direct him to stand by its entrance and see that the flap is kept down. Under no circumstances is he to let either of its occupants out. It's not a spectacle for women—above all, one of them. Never mind; we can't help that I'm sorry myself, but duty demands this rigorous measure. Now go. First give Galvez his orders; then to the men and get them ready. Make no more noise than is necessary. Let your lancers be drawn up in line; afoot, of course, and single file."

"Where am I to place the prisoners, colonel?"

"Ah! true; I did not think of that."

Uraga steps to the entrance of the tent, and, looking forth, takes a survey of the camp-ground. His eyes seek the spot occupied by the prisoners. They are both again together, under the same tree where first placed, a sentry keeping guard over them. The tree is a cottonwood, with smooth stem and large limbs extending horizontally. Another is near, so similar as to seem a twin; both being a little out from the thick timber, which forms a dark background behind them.

After regarding them a moment, scanning them as a lumberman would a log intended for a saw-mill, Uraga directs.

"Raise the prisoners upright, and tie one to each of those two trees. Set their backs to the trunk. They've both been army men, and we won't disgrace the cloth by shooting them from behind. That's grace enough for rebels."

The sergeant, saluting, is again about to go, only staying to catch some final words of direction. They are—

"In ten minutes I shall expect you to have everything ready. When you've got the stage set I shall myself appear upon it as an actor—the Star of this pretty play!"

And with a hoarse laugh at his horrid jest, the ruffian retires within his tent.

Chapter Seventy Three.
The Hand of God.

The sun is descending towards the crest of the Cordillera, his rays becoming encrimsoned as twilight approaches. They fall like streams of blood between the bluffs enclosing the valley of the Arroyo de Alamo, their tint in unison with a tragedy there about to be enacted—in itself strangely out of correspondence with the soft, tranquil scene.

The stage is the encampment of Uraga and his detachment of lancers, now set for the terrible spectacle soon to take place.

The two tents are still standing as pitched, several paces apart. At the entrance of the square one, with its flap drawn close and tied, a soldier keeps sentry; that of conical shape being unguarded.

Rearward, by the wood edge, are three horses and a mule, all four under saddle, with bridles on; these attached to the branches of a tree. There is no providence in this, but rather neglect. Since the purpose for which they were caparisoned has proved abortive, they remain so only from having been forgotten.

The other troop-horses have been stripped, and, scattered over the mead, are browsing at the length of their lariats.

It is in the positions and attitudes of the men that a spectator might read preparation; and of a kind from which he could not fail to deduce the sequence of a sanguinary drama. Not one accompanied by much noise, but rather solemn and silent; only a few words firmly spoken, to be followed by a volley; in short, a military execution, or, as it might be more properly designated, a military murder.

The victims devoted are seen near the edge of the open ground—its lower edge regarding the direction of the stream. They are in erect attitude, each with his back to the trunk of a tree, to which with raw-hide ropes they are securely lashed. No need telling who they are. The reader knows them to be the prisoners lately lying prostrate near the same place.

In their front, and scarce ten paces distant, the lancers are drawn up in line and single file. There are ten of them, the tenth a little retired to the right, showing chevrons on his sleeve. He is the sergeant in immediate command of the firing party. Farther rearward, and close by the conical tent, and two in the uniform of officers, Uraga and his adjutant. The former is himself about to pronounce the word of command, the relentless expression upon his face, blent with a grim smile that overspreads it, leading to believe that the act of diabolical cruelty gives him gratification. Above, upon the cliff's brow, the black vultures also show signs of satisfaction. With necks craned and awry, the better to look below, they see preparations which instinct or experience has taught them to understand. Blood is about to be spilled; there will be flesh to afford them a feast.

There is now perfect silence, after a scene which preceded; once more Uraga having made overtures to Miranda, with promise of life under the same scandalous conditions; as before, to receive the response, firmly spoken,—

"No—never!"

The patriot soldier prefers death to dishonour.

His choice taken, he quails not. Tied to the trunk of the tree, he stands facing his executioners without show of fear. If his cheeks be blanched, and his bosom throbbing with tumultuous emotion, 'tis not at sight of the firing party, or the guns held loaded in their hands. Far other are his fears, none of them for himself, but all for his dear sister—Adela. No need to dwell upon or describe them. They may be imagined.

And Don Prospero, brave and defiant too. He stands backed by the tree, his eyes showing calm courage, his long silvered beard touching his breast, not drooping or despairingly, but like one resigned to his fate, and still firm in the faith that has led to it—a second Wickliffe at the stake.

The moment has arrived when the stillness becomes profound, like the calm which precedes the first burst of a thunderstorm. The vultures above, the horses and men below, are all alike silent.

The birds, gazing intently, have ceased their harsh croaking; the quadrupeds, as if startled by the very silence, forsaking the sweet grass, have tossed their heads aloft, and so hold them. While the men, hitherto speaking in whispers, no more converse, but stand mute and motionless. They are going to deal death to two of their fellow-creatures; and there is not one among them who does not know it is a death undeserved—that he is about to commit murder!

For all this, not one has a thought of staying his hand. Along the whole line there is no heart amenable to mercy, no breast throbbing with humanity. All have been in a like position before—drawn up to fire upon prisoners, their countrymen. The patriots of their country, too; for the followers of Gil Uraga are all of them picked adherents of the *parti preter*.

"*Sergente!*" asks Uraga, on coming forth from his tent, "is everything ready?"

"All ready," is the prompt reply.

"Attention!" commands the Colonel, stepping a pace or two forward, and speaking in a low tone, though loud enough to be heard by the lancers.

"Make ready!"

The carbines are raised to the ready.

"Take aim!"

The guns are brought to the level, their bronzed barrels glistening under the rays of the setting sun, with muzzles pointed at the prisoners. They who grasp them but wait for the word "Fire!"

It is forming itself on Gil Uraga's lips. But before he can speak there comes a volley, filling the valley with sound, and the space around the prisoners with smoke. The reports of more than forty pieces speak almost simultaneously, none of them with the dull detonation of cavalry carbines, but the sharper ring of the rifle!

While the last crack is still reverberating from the rocks, Uraga sees his line of lancers prostrate along the sward; their guns, escaped from their grasp, scattered beside them, still undischarged!

Chapter Seventy Four.
"Sauve Qui Peut."

At sight of his soldiers cut down like ripe corn before the reaper, Uraga stands in stupefied amaze; his adjutant the same. Both are alike under the spell of a superstitious terror. For the blow, so sudden and sweeping, seems given by God's own hand. They might fancy it a *coup d'éclair*. But the jets of fire shooting forth from the forest edge, through a cloud of sulphurous smoke, are not flashes of lightning; nor the rattle that accompanies them the rolling of thunder, but the reports of firearms discharged in rapid succession. While in shouts following the shots there is no accent of Heaven; on the contrary, the cries are human, in the voices of men intoned to a terrible vengeance.

Though every one of the firing party has fallen, sergeant as well as rank and file, the two officers are still untouched. So far they have been saved by the interposition of the formed line. But straggling shots succeed, and bullets are whizzing past their ears.

These, quickening their instincts, rouse them from their stupefaction; and both, turning from the direction of the danger, looked to the other side for safety.

At first wildly and uncertain, for they are still under a weird impression, with senses half bewildered.

Neither has a knowledge of the enemy that has made such havoc among their men; only an instinct or intuition that the blow has been struck by those terrible *Tejanos*, for the shots heard were the cracks of rifles, and the shouts, still continued, are not Indian yells nor Mexican vivas, but the rough hurrahs of the Anglo-Saxon.

While standing in hesitancy, they hear a voice raised above the rest— one which both recognise. Well do they remember it, pealing among the waggons on that day of real ruthless carnage.

Glancing back over their shoulders, they see him who sends it forth— the giant guide of the caravan. He has just broken from the timber's edge, and in vigorous bounds is advancing towards them. Another is by his side, also recognised. With trembling frame, and heart chilled by fear, Uraga identifies his adversary in the duel at Chihuahua.

Neither he nor his subordinate remains a moment longer on the ground. No thought now of carrying off their female captives, no time to think of them. Enough, and they will be fortunate, if they can themselves escape.

Better for both to perish there by the sides of their slain comrades. But they know not this, and only yield to the common instinct of cowardice, forcing them to flee.

Fortune seems to favour them. For animals fully caparisoned stand behind the conical tent. They are these that were in readiness for a flight of far different kind, since unthought of—altogether forgotten.

Good luck their being saddled and bridled now. So think Uraga and Roblez as they rush towards them. So thinks Galvez, who is also making to mount one. The sentry has forsaken his post, leaving the marquee unguarded. When a lover no longer cares for his sweetheart, why should he for a captive.

And in the *sauve-qui-peut* scramble there is rarely a regard for rank, the colonel counting for no more than the corporal. Obedient to this levelling instinct, Galvez, who has arrived first on the ground, selects the best steed of the three—this being the horse of Hamersley.

Grasping the bridle, and jerking it from the branch, he springs upon the animal's back and starts to ride off. Almost as soon the two officers get astride, Roblez on his own charger, the mustang mare being left to Uraga. From her mistress he must part thus unceremoniously, covered with ignominious shame!

The thought is torture, and for a time stays him.

A dire, damnable purpose flashes across his brain, and for an instant holds possession of his heart. It is to dismount, make for the marquee, enter it, and kill Adela Miranda—thrust her through with his sword.

Fortunately for her, the coward's heart fails him.

He will not have time to do the murder and remount his horse. The Rangers are already in the open ground and rushing towards him, Wilder and Hamersley at their head. In a minute more they will be around him.

He hesitates no longer, but, smothering his chagrin and swallowing his unappeased vengeance, puts whip and spur to the mustang mare, going off as fast as she can carry him.

Chapter Seventy Five.
Divided by Duty.

But for a half-score men lying dead along the earth, their warm blood welling from wounds where bullets have passed through their bodies, the gory drops here and there like dew bedecking the blades of grass, or in fuller stream settling down into the sand—but for this, the too real evidence of death, one who entered the camp of Uraga as the Mexican Colonel is riding out of it might fancy himself spectator of a pantomime during the scene of transformation. In the stage spectacle, not quicker or more contrasting could be the change.

The gaily-apparelled lancers, with their plumes, pennons, and tassels, representing the sprites and sylphides of the pantomime, are succeeded by men who look real life. Big bearded men, habited in homespun; some wearing buckskin, others blanket coats; all carrying guns, bowie-knives, and pistols; the first smoking at the muzzles, as freshly fired, the last held in hand, ready to be discharged as soon as somebody worth shooting at shows himself.

Entering the open ground ahead of the others, Hamersley and Wilder glance around in search of this somebody, both thinking of the same. They see stretched along the sward ten soldiers dead as herrings on a string, but among them no one wearing the uniform of an officer—certainly not him they are after.

Their first glance is unrewarded, but their second gives all they seek. Behind a tent, and partially screened by the trees, three men are in the act of mounting three horses. One is already in the saddle and moving away, the other two have just set foot in the stirrup. The roan mounted is unknown to the pursuers; but his animal is recognised by them. It is Hamersley's own horse! Of the other two but one is identified, and him only by Hamersley. He sees Gil Uraga.

A cry from the Kentuckian expresses disappointment. For on the instant after sighting the Mexican officers the latter have leaped into their saddles and gone off at a full gallop. A rifle shet might yet reach them; but the guns of both Kentuckian and Texan are empty. Their revolvers are loaded to no purpose. The retreating horsemen are beyond pistol range!

Sure of this, they do not think of firing. And afoot, as all the Rangers are—having left the horses behind to steal forward—they feel helpless to pursue for the present. While hesitating, a circumstance occurs giving Hamersley a hope. The man who has mounted his horse finds a difficulty in managing him. As a Mexican he sits the saddle to perfection, but cannot make the animal go the way he wants.

From behind the horse has heard neighing, which he knows to come from the steeds of his own race, and, knowing this, has resolved to rub noses with them.

In vain Galvez kicks against his ribs, beats him about the head, and makes frantic efforts to urge him on. He but rears in the opposite direction, backing so far as to bring his rider within reach of the revolver held in the hands of Hamersley. Its crack rings clear—not needing to be repeated or the cylinder turned. At the first explosion the soldier is seen to spring from the saddle, dropping dead without kick or cry, while the steed, disembarrassed, sheers round and comes trotting towards the place whence the shot proceeded.

In a moment more its real master has hold of the bridle-rein, his shout of joy answered by a whimper of recognition.

Seeing how matters stand, the Rangers hasten back to get possession of their horses; others make for those of the fallen lancers, that now in affright are rearing and straining at the end of their trail-ropes in a vain endeavour to break loose.

For neither can Hamersley wait. It will take time, which his impatience—his burning thirst for vengeance—cannot brook. He is thinking of his slain comrades, whose bones lie unburied on the sands of the Canadian; also of the outrage so near being perpetrated, so opportunely interrupted.

But one thought stays him—Adela. Where is she? Is she safe? He turns towards the marquee late guarded by Galvez. A very different individual is now seen at its entrance. Walt Wilder, with bowie-knife bared, its blade cutting the cords that kept the tent closed. In an instant they are severed, the flap flies open, and two female forms rush forth. In another instant one of them is lying along Hamersley's breast, the other in the embrace of Wilder. Kisses and words are exchanged. Only a few of the latter, till Hamersley, withdrawing himself from the arms that softly entwine him, tells of his intention to part.

"For what purpose?" is the interrogatory, asked in tremulous accents, and with eyes that speak painful surprise.

"To redress my wrongs and yours, Adela," is the response firmly spoken.

"*Santissima!*" she exclaims, seeing her lover prepare to spring into the saddle. "Francisco! Stay with me. Do not again seek danger. The wretch is not worthy of your vengeance."

"'Tis not vengeance, but justice. 'Tis my duty to chastise this crime—the greatest on earth. Something whispers me 'tis a destiny, and I shall succeed. Dearest Adela, do not stay me. There is no danger. I shall be back soon, bringing Uraga's sword, perhaps himself, along with me."

"Thar's odds again ye, Frank," interposes Wilder. "Two to one. If I foller afoot I mayn't be up in time. An' the boys that's gone arter thar critters, they'll be too late."

"Never mind the odds! I'll make it up with the five shots still in my revolver. See, dearest, your brother is coming this way. Go meet and tell him I shall soon return with a prisoner to be exchanged for him. Another kiss! *Adios! hasta luego!*"

Tearing himself from arms so reluctant to release him, he bounds upon the back of his horse and spurs off, soon disappearing among the trees.

Scarce is he out of sight when another quadruped is seen galloping after—not a horse, but a hybrid.

Walt Wilder has espied the saddled mule hitched up behind the tent—that intended for Conchita. It is now ridden by the ex-Ranger, who, prodding it with the point of his bowie, puts it to its best speed.

And soon after go other horsemen—the Texans who have recovered their steeds, with some who have caught those of the troopers, rapidly bridled and mounted them bare-back.

They who stay behind become spectators of a scene strange and tender. Two male prisoners unexpectedly rescued—snatched, as it were, from the jaws of death—two female captives alike saved from dishonour. A brother embracing his sister, whose noble affection but the moment before prompted her to share with him the first sooner than submit to the last.

Chapter Seventy Six.
The Chase.

Hamersley has his horse fairly astretch ere the fugitives, though out of sight, are many hundred yards ahead; for the scenes and speeches recorded occupied but a few seconds of time.

He is confident of being able to overtake them. He knows his Kentucky charger is more than a match for any Mexican horse, and will soon bring him up with Uraga and the other officer. If they should separate he will follow the former.

As he rides on he sees they cannot go far apart. There is a sheer precipice on each side—the bluffs that bound the creek bottom. These will keep the pursued men together, and he will have both to deal with.

The ground is such that they cannot possibly escape him except by superior speed. He can see the cliffs on each side to their bases. There is not enough underwood for a horseman to hide in.

He hastens on, therefore, supposing them still before him.

In ten minutes more he is sure of it—they are in sight!

The timber through which the chase has hitherto led abruptly terminates, a long grassy mead of over a mile in length lying beyond; and beyond it the trees again obstruct the vista up the valley. The retreating horsemen have entered upon this open tract, but not got far over it, when Hamersley spurs his horse out of the timber tract, and pursuer and pursued are in sight of other.

It is now a tail-on-end chase, all three horses going at the greatest speed to which their riders can press them. It is evident that the large American horse is rapidly gaining upon the Mexican mustangs, and, if no accident occur, will soon be alongside them.

Hamersley perceives this, and, casting a glance ahead, calculates the distance to where the timber again commences. To overtake them before they can reach it is the thought uppermost in his mind. Once among the tree-trunks they can go as fast as he, for there the superior fleetness of his horse will not avail. Besides, there may be a thick underwood, giving them a chance of concealment.

He must come up with them before they can reach the cover, and to this end he once more urges his animal both with spur and speech.

At this moment Roblez looking back, perceives there is but one man in chase of them. A long stretch of open plain in his rear, and no other pursuer upon it. Brigand though he be, the adjutant possesses real courage. And there are two of them, in full health and strength, both armed with sabres, himself carrying a pair of dragoon pistols in his holsters. Those belonging to Uraga are nearer to the hand of Hamersley—having been left upon the saddle which the colonel, in his hasty retreat, had been hindered from occupying.

"*Carajo!*" exclaims Roblez, "there's but one of them after us. The others haven't had time to get mounted, and won't be up for a while. It's some rash fool who's got your horse under him. Let's turn upon him, colonel."

The coward thus appealed to cannot refuse compliance. In an instant the two wheel round, and, with blades bared, await the approach of the pursuer.

In a dozen more strides of his horse Hamersley is on the ground. Uraga now recognises his antagonist in the Chihuahua duel—the man he hates above all others on earth.

This, hatred, intense as it is, does not supply him with courage. In the eye of the pursuer coming on, when close up, Uraga reads a terrible expression—that of the avenger!

Something whispers him his hour has come, and with shrinking heart and palsied arm he awaits the encounter.

As said, the two Mexican officers carry swords, cavalry sabres. Against these the Kentuckian has no weapon for parrying or defence. He is but ill-armed for the unequal strife, having only a Colt's revolver with one chamber empty, and, as a *dernier ressort*, the single-barrelled pistols in the holsters.

Quickly perceiving his disadvantage, he checks up before coming too close, and with his revolver takes aim, and fires at the nearest of his antagonists, who is Roblez.

The shot tells, tumbling the lancer lieutenant out of his saddle, and making more equal the chances of the strife.

But there is no more fighting, nor the show of it, for Uraga, on seeing his comrade fall, and once more catching sight of that avenging glance that glares at him as if from the eyes of Nemesis, wrenches the mustang round, and rides off in wild retreat; his sword, held loosely, likely to drop from his grasp.

Soon it does drop, for Hamersley, following in close pursuit, delivers a second shot from the revolver. The bullet hits the extended sword arm; the naked blade whirls out, and falls with a ring upon the meadow turf.

Uraga rides on without looking back. He has not even courage to turn his face towards his antagonist. He thinks only of reaching the timber, in a despairing hope he may there find shelter and safety.

It is not his destiny to reach it; the pursuer is too close upon his heels. The head of Hamersley's horse is swept by the mustang's tail, its long, white hair spread comet-like behind.

Once more the revolver is raised, its muzzle pointed at the retreating coward. The pressing of its trigger would send a bullet into his back. It is not pressed.

As if from mercy or mere caprice Hamersley suddenly transfers the pistol to his left hand. Then, forcing his horse to a long leap forward, he lays hold of Uraga with his right.

Grasping the Mexican by the sword-belt and jerking him out of the saddle, he dashes him down to the earth. Then reining up, with the revolver once more in his right hand, he cries out—

"Lie still, you ruffian! Don't move an inch! I have four shots to spare, and if you attempt to stir, one of them will quiet you."

The admonition is not needed. Uraga, stunned by the shock for a time, makes no movement. He is insensible.

Before he comes to himself the Rangers have ridden up, with Walt Wilder at their head. They proceed to make prisoners of the two men, neither of whom has been killed in the encounter.

Better for both if they had. For they are now in the hands of men who will surely doom them to a death less easy thar that they had escaped.

Their fate is inevitable.

Chapter Seventy Seven.
The Camp Transformed.

Another sun rises over the Llano Estacado, his beams gilding with ruddy glow the brown basaltic cliffs that enclose the valley of the Arroyo de Alamo.

On projecting points of these, above the spot chosen by Uraga for his camp, the black vultures are still perched. Though 'tis not their usual roosting-place, they have remained there all night, now and then giving utterance to their hoarse, guttural croaks, when some howling, predatory quadruped—coyote or puma—approaching too near, has startled them from their dozing slumbers. As the first rays of the sun rouse them to activity, their movements tell why they have stayed. No longer at rest, or only at intervals, they flit from rock to rock, and across the valley from cliff to cliff, at times swooping so low that their wings almost touch the topmost twigs of the trees growing upon the banks of the stream. All the while with necks astretch, and eyes glaring in hungry concupiscence. For below they perceive the materials of a repast—a grand, gluttonous feast—no longer in doubtful expectation, but now surely provided for them.

Ten men lie prostrate upon the sward; not asleep, as the vultures well know—nor yet reclining to rest themselves. Their attitudes are evidence against this. They lie with bodies bent and limbs stiff, some of them contorted to unnatural postures. Besides, on the grass-blades around are drops and gouts of blood, grown black during the night, looking as if it had rained ink; while little pools of the same are here and there seen, dull crimson and coagulated.

From these sanguinary symbols the vultures are well aware that the recumbent forms are neither asleep nor reposing. Every bird knows that every man of them is dead; and, though still clad in the uniform of soldiers, with all the gay insignia of lancers, they are but clay-cold corpses.

It is the firing party, still lying as it fell; not a figure disturbed, not a coat stripped off nor pocket rifled; no strap, plume, or pennon displaced since the moment when all dropped dead almost simultaneously at the detonation of the Rangers' rifles.

Except the tents, which are still set as before, this cluster of corpses is the only thing seeming unchanged since yesterday's sun went down. For it was after sunset when the pursuers returned, bringing their prisoners along with them. As on yesterday, two captives are seen under the same tree, where late lay Don Valerian and the doctor. But different men, with quite another style of sentry standing over them. The latter, a rough-garbed, big-bearded Texan, full six feet in height, shouldering a gun whose butt, when rested on the ground, places the muzzle within an inch of his chin. No need to say who are the two he is guarding. At his feet Uraga lies, crestfallen, with a craven look upon his face, like a fox in the trap; his splendid habiliments torn, mud-bedaubed, bedraggled. Besides him his adjutant, Roblez—his confederate in many a crime—also showing signs of having received rough treatment, but not without resenting it. His aspect is that of a tiger encaged, chafing at the torture, regardless of what may be the end. On the camp ground are seen some sixty horses with half-a-dozen mules. About fifty of the former are under saddle and bridle, as if soon to be mounted. The others have lariats around their necks, intended to be led.

A few men—those of inferior standing—look after the animals; while the larger number is gathered into a group near the centre of the camp ground. Their air, attitudes, earnest speech, and excited gesticulations tell they are taking counsel on some matter of serious import.

Walt Wilder is among them, Hamersley being absent. The latter is inside the square tent, in pleasanter companionship.

He is seated upon a *catré*, Adela by his side, her hand clasping his. This without any bashfulness or reserve at her brother being present. Which he is, along with the dear old doctor, both now released from their bonds. It is a tableau of true love, wreathed with fraternal affection.

With devotion also, of an humbler kind, Conchita is passing out and in, rejoicing in a general way. She pays no attention to a peon who lies tied behind the tent—José; and gives only scorn to another seen fast bound beside him—Manuel.

Notwithstanding her knowledge that this man is madly in love with her—for she now also knows how much he has been a traitor—her thoughts, as her eyes, are upon one more true—on her grand, gallant *Tejano*! She is proud to observe the distinguished part he plays among his *compaisanos*. For, in truth, Walt is doing this. Standing a half head taller than any of the Rangers around him, he is alike leader in their deliberations, those the most serious in which men can be engaged.

No question of life and death. It has been, but is no longer. The latter has been unanimously decreed, the verdict declared, the sentence pronounced. Their talk now only relates to the manner of execution.

The Ranger Captain, who presides, puts the interrogatory thus:

"Well, boys, what are we to do with them? Shoot or hang?"

"Hang!" is the response from more than a majority of voices.

"Shootin' is too clean a death for scoundrels sech as them," is the commentary of a voice recognisable as that of Nat Cully.

"They ought to be scalped, skinned, an' quartered," adds a man disposed to severer punishment.

"Yes!" affirms another of the like inclining. "A bit of torture wouldn't be more than the rascals deserve."

"Come, comrades!" cries the Ranger Captain. "Remember, we are Texans, and not savages like those we're about to punish. Sufficient to send them out of the world without acting inhumanly. You all declare for hanging?"

"All!"

"Enough! Where shall we string them up?"

"Yonner's a pick spot," responds Wilder, pointing out the two trees to which Don Valerian and the doctor had been lately lashed. "They kin each hev a branch separate, so's not to crowd one the t'other in makin' tracks to etarnity."

"Jest the place!" endorses Cully. "Kedn't be a better gallis if the sheriff o' Pike County, Massoury, had rigged it up hisself. We'll gie 'em a tree apiece, as they war about to do wi' thar innocent prisoners. Takin' their places'll be turn an' turn about. That's fair, I reckin."

"Boys!" cries Walt, "look out a cupple o' layvettes, an' fetch 'em this way."

Several start towards the horse-drove, and soon return with the trail-ropes. Then all proceed towards the two trees. Each chances to have a large limb extending horizontally outward from the trunk. Over each a tazo is flung, one end left loose, the other remaining in the hand of him who pitched it. Before flinging them the rope has been passed through the iron ring with which all lariats are provided, thus furnishing a ready-made running noose.

"Who's to haul up?" asks the Ranger Captain; adding, "Boys! 'Taint a nice business, I know; but I suppose there's some of you willing to undertake it."

Some of them!

Forty voices, nearly all present, are heard crying out with one accord—

"I'm willing!"

In fact, every man upon the ground seems eager to take part in a duty which, under other circumstances, would be not only disagreeable, but disgusting to them. Rough, rude men as most of the Rangers are, little prone to delicate sentimentalism, they are, nevertheless, true to the ordinary instincts of humanity. Accustomed to seeing blood spilled, and not squeamish about spilling it if it be that of a red-skinned foe, it is different when the complexion is white.

In the present case they have no scruples on the score of colour. What has been told them about their two prisoners—the atrocities these have committed—puts all this aside. The tale has made a profound impression upon their minds; and, beyond any motive of mere revenge, they are stirred by a sense of just retribution. Every man of them feels as if it were his sacred duty to deal out justice, and administer the punishment of death to criminals so surely deserving it.

Chapter Seventy Eight.
A Living Scaffold.

Captain Haynes, seeing there will be no difficulty in obtaining executioners, deems everything settled, and is about ordering the prisoners to be brought up. Being a man of humane feelings, with susceptibilities that make him somewhat averse to performing the part of sheriff, it occurs to him that he can avoid the disagreeable duty by appointing a deputy.

For this he selects Walt Wilder, who in turn chooses Nat Cully to assist him. The two assume superintendence of the ceremony, and the Ranger Captain retires from the ground.

After communing for some seconds between themselves, and in *sotto voce*, as if arranging the mode of execution, Walt faces round to the assembled Texans, saying—

"Wal, boys, thar 'pears to be no stint o' hangmen among ye. This chile niver seed so many o' the Jack Ketch kind since he fust set foot on the soil o' Texas. Maybe it's the smell o' these Mexikins makes ye so savagerous."

Walt's quaint speech elicits a general laugh, but suppressed. The scene is too solemn for an ebullition of boisterous mirth. The ex-Ranger continues—

"I see you'll want to have a pull at these ropes. But I reckon we'll have to disapp'int ye. The things we're agoin' to swing up don't desarve hoistin' to eternity by free-born citizens o' the Lone Star State. 'Twould be a burnin' shame for any Texan to do the hangin' o' sech skunks as they."

"What do you mean, Walt?" one asks. "Somebody must hoist them up!"

"'Taint at all necessary. They kin be strung 'ithout e'er a hand techin' trail-rope."

"How?" inquire several voices.

"Wal, thar's a way Nat Cully an' me hev been speaking o'. I've heern o' them Mexikins practisin' themselves on thar Injun prisoners for sport. We'll gie' 'em a dose o' their own medicine. Some o' you fellows go an' fetch a kupple o' pack mules. Ye may take the saddles off—they won't be needed."

Half-a-dozen of the Rangers rush out, and return leading two mules, having hastily stripped off their alparejas.

"Now!" cries Walt, "conduct hyar the kriminals!"

A party proceeds to the spot where the two prisoners lie; and taking hold, raise them to an erect attitude. Then, half carrying, half dragging, bring them under the branches designed for their gallows-tree.

With their splendid uniforms torn, mud-bedaubed, and stained with spots of blood, they present a sorry spectacle. They resemble wounded wolves, taken in a trap; nevertheless, bearing their misfortune in a far different manner. Roblez looks the large, grey wolf—savage, reckless, unyielding; Uraga, the coyote—cowed, crestfallen, shivering; in fear of what may follow.

For a time neither speaks a word nor makes an appeal for mercy. They seem to know it would be idle. Regarding the faces around, they may well think so. There is not one but has "death" plainly stamped upon it, as if the word itself were upon every lip.

There is an interval of profound silence, only broken by the croak of the buzzards and the swish of their spread wings. The bodies of the dead lancers lie neglected; and, the Rangers now further off, the birds go nearer them. Wolves, too, begin to show themselves by the edge of the underwood— from the stillness thinking the time arrived to commence their ravenous repast. It has but come to increase the quantity of food soon to be spread before them.

"Take off thar leg fastenin's!" commands Wilder, pointing to the prisoners.

In a trice the lashings are loosed from their ankles, and only the ropes remain confining their wrists—these drawn behind their backs, and there made fast.

"Mount 'em on the mules!"

As the other order, this is instantly executed; and the two prisoners are set astride on the hybrids, each held by a man at its head.

"Now fix the snares roun' thar thrapples. Make the other eends fast by giein' them a wheen o' turn over them branches above. See as ye draw 'em tight 'ithout streetchin'."

Walt's orders are carried out quickly, and to the letter, for the men executing them now comprehend what is meant. They also, too well, who are seated upon the backs of the mules. It is an old trick of their own. They know they are upon a scaffold—a living scaffold—with a halter and running noose around their necks.

"Now, Nat!" says Walt, in undertone to Cully. "I guess we may spring the trap? Git your knife riddy."

"It's hyar."

"You take the critter to the left. I'll look arter that on the right."

The latter is bestridden by Uraga. With Walt's ideas of duty are mingled memories that prompt to revenge. He remembers his comrades slaughtered upon the sands of the Canadian, himself left buried alive. With a feeling almost jubilant—natural, considering the circumstances, scarce reprehensible—he takes his stand by the side of the mule which carries Colonel Uraga. At the same time Cully places himself beside that bestridden by Roblez.

Both have their bowie-knives in hand, the blades bare. One regarding them, a stranger to their intent, might think they meant slaughtering either the mules or the men on their backs.

They have no such thought, but a design altogether different, as declared by Wilder's words—the last spoken by him before the act of execution.

"When I gie the signal, Nat, prod yur critter sharp, an' sweep the support from unner them. They've been thegither in this world in the doin' o' many a rascally deed. Let's send 'em thegither inter the next."

"All right, ole hoss! I'll be riddy," is the laconic rejoinder of Cully.

After it another interval of silence, resembling that which usually precedes the falling of the gallows drop. So profound, that the chirp of a tree cricket, even the rustling of a leaf, would seem a loud noise. So ominous, that the vultures perched upon the summit of the cliff crane out their necks to inquire the cause.

The stillness is interrupted by a shout; not the signal promised by Wilder, but a cry coming from the lips of Uraga.

In the last hour of anguish his craven heart has given way, and he makes a piteous appeal for mercy. Not to those near him, knowing it would scarce be listened to; but to the man he has much wronged, calling out his name, "Colonel Miranda."

On hearing it Don Valerian rushes forth from the tent, his sister by his side, Hamersley with the doctor behind. All stand in front regarding the strange spectacle, of which they have been unconscious, seemingly prepared for them. There can be no mistaking its import. The *mise en scène* explains it, showing the stage set for an execution.

If they have a thought of interfering it is too late. While they stand in suspense, a shout reaches them, followed by explanatory words.

They are in the voice of Walt Wilder, who has said —

"Death to the scoundrels! Now, Nat, move your mule forrard!"

At the same instant he and Cully are seen leaning towards the two mules, which bound simultaneously forward, as if stung by hornets or bitten by gadflys.

But neither brings its rider along. The latter—both of them—stay behind; not naturally, as dismounted and thrown to the earth; but, like the cradle of Mahomet, suspended between earth and heaven.

Chapter Seventy Nine.
After the Execution.

It is mid-day over the Arroyo de Alamo.

The same sun whose early morning rays fell around the deliberating lynchers, at a later hour lighting up a spectacle of execution, has mounted to the meridian, and now glares down upon a spectacle still sanguinary, though with tableaux changed.

The camp is deserted. There are no tents, no Texans, no horses, nor yet any mules. All have disappeared from the place.

True, Uraga and his lancers are still there—in body, not in spirit. Their souls have gone, no one may know whither. Only their clay-cold forms remain, us left by the Rangers—the common soldiers lying upon the grass, the two officers swinging side by side, from the trees, with broken necks, drooping heads, and limbs dangling down—all alike corpses.

Not for long do they stay unchanged—untouched.

Scarce has the last hoof-stroke of the Texan horses died away down the valley, when the buzzards forsake their perch upon the bluff, and swoop down to the creek bottom.

Simultaneously the wolves—grand grey and coyote—come sneaking out from the thicket's edge; at first cautiously, soon with bolder front, approaching the abandoned bodies.

To the bark of the coyote, the bay of the bigger wolf, and the buzzard's hoarse croak, a *caracara* adds its shrill note; the fiend-like chorus further strengthened by the scream of the white-headed eagle—for all the world like the filing of a frame saw, and not unlike the wild, unmeaning laughter of a madman.

Both the predatory birds and the ravening beasts, with instincts in accord, gather around the quarry killed for them. There is a grand feast—a banquet for all; and they have no need to quarrel over it. But they do—the birds having to stand back till the beasts have eaten their fill.

The puma, or panther, takes precedence—the so-called lion of America. A sorry brute to bear the name belonging to the king of quadrupeds. Still, on the Llano Estacado, lord of all, save when confronted by the grizzly bear—then he becomes a cat.

As no grizzly has yet come upon the ground, and only two panthers, the wolves have it almost their own way, and only the vultures and eagles have to hold back. But for the birds there is a side dish on which they may whet their appetites, beyond reach of the beasts. To their share fall the two suspended from the trees; and, driven off from the others, they attack these with beak and talon, flapping around, settling upon the branches above, on the shoulders of the corpses, thick as honey-bees upon a branch, pecking out eyes, tearing at flesh, mutilating man—God's image—in every conceivable mode.

No; there is one left, peculiar to man himself. Strange, at this crisis, he should appear to give exhibition of it. By pure chance—a sheer contingency—though not less deserving record.

The beasts and birds while engaged in devouring the dead bodies are interrupted and scared away from their filthy repast, retreating suddenly from the ground at sight of their masters—men, who unexpectedly appear upon it.

These are not the Rangers returning, but a band of Jicarilla Apaches—young braves out on a roving excursion. They have come down the creek, making for the Pecos, and so chanced to stray into the deserted camp.

Surprised at the spectacle there presented to their eyes, they are not the less delighted. More than a dozen dead men, with scalps untaken! They can see there has been a fight, but do not stay to think who have been the victors. Their thoughts are turned towards the vanquished, their eyes resting on heads that still carry their covering of hair. In a trice their blades are bare, and it is cut off—the skin along with it—to the skull of the last lancer!

Neither does Uraga nor his lieutenant escape the scalping-knife. Before the savages part from the spot, the crowns of both show crimson, while the scalps stripped off appear as trophies on the points of two Apache spears.

Not long do the Indians dally on the ghastly ground. Soon forsaking it, they continue on down the creek. Not in pursuit of the party which has so opportunely furnished them with spear-pennons and fringes for their leggings. The testimony of so many dead men, with the tracks of so many horses—horses with large hoofs, evidently not ridden by Mexicans, whom they contemn, but Texans they terribly fear; these evidences make the Apaches cautious, and, keeping on towards the Pecos, they go not as pursuers, but men trying to shun the party that has passed before.

In this they are successful. They never sight the returning Texans, nor these them. The Rangers go down the river; the savages up stream. Of all Apaches, of all Indians, the Jicarillas are the most contemptible cowards. Dastards to the last degree, the young "braves" who mutilated the slain lancers will return to their tribe to tell of scalps fairly taken in fight!

And while they are boasting, the wolves, eagles, and vultures will be back among the dead bodies, strip them of their flesh, and leave nought but their bones to bleach white; in time to become dust, and mingle with the earth on which they once moved in all the pride of manhood and panoply of war!

Chapter Eighty.
Tranquil Scenes.

The last act of our drama is recorded, the last sanguinary scene. All red enough, the reader will say, while the keenly susceptible one may deem them too red. Alas! the writer is not answerable for this. He but depicts life as it exists on the borderland between Mexico and Texas. Those who doubt its reality, and would deem him drawing upon imagination, should read the Texan newspapers of that time, or those of this very day. In either he will find recorded occurrences as strange, incidents as improbable, episodes as romantic, and tragedies of hue sanguinary as any recorded in this mere romance.

Not always with such a satisfactory termination. Fortunately for our tale and its readers, Nemesis, in dealing out death and meting vengeance, has necessarily allied herself with Justice. The fallen deserved their fate— all, save the teamsters of the caravan, and those Texans who on Pecan Creek succumbed to the Comanche spears.

These victims, like stage supernumeraries, living nameless and dying unknown, though their fate may stir our sympathy it does not appeal to the painful depths of sorrow. More easily can it be borne, reflecting on the brighter fate of the survivors.

It can give no painful sensation to tell that Colonel Miranda and his sister accompanied Frank Hamersley on his return to the States, Don Prospero and the New Mexican damsel, Conchita, being of the party, which had for escort across the plains Captain Haynes and his company of Texan Rangers, their old comrade, Walt Wilder, travelling along, and, with Nat Cully, narrating around their nightly camp fires many a strange "scrape" of the mountains and prairies. Two subsequent scenes alone seem worthy of record, both fairly deserving it.

The first occurs in a little country church in the celebrated "Blue Grass district" of Kentucky. Within its walls have assembled some scores of the very bluest blood of this blue grass country—stalwart, handsome men, alongside a like number of lovely women. They are assisting at a marriage ceremony, not an uncommon occurrence in a church. But in the Kentuckian place of worship—a little rural edifice, far away from any town—it is something unusual to see three couples standing before the altar. In the present case there is this number, none of the pairs strangers to the other two, but all three, by mutual agreement and understanding, to take Hymen's oath at the same time.

Foremost and first to put the ring on his bride's finger is Frank Hamersley. She who holds out her hand to receive it is Adela Miranda.

Of the couple coming next, the bridegroom is known to the reader. A handsome man, of dark complexion and pure Spanish features, remarked by the spectators as having resemblance to those of Hamersley's new-made bride. Not strange, he being her brother.

But who is the lady, the tall, fair girl consenting to make Don Valerian happy, so like Hamersley himself.

No one asks this question, all present knowing she is his sister.

A fair exchange between the brothers of the bride; each equally quick to fall in love with the sister of the other. On the sterile Llano Estacado it took scarce a minute for the dark Mexican maiden to subdue the heart of Hamersley. Almost as soon, in the fertile State of Kentucky, has his bright-skinned, blonde-haired sister made conquest of the Mexican Colonel.

The third pair that presents itself to be made man and wife—who are they? The bridegroom stands six feet two in his boots; the bride, in her satin slippers, far under five. Without thinking of the disproportion in their stature, the reader will recognise Walt Wilder and Conchita.

As the ex-Ranger puts the ring on the finger of his blushing bride, he accompanies the act with certain ludicrous protestations of fidelity not to be found in the printed ritual of the Church.

Another scene ends our tale; a simple episode of every-day life; but life in a strange land, remote from the ordinary centres of civilisation.

It occurs in New Mexico, in itself a sort of oasis in the great middle desert of North America. Locally, the scene takes place near Albuquerque, on the azotea of a handsome house, which commands a view of the town.

It is the mansion once belonging to Don Valerian Miranda.

That its former master has retained possession of it is evident from the fact of his being again on its roof, tranquilly smoking a cigaretto; while near by him is his sister. Though one dearer stands between—his wife. Adela is not distressed by her brother's preference for the new mistress of the mansion. She has a mansion of her own, independent. Though far off, its master, Frank Hamersley, is near.

Near, also, in the court-yard below is Walt Wilder, in his grotesque way playing Benedict to Conchita. While up and down moves the doctor, sharing the general joy.

Outside, upon the plain, the white tilts of twenty waggons, with the smoke of camp-fires rising over them, tell of a trader's caravan. It is Hamersley's—late arrived—*en route* for the Rio Abajo and El Paso del Norte.

Its teamsters take their siesta, reposing in full confidence. No fear of Indian attacks now, nor impost exactions from the tyrant Governor of New Mexico, Don Manuel Armijo!

A war has swept the land; a new flag floats over it. Seen streaming above the towers of Albuquerque, it promises security to all. For it is the banner of the "Stars and Stripes!"